The Walled-Up Wife

Edited by

ALAN DUNDES

The Walled-Up Wife

A Casebook

The University of Wisconsin Press

The University of Wisconsin Press
114 North Murray Street
Madison, Wisconsin 53715

3 Henrietta Street
London WC2E 8LU, England

Printed in the United States of Amerca

Cover illustration: The picture of the "Bridge of Arta" is reprinted by kind
permission of Crete University Press. It was painted by Spyros Kardamakis
for the double CD "Tunes and Songs of Thrace" (published in Greece in
1994; editor Nikos Dionyssopoulos) to illustrate the homonymous ballad.

Library of Congress Cataloging-in-Publication Data
The walled-up wife: a casebook / edited by Alan Dundes.
                   222 p.   cm.
Includes texts of the ballad of the Walled-up wife from
Bulgaria, Greece, India, Romania, and former Yugoslavia.
Includes bibliographical references and index.
ISBN 0-299-15070-4 (cloth: alk. paper).
ISBN 0-299-15074-7 (pbk.: alk. paper).
     1. Ballads—History and criticism.
     2. Foundation sacrifices in literature.
I. Dundes, Alan.   II. Walled-up wife. Polyglot.
     PN1376.W35   1996
     809.1'44—dc20   96-1225

This casebook is lovingly dedicated to my wife, Carolyn, whose many sacrifices made my career as a folklorist possible.

Contents

Contents

Preface

The study of folklore is in large measure the study of folklore genres or subgenres. Among the major genres of folklore are epic, myth, folktale, legend, and folksong. Most of these genres can be subdivided. Folksong, for example, includes a number of important types or subgenres: lullabies, rounds, dirges or laments, drinking songs, and the like. Historically speaking, however, perhaps the best-studied form of folksong is the traditional ballad.

The ballad is a narrative song whose story is told succinctly and whose drama often depends upon acts of love and violence. The plot may develop in a series of striking scenes, a process sometimes referred to as "leaping and lingering." It is no doubt the exquisite literary (and musical) qualities of the traditional ballad which have endeared it to devotees of national literatures. Early investigations of the ballad (e.g., in the sixteenth and seventeenth centuries in Europe) tended to limit discussion to the text only, typically ignoring the tune altogether. The textual bias of ballad scholarship unfortunately continues. Instructors in English literature, for instance, often analyze ballad texts such as *Edward* and *Lord Randal* strictly as poems, written poems, with little or no reference to the melodies to which these orally transmitted ballads were originally sung. Generally speaking, the musicological aspect of ballads has lagged well behind the purely textual explorations of the genre, and this is true across the board for ballads in both western and eastern Europe. One need only compare the canonical collection of Francis James Child, *The English and Scottish Popular Ballad* (1882–1898), with Bertrand Bronson, *The Traditional Tunes of the Child Ballads* (1959–1972), to appreciate the disparity between considering ballads *as texts* as opposed to treating ballads *as songs* including music.

The ballad may or may not be derived originally from songs accompanying dances; the word *ballad* itself seems to be related to the word *ballare*, meaning "to dance." In some ballads, there are commonplaces or formulas in the burden or refrain which could be construed as referring to dance instructions. What is more certain is that the ballad as a specific genre or subgenre appears to be confined to Indo-European peoples. Native peoples in North and South America do not have ballads (although they certainly have folksongs). Nor do indigenous peoples in Africa or Oceania have ballads as such (though they too have no lack of traditional songs). Part of the definitional problem may simply stem from the Eurocentric bias in ballad scholarship.

In any event, international ballad scholarship has tended to favor ballads reported from western Europe. There are historical reasons for this. Danish pioneer folklorist Svend Grundtvig (1824–1883), one of the founders of ballad studies, published a Danish translation of English and Scottish ballads in 1842, a precursor of his remarkable monumental compilation of Danish ballads, the first volume of which appeared in 1853. The last of the twelve volumes of *Danmarks gamle Folkeviser* (Denmark's old ballads) was not published until 1976, nearly one hundred years after Grundtvig's death. Grundtvig's presentation of Danish ballads was a direct and explicit model for Francis J. Child's multivolume assemblage of 305 English and Scottish ballads. For synopses of some 838 Scandinavian ballad types based upon more than 15,000 texts, see Bengt R. Jonsson et al., eds., *The Types of the Scandinavian Medieval Ballad* (Oslo: Universitetsforlaget, 1978); for a helpful entrée into the substantial literature consecrated to ballad study, see W. Edson Richmond, *Ballad Scholarship: An Annotated Bibliography* (New York: Garland, 1989); for a useful sampling of Child ballad scholarship, see Dianne Dugaw, ed., *The Anglo-American Ballad: A Folklore Casebook* (New York: Garland, 1995).

Despite the overwhelming preponderance of studies of ballads popular in Western Europe, there is also a strong interest in the genre in eastern Europe. Indeed, the present volume is devoted to one particular ballad which has attracted the attention of many, if not most, ballad specialists in that part of the world. The ballad of "The Walled-Up Wife," like its counterparts in western Europe, has a long and complex history of scholarly investigations. The story concerns the sacrifice of a female victim usually in connection with ensuring the construction of a building, bridge, or spring. Early discussions of the ballad focussed on possible points of origin, usually with each country claiming the distinctive folksong as its very own, much to the consternation of ballad scholars in neighboring countries, who were making similar nationalistic proprietary claims. Later studies tended to be more interested in interpreting the possible ritual origin of the ballad in terms of a presumed construction-site sacrifice. Most often the plot occurred in ballad form, that is, as a song, but it was also reported as a spoken, unsung narrative, that is, as a legend or folktale. It is not that unusual for a given plot to exist in both ballad and folktale form. See Archer Taylor, "The Parallels between Ballads and Tales," *Jahrbuch für Volksliedforschung* 9 (1964): 104–15.

This volume contains eighteen contributions to the study of "The

Walled-Up Wife." The name of the ballad varies from country to country: "The Building of Skadar," or Scutari, in the former Yugoslavia; "The Bridge of Arta" in Greece; "Master Manole" in Romania, and so forth. The essays, some short, some long, range from the presentation of typical texts from Yugoslavia, Greece, Romania, Bulgaria, and India all the way to specialized literary, ritual, structuralist, or feminist interpretations of the ballad. The intent is to demonstrate some sense of the century-long debate about the provenience of the ballad as well as some of the diverse theoretical and methodological approaches employed in analyzing the ballad. The emphasis on the versions of the ballad from South Asia provides a new direction in the study of this particular folksong, a direction which will presumably have to be taken into account in future scholarship concerned with the ballad, which was previously wrongly thought to be limited to the Balkans area.

The multiplicity of approaches and hence interpretations of one ballad should give pause to all students of folklore, making them more cautious about accepting *in toto* any monolithic school of analysis. Just as literary criticism reveals genuine and legitimate differences of opinion about the meaning(s) of a short story or novel, so folkloristics must similarly encourage diversity in seeking to understand some of the finest specimens of human creativity, namely, folklore. "The Walled-Up Wife" surely qualifies as a prime example of the sublime nobility and delicate poignancy of folk creation.

The Walled-Up Wife

"The Building of Skadar"

One of the earliest recorded versions of "The Walled-Up Wife" was recorded by Vuk Karadžić (1787–1864), who is generally regarded as the pioneering figure in Serbian folkloristics. One of the reasons the ballad became well known was that Jacob Grimm (1785–1863) admired it. When Karadižić sent a copy of his folksong collection to Grimm in 1824, the latter was so enthralled by this particular ballad that he made a translation of it into German and sent it on to Goethe the same year. Goethe's reaction was, however, quite different from that of Grimm. He was disgusted by what he considered the barbarity of human sacrifice. Nevertheless, it was Grimm's opinion which prevailed, and the ballad has continued to be admired by generations of folksingers and ballad scholars ever since.

Karadžić recorded one version of the ballad from one of his prize informants, a man called Old Rashko, who was born in old Herzegovina, but who later came to Serbia, specifically the town of Kolašin. The ballad was first published in 1815. It has occupied a prominent place in Serbian ballad scholarship for nearly two hundred years, and almost all discussions begin with the version initially reported by Karadžić.

For details of Karadžić's career as a self-educated folklorist, see Duncan Wilson, The Life and Times of Vuk Stefanović Karadžić 1787–1864 *(Oxford: Oxford University Press, 1970). For some sense of his continuing importance, one should consult the papers presented at international symposia devoted to appreciations of his scholarship in linguistics and folkloristics, symposia held in Göttingen and Trieste in 1987, the bicentennial of his birth. See, for example, Gabriella Schubert, "Vuk Karadžić—Der Volkskundler," in Reinhard Lauer, ed.,* Sprache, Literatur, Folklore bei Vuk Stefanović Karadžić, *Opera Slavica 13 (Wiesbaden: Otto Harrassowitz, 1988), pp. 309–22; and Vojislav Đurić, "Die nationale und internationale Bedeutung von Vuk Stefanović Karadžić," in Walter Lukan and Dejan Madaković,*

Reprinted from Zora Devrnja, "The Functions of Metaphor in Traditional Serbian Narrative," unpublished doctoral dissertation, State University of New York at Buffalo, 1974, pp. 156–170, by permission of the author.

eds., Vuk Karadžić, 1787–1987: Festschrift zu seinem 200 Geburt-
stag, *published as a special supplement* (Sonderheft) *to* Österre-
ichische Osthefte 29 (1987): 30–46.

Three brothers build a citadel:
Mrljavčevići,[1] brothers three:
The eldest is Vukašin King,
The second is Duke Uglješa,
5   And Gojko[2] is the youngest one.

Three years on River Bojana
Three hundred men build Skadar's[3] walls,
The workmen labor three long years,
In vain they try to raise the walls,
10 In vain they try to build the fort:
What workmen raise throughout the day,
The vila razes in the night.

Now when the fourth year had begun
The vila calls from mountains high:
15 "Vukašin, King, your torment end,
Your torment end, no treasure waste,
You cannot lay foundations, King,
Or ever raise Fort Skadar's walls,
Until you find two matching names,
20 Stojan and Stoja[4] you must find:
Stojan the brother of Stoja.
Immure them in the tower walls;
At once the groundwork will be strong,
At once your citadel can grow."

25 When King Vukašin heard these words,
He calls his servant Desimir:
"O Desimir, my dearest son!
With faithful heart, you've always served—
Be loyal now, my dearest son:
30 Go fasten horses to my coach,
And take with you six treasure loads,
Then go, my son, throughout the world

And find for me two matching names,
Stojan and Stoja, find for me;
35   Stojan the brother of Stoja.
And if for gold they will not come,
Then seize them, bring them back by force,
To be immured in Skadar's walls,
For then will Skadar's walls be strong,
40   And then our citadel can grow."

When Desimir had heard these words,
He fastens horses to the coach
And takes with him six treasure loads.
Throughout the world, the servant goes,
45   He searches for two matching names:
Stojan and Stoja must be found.
The servant searches three long years,
But does not find two matching names:
Stojan and Stoja can't be found.

50   To Skadar he returns at last;
He gives the king his steeds and coach,
He gives to him six treasure loads:
"Receive, my king, your steeds and coach,
Receive again, six treasure loads.
55   I cannot find two matching names:
Stojan and Stoja can't be found."

When King Vukašin heard these words,
His master builder,[5] Rada, comes,
And calls upon three hundred men:
60   Bojana's Skadar will be raised!
By day he builds, by night it falls.
In vain they try to raise the walls,
In vain they try to build the fort.

65   From mountains high, the vila calls:
"Vukašin, listen, you must hear,
Your torment end, no treasure waste.
You cannot lay foundations, King,
Or ever raise Fort Skadar's walls.
There are three royal brothers here,[6]

5

70 And each one has a faithful wife:
  Tomorrow whosoever comes
  To bring the men their daily meal,
  Immure her in the tower walls:
  At once the groundwork will be strong,
75 At once the citadel can grow."

  When King Vukašin heard these words,
  At once he calls his brothers two:
  "O brothers, you must hear me now,
  From mountains high the vila calls:
80 We waste our treasure all in vain,
  In vain we try to raise the walls,
  In vain we try to build the fort!

  The mountain vila tells us more:
  If we, in truth, are brothers three,
85 Then each one has a faithful wife:
  Tomorrow whosoever comes
  To bring the men their daily meal,
  Immure her in the tower walls:
  At once the groundwork will be strong,
90 At once the citadel can grow.

  In God's high presence, let each swear,
  To keep this secret from his love,
  To leave to chance whose fate 'twill be
  To come at noon to Skadar's walls!"
95 In God's high presence each did swear,
  To keep this secret from his love.
  This done, night interrupted them,
  They hasten to their own white halls,
  And sup befitting such great lords.
100 Each seeks his chamber with his love.

  Had you but seen the wondrous change!
  Vukašin tramples on his oath,
  He is the first to tell his love:
  "Take care, my faithful love, take care:
105 Tomorrow neither come to me,
  Nor bring the men their daily meal,

Or else, my love, you'll lose your head;
They will immure you in the walls!"

And Uglješa his oath defiles.
110   He too reveals the awful fate:
"Do not deceive yourself, my love:
Tomorrow neither come to me,
Nor bring the men their daily meal,
Unless you wish to die in youth:
115   They will immure you in the walls!"

Young Gojko tramples not his oath,
He keeps the secret from his love.
When in the morning day had dawned,
The three Mrljavčevići rise
120   And hasten to the Bojana.

The time has come to bring the meal:
It is the young queen's turn to go.
She hastens to Uglješa's home,
To beg the wife of Uglješa:
125   "O sister, wife of Uglješa!
My head aches so! The pain is great!
Good health to you! I am too ill
To go and bring the men their meal."
The bride of Uglješa replies:
130   "O listen now, my dear young queen!
My arm aches so! The pain is great!
Good health to you! This cannot heal;
Our youngest sister go and find."

She hastens to young Gojko's home:
135   "O bride of Gojko, hear my plea!
My head aches so! The pain is great!
Good health to you! I am too ill
To go and bring the men their meal."
The bride of Gojko answers her:
140   "O listen now, my dear young queen!
With joy would I grant your request,
But I must bathe my infant son,
And I must wash his fine white clothes."

7

Then speaks to her Vukašin's queen:
145   "My dear young sister, go at once,
And bring the men their daily meal.
For I will wash your son's white clothes,
And bathe with care your infant son."

The bride of Gojko falters not,
150   She brings the men their daily meal.
When she does reach Bojana's shore,
Young Gojko sees his young love there.
The hero's heart is filled with pain,
He sorrows for his faithful wife,
155   He sorrows for his cradled son—
An orphan of a month of days—
And from his face the tears spill down.
Upon him looks his slender bride,
With slow, shy steps she reaches him,
160   With slow, shy steps; then softly speaks:
"What ails you so, my dearest lord,
That down your cheek those tears should flow?"
Then Gojko answers his young bride:
"An evil day, my faithful love!
165   A golden apple I once had,
Into Bojana's depths it fell.
I grieve for this—my pain won't heal."
She fathoms not, his slender bride,
And to her young lord gently speaks:
170   Ask God instead to grant you health.
A better apple—you will find."
In deepest grief the hero then,
In pain, must turn his face away,
To look no more upon his love.

175   Here two Mrljavčevići come—
Young Gojko's older brothers come.
They take the bride by her white hand;
They lead her off to be immured.

Now Rada, master builder comes,
180   And calls to him three hundred men.
Yet still she smiles, the slender bride,
She thinks it all a playful jest.

They place her in a gaping hole,
Three hundred artisans beat down,
185   Beat down the wood, and beat the stones,
And build a wall up to her knees:
But still she smiles, the slender bride:
Believes it all to be a jest.

Three hundred artisans beat down,
190   Beat down the wood, and beat the stones,
And build the wall up to her waist;
When heavy grew the wood and stones,
She sees, poor one, what they will do:
An angry snake in anger screams!
195   She begs young Gojko's brothers two:
"Do not give me, if you know God!
Do not immure a green young bride!"
She pleads but all to no avail,
Upon her they refuse to look.

200   Now shame and modesty are gone,[7]
Her own young lord she now implores.
"Do not give me, my dearest lord!
I am so young, immure me not!
To my old mother go instead,
205   My mother has great stores of gold,
A slave or slave girl she will buy,
To be immured in Skadar's walls."
She pleads but all to no avail.

And when the slender bride has seen
210   That all her pleas will bring no change,
She begs the master builder then:
"O brother, Rada, hear, by God!
A window for my bosom leave,
Draw out for me my two white breasts,
215   So when my tiny Jovo comes,
He still can suckle from my breasts."
As brother, Rada grants her plea,
And leaves a window for her breasts;
Into the light he draws her breasts,
220   So when her tiny Jovo comes,
He still can suckle from her breasts.

9

Once more the grieved one speaks to him:
"O brother Rada, hear, by God!
And leave a window for my eyes.
225   My own white dwelling I would see,
To see when Jovo comes to me
And when they carry him back home."
And this in brotherhood he grants.
He leaves a window for her eyes.
230   Her own white dwelling she can see,
Can see when Jovo comes to her,
And when they carry him back home.

The slender bride was then immured.
Her cradled son was brought to her,
235   And he did nurse a week of days;
After a week, her voice was gone,
But for her child there still was milk:
She nursed him for a year of days!
As it was then, so it is now,
240   Today, as then, the milk does flow,
It works great wonders and great cures,
For every woman with no milk.[8]

Lines 121–179, Version II[9]

Behold! the fair young women now,
The noble ones, the eldest two:
One takes her snow-white linen up,
To bleach again in summer sun.
125   To bleaching meadows she does go,
With little thought of coming home.
The second takes her fine gold jug,
And hurries toward the village well.
She lingers there among the talk,
130   With little thought of coming home.
But Gojko's bride is not so free:
She cradles yet an infant son—
So very young—a month of days.

The time for dinner now has passed,
135   The aged mother rises up,
And calls young serving maids to go,

For she will bring the men their food.
The bride of Gojko speaks to her:
"O Mother, sit in peace," she cries,
140   "And rock the cradle of my child!
To Skadar I will bring the food;
A sin within the sight of God,
Great shame and scandal to our name,
If you should go, when we are here."

145   And so the aged mother stays
To rock the cradle of the child.
Then rises Gojko's bride and calls
The serving maids to gather round:
To Skadar they will bring the food.
150   When she does reach Bojana's shore,
Young Gojko looks upon his bride,
About her throws his strong right arm,
With kisses covers her white face,
While from his eyes the tears stream down.
155   To his own love, he then must speak:
"My love, my own! What pain and grief!
Do you not see where you must die?
Now who will mother our young child?
Now who will bathe our little son?
160   And whose white breasts will give him milk?"
Far more would Gojko tell his bride,
Vukašin, though, allowed no more.
He takes the bride by her right hand,
And calls the master-builder then.

(Vuk II:25)
Raško[10]

Notes

1. The correct name of the family is Mrnjavčević; Vuk preserved the local error in the name.
2. Although the two elder brothers are historical personages, Gojko is invented.
3. Scutari, now in Albania.
4. Stojan and Stoja are the masculine and feminine proper names derived from *stojati*, "to stand; to be erect; to be immovable."

11

5. The master builder was a skilled craftsman, the chief architect, and the head engineer. Historically, Rada appears to have been a noted architect.

6. The conditions by which the fortress may be built have now become more severe. The vila asks that one of the royal wives be sacrificed as punishment for disobeying her first conditions (the men began to build again when the search for Stojan and Stoja failed).

7. In this period, it was considered improper and immodest for a woman to accost her husband publicly.

8. People say that a chalky liquid oozes from Skadar's walls, from the holes through which Gojko's bride nursed her son. Women mix this chalky substance with water and drink it. The liquid purportedly restores milk to women who cannot nurse, and relieves the pain of full breasts.

Even in Vuk's time people believed that no great building could be erected without the immurement of a human being. People avoided building sites whenever possible, for it was also believed that even a man's shadow could be immured, whereupon the man would die (Vuk II:123).

9. Vuk includes this second rendering of part of the plot, noting that he collected it from the same singer: Raško. Raško's only explanation for this version was: "some sing it this way" (Vuk II:118).

10. Raško originally lived in the old town of Kolašin, but when the Karadjordje uprising against the Turks (1804–1805) began, he escaped to other parts of Serbia. This was where Vuk found him and transcribed this song (Vuk II:665).

Reference

Vuk II: Vuk Stefanović Karadžić. *Srpske Narodne Pjesme.* Vol. 2. 2nd ed. 4 vols. 1823; reprint, Belgrade: Prosveta, 1953.

Three Santal Tales

Although the ballad or legend concerning the sacrifice of a woman to facilitate the building of a castle, bridge, or monastery has traditionally been associated with the Balkans, there is reason to believe that the plot is also popular in India. In India, however, it is typically a spring or well which requires a female sacrifice.

The three versions of the plot presented here come from the Santals, one of the so-called tribal peoples of India. The Santals live in areas of Orissa, Bihar, and West Bengal. They are one of the largest of the "tribal" groups in India, numbering more than four million in 1971.

The first two versions of the story come from an 1891 collection of Santal Folk Tales *compiled by G. A. Campbell, while the third version, entitled "How Sabai Grass Grew," was contained in* Folklore of the Santal Parganas, *a collection made by Cecil Henry Bompas and published in 1909. The presentation of these three texts will allow the reader to draw his or her own conclusions about whether the Indic texts are or are not cognate with the Balkans ballad.*

For more about the Santals, see W. J. Culshaw, Tribal Heritage: A Study of the Santals *(London: Lutterworth Press, 1949). For further references to Santal folklore, see the entries under "Santal" in Edwin Capers Kirkland,* A Bibliography of South Asian Folklore, *Indiana University Folklore Series No. 21 (Bloomington: Indiana University Research Center in Anthropology, Folklore, and Linguistics, 1966).*

The tale would appear to be an example of Aarne-Thompson 780A, The Cannibalistic Brothers, a tale reported only from India, but which is likely related to Aarne-Thompson tale type 780, The Singing Bone. The key motif of a singing bone, flower, fiddle, and so forth, which reveals a murder suggests a possible linkage to the Child Ballad 10, "The Two Sisters," in which typically older sisters drown an envied younger sister but the murder is revealed by a singing harp or the like. It is tempting to speculate about a possible connection between "The Two Sisters" and "The Walled-Up Wife," especially

Reprinted from G. A. Campbell, *Santal Folk Tales* (Pokhuria: Santal Mission Press, 1891), pp. 52–56, 106–10; and from Cecil Henry Bompas, *Folklore of the Santal Parganas* (London: David Nutt, 1909), pp. 102–6.

since in some versions of "The Two Sisters" the victim jumps into the river to retrieve a ring, a motif similar to one found in many versions of "The Walled-Up Wife."

For relevant scholarship, see Lutz Mackensen, Der Singende Knochen, *FF Communications 49 (Helsinki: Academia Scientiarum Fennica, 1923); Paul G. Brewster,* The Two Sisters, *FF Communications 147 (Helsinki: Academia Scientiarum Fennica, 1953); and Christina Jaremko, "Baltic Ballads of the 'Singing Bone': Prototype and Oicotype," in Georgina Boyes, ed.,* The Ballad Today, *Proceedings of the 13th International Folk Ballad Conference (Doncaster: January Books, 1985), pp. 66–71.*

"The Magic Fiddle"

Once upon a time there lived seven brothers and a sister. The brothers were married, but their wives did not do the cooking for the family. It was done by their sister. The wives for this reason bore their sister-in-law much ill will, and at length they combined together to oust her from the office of cook and general provider, so that one of themselves might obtain it. They said, "She does not go out to the fields to work, but remains quietly at home, and yet she has not the meals ready at the proper time." They then called upon their *Bad Bonga*,[1] and vowing vows unto him they secured his good will and assistance; then they said to the *Bad Bonga*,

> "At midday when our sister-in-law goes to bring water, cause it thus to happen, that on seeing her pitcher the water shall vanish, and again slowly reappear. In this way she will be delayed. May the water not flow into her pitcher, and you keep the maiden as your own."

At noon when she went to bring water, it suddenly dried up before her, and she began to weep. Then after a while the water began slowly to rise. When it reached her ankles she tried to fill her pitcher, but it would not go under the water. Being frightened she began to wail as follows:

> "Oh! my brother, the water reaches to my ankles,
> Oh! my brother, the water reaches to my ankles,
> Still, Oh! my brother, the pitcher will not dip,
> Still, Oh! my brother, the pitcher will not dip."

14

The water continued to rise until it reached her knee, when she began to wail as follows:

> "Oh! my brother, the water reaches to my knee,
> Oh! my brother, the water reaches to my knee,
> Still, Oh! my brother, the pitcher will not dip,
> Still, Oh! my brother, the pitcher will not dip."

The water continued to rise, and when it reached her waist, she wailed as follows:

> "Oh! my brother, the water reaches to my waist,
> Oh! my brother, the water reaches to my waist,
> Still, Oh! my brother, the pitcher will not dip,
> Still, Oh! my brother, the pitcher will not dip."

The water in the tank continued to rise, and when it reached her breast, she wailed as follows:

> "Oh! my brother, the water reaches to my breast,
> Oh! my brother, the water reaches to my breast,
> Still, Oh! my brother, the pitcher will not fill,
> Still, Oh! my brother, the pitcher will not fill."

The water still rose, and when it reached her neck she wailed as follows:

> "Oh! my brother, the water reaches to my neck,
> Oh! my brother, the water reaches to my neck,
> Still, Oh! my brother, the pitcher will not dip,
> Still, Oh! my brother, the pitcher will not dip."

At length the water became so deep that she felt herself to be drowning, then she wailed as follows:

> "Oh! my brother, the water measures a man's height,
> Oh! my brother, the water measures a man's height,
> Oh! my brother, the pitcher begins to fill,
> Oh! my brother, the pitcher begins to fill."

The pitcher filled with water, and along with it she sank and was drowned. The *bonga* then transformed her into a *bonga* like himself, and carried her off.

After a time she reappeared as a bamboo growing on the embankment of the tank in which she had been drowned. When the bamboo had grown to an immense size, a *Jugi*, who was in the habit of passing that way, seeing it said to himself, this will make a splendid fiddle. So one day he brought an axe to cut it down; but when he was about to begin, the bamboo exclaimed, "Do not cut at the root, cut higher up." When he lifted his axe to cut high up the stem, the bamboo cried out, "Do not cut near the top, cut at the root." When the *Jugi* again prepared himself to cut at the root as requested, the bamboo said, "Do not cut at the root, cut higher up"; and when he was about to cut higher up, it again called out to him, "Do not cut high up, cut at the root." The *Jugi* by this time was aware that a *bonga* was trying to frighten him, so becoming angry he cut down the bamboo at the root, and taking it away made a fiddle out of it. The instrument had a superior tone and delighted all who heard it. The *Jugi* carried it with him when he went a-begging, and through the influence of its sweet music he returned home every evening with a full wallet.

He now and again visited, when on his rounds, the house of the *bonga* girl's brothers, and the strains of the fiddle affected them greatly. Some of them were moved even to tears, for the fiddle seemed to wail as one in bitter anguish. The elder brother wished to purchase it, and offered to support the *Jugi* for a whole year, if he would consent to part with his magical instrument. The *Jugi*, however, knew its value, and refused to sell it.

It so happened that the *Jugi* sometime after went to the house of a village chief, and after playing a tune or two on his fiddle asked something to eat. They offered to buy his fiddle and promised a high price for it, but he rejected all such overtures, his fiddle being to him his means of livelihood. When they saw that he was not to be prevailed upon, they gave him food and a plentiful supply of liquor. Of the latter he partook so freely that he presently became intoxicated. While he was in this condition, they took away his fiddle, and substituted their own old one for it. When the *Jugi* recovered, he missed his instrument, and suspecting that it had been stolen requested them to return it to him. They denied having taken it, so he had to depart, leaving his fiddle behind him. The chief's son being a musician, used to play on the *Jugi's* fiddle, and in his hands the music it gave forth delighted the ears of all within hearing.

When all the household were absent at their labors in the fields, the *bonga* girl emerged from the bamboo fiddle, and prepared the family meal. Having partaken of her own share, she placed that of the chief's son under his bed, and covering it up to keep off the dust, reentered the fiddle. This happening every day the other members of the household were under the impression that some female neighbor of theirs was in this manner showing her interest in the young man, so they did not trouble themselves to find out how it came about. The young chief, however, was determined to watch, and see which of his lady friends was so attentive to his comfort. He said in his own mind, "I will catch her today, and give her a sound beating; she is causing me to be ashamed before the others." So saying, he hid himself in a corner in a pile of firewood. In a short time the girl came out of the bamboo fiddle, and began to dress her hair. Having completed her toilet, she cooked the meal of rice as usual, and having partaken herself, she placed the young man's portion under his bed, as she was wont, and was about to enter the fiddle again, when he, running out from his hiding place, caught her in his arms. The *bonga* girl exclaimed, "Fie! Fie! you may be a Dom, or you may be a Hadi."[2] He said, "No. But from today, you and I are one." So they began lovingly to hold converse with each other. When the others returned home in the evening, they saw that she was both a human being and a *bonga*, and they rejoiced exceedingly.

Through course of time the *bonga* girl's family became very poor, and her brothers on one occasion came to the chief's house on a visit.

The *bonga* girl recognized them at once, but they did not know who she was. She brought them water on their arrival, and afterwards set cooked rice before them. Then sitting down near them, she began in wailing tones to upbraid them on account of the treatment she had been subjected to by their wives. She related all that had befallen her, and wound up by saying, "It is probable that you knew it all, and yet you did not interfere to save me."

After a time she became reconciled to her sisters-in-law, and no longer harbored enmity in her mind against them, for the injury they had done her.

"Seven Brothers and Their Sister"

In a certain village there lived seven brothers and a sister. Their family was wealthy. Their father was dead. The brothers agreed to dig a tank so that whatever happened their name would continue. So they began the work, but although they dug deep they found no water. Then they said to each other, "Why is there no water?" While they were speaking thus among themselves a jugi gosae on his rounds, came to the tank in the hope of finding water, but he was disappointed. The seven brothers on seeing the jugi gosae went and sat down near him, and said, "We have been working for many days, and have dug so deep, still we have not reached water. You, who are a jugi gosae, tell us why water does not come." He replied, "Unless you give a gift you will never get water." They inquired, "What should we give?" The jugi gosae replied, "Not gold, or silver, or an elephant, or a horse, but you have a sister?" They said, "Yes, we have one sister." He replied, "Then make a gift of her to the spirit of the tank." The girl was betrothed, and her family had received the amount that had been fixed as her price. The brothers argued thus, "We have labored so long to make a name for ourselves, but have not found water, so where is our name? If we do not sacrifice our sister we shall never obtain the fulfilment of our wishes, let us all agree to it." So they all said, "Agreed," but the youngest did not fully approve of their design.

In the evening they said to their mother, "Let our sister wash her clothes, dress her hair, and put on all her ornaments tomorrow when she brings us our breakfast to the tank." They did not, however, enlighten their mother as to why they desired their sister to be so careful with her toilet.

The following day the mother addressed her daughter as follows, "Oh! my daughter, your brothers yesterday said to me, 'Let the daughter, when she brings us our breakfast, come with clean clothes, her hair dressed, and all her ornaments on.' So as it is nearly time, go and dress, and put on all your ornaments, and take your brothers' breakfast to where they are working." She complied with her mother's order, and set out for the tank, dressed in her best with all her ornaments on, carrying boiled rice in a new basket.

When she arrived at the tank her brothers said to her, "Oh! sister, set down the basket under yonder tree." She did so, and the brothers came to where she was. They then said to her, "Go bring us water from the tank to drink." She took her water-pot under her arm, and went into the tank, but did not at once find water. Presently, however, she saw the sheen of water in the center, and went to fill her pitcher, but she could not do so, as the water rose so rapidly. The tank was soon full to the brim, and the girl was drowned.

The brothers having seen their sister perish, went home. Their mother inquired, "Oh! my sons, where is the daughter?" They replied, "We have given her to the tank. A certain jugi gosae said to us, 'Unless you offer up your sister you will never get water.'" On hearing this she loudly wailed the loss of her daughter. Her sons strove to mitigate her grief by saying, "Look mother, we undertook the excavation of the tank to perpetuate our name, and to gain the fruit of a meritorious work. And unless there be water in the tank for men and cattle to drink, where is the perpetuation of our name? By our offering up the daughter the tank is full to overflowing. So the cattle can now quench their thirst, and travellers, when they encamp nearby and drink the water, will say, 'The excavators of this tank deserve the thanks of all. We, and others who pass by are recipients of their bounty. Their merit is indeed great.'" In this way with many such like arguments they sought to allay their mother's grief.

Right in the center of the tank, where the girl was drowned, there sprang up an Upel flower, the purple sheen of which filled the beholder with delight.

It has already been stated that the girl had been betrothed, and that her family had received the money for her. The day appointed for the marriage arrived, and the bridegroom's party, with drums, elephants, and horses, set out for the bride's house. On arrival they were informed that she had left her home, and that all efforts to trace her had proved fruitless. So they returned home greatly disappointed. It so happened that their way lay past the tank in which the girl had been sacrificed, and the bridegroom, from his palki, saw the Upel flower in the center. As he wished to possess himself of it, he ordered his bearers to set down the palki, and stepping out prepared to swim out to pluck the flower. His companions tried to dissuade him, but as he insisted he was permitted to enter the water. He swam to within a short distance of the flower, but as he stretched out his hand to pluck it, the Upel flower, moving away, said, "Chi! Chi! Chi! Chi! You may be either a Dom or a Hadi, do not touch me." The bridegroom replied, "Not so. Are not we two one?" He made another effort to seize the flower, but it again moved away, saying, "Chi! Chi! Chi! Chi! you may be a Dom or a Hadi, so do not touch me." To which he replied, "Not so. You and I are one." He swam after it again, but the flower eluded his grasp, and said, "Chi! Chi! Chi! Chi! You may be a Dom, or you may be a Hadi, so do not touch me." He said, "Not so. You and I are bride and bridegroom for ever." Then the Upel flower allowed itself to be plucked, and the bridegroom returned to his company bearing it with him.

He entered his palki and the cortege started. They had not proceeded far before the bearers were convinced that the palki was increasing in weight. They said, "How is it that it is now so heavy? A short time ago it was light." So they pushed aside the panel, and beheld the bride and bridegroom sitting side by side. The marriage party on hearing the glad news rejoiced exceedingly. They beat drums, shouted, danced, and fired off guns. Thus they proceeded on their homeward way.

When the bridegroom's family heard the noise, they said, one to the other, "Sister, they have arrived." Then they went forth to meet the bridegroom, and brought them in with great rejoicing. The bride was she who had been the Upel flower, and was exceedingly beautiful. In form she was both human and divine. The village people, as well as the marriage guests, when they saw her, exclaimed, "What a beautiful bride! She is the fairest bride that we have seen. She has no peer." Thus they all praised her beauty.

It so happened that in the meantime the mother and brothers of the girl had become poor. They were reduced to such straits as to be compelled to sell firewood for a living. So one day the brothers went to the bridegroom's village with firewood for sale. They offered it to one and another, but no one would buy. At last someone said, "Take it to the house in which the marriage party is assembled. They may require it." So the brothers went there, and asked, "Will you buy firewood?" They replied, "Yes. We will take it." Someone informed the bride that some men from somewhere had brought firewood for sale. So she went out, and at once recognized her brothers, and said to them, "Put down your loads." And when they had done so she placed beds for them to sit on, and brought them water; but they did not know that she was their sister, as she was so greatly changed. Then she gave them vessels of oil, and said, "Go bathe, for you will dine here today." So they took the oil, and went to bathe, but they were so hungry that they drank the oil on the way. So they bathed, and returned to the house. She then brought them water to wash their hands, and they sat down in a row to eat. The bride gave her youngest brother food on a brass plate, because he had not approved of what had been done to her, but to the others she gave it on leaf plates.

They had only eaten one handful of rice when the girl placed herself in front of them, and putting a hand upon her head, began to weep bitterly. She exclaimed, "Oh! my brothers, you had no pity upon me. You threw me away as an offering to the tank. You saw me lost, and then went home." When the brothers heard this they felt as if their breasts were torn open. If they looked up to heaven, heaven was high. Then they saw an axe, which they seized, and with it they struck the ground with all their might. It opened like the mouth of a large tiger, and the brothers plunged in. The girl caught the youngest brother by the hair to pull him up, but it came away in her hand, and they all disappeared into the bowels of the earth, which closed over them.

The girl held the hair in her hand and wept over it. She then planted it, and from it sprang the hair like Bachkom[3] grass, and from that time Bachkom grass grows in the jungles.

The sister had pity on her youngest brother because he did not join heartily with the others in causing her death. So she tried to rescue him from the fate which was about to overtake him, but in this she failed, and he suffered for the sins of his brothers.

"How Sabai Grass Grew"

Once upon a time there were seven brothers who had an only sister. These brothers undertook the excavation of a large tank; but although they spent large sums and dug very deep they could not reach water and the tank remained dry.

One day as they were consulting what to do to get the tank to fill, they saw a Jogi coming towards them with a lota in his hand; they at once called to him to come and advise them, for they thought that, as he spent his time wandering from country to country, he might somewhere have learned something which would be of use to them. All the Jogi said to them was, "You have a sister: if you sacrifice her, the tank will fill with water." The brothers were fond of the girl, but in their despair at seeing their labor wasted they agreed to give the advice of the Jogi a trial. So they told their mother the next day that, when their sister brought them out their midday meal, she was to be dressed in her best and carry the rice in a new basket and must bring a new water-pot to draw their water in. At midday the girl went down to her brothers with her best cloth and all her jewelry on; and when they saw their victim coming they could not keep from tears. She asked them what they were grieving for; they told her that nothing was the matter and sent her to draw water in her new water-pot from the dry tank. Directly the girl drew near to the bank the water began to bubble up from the bottom; and when she went down to the water's edge it rose to her instep. She bent down to fill her pot but the pot would not fill though the water rose higher and higher; then she sang:

> "The water has risen, brother,
> And wetted my ankle, brother,
> But still the lota in my hand
> Will not sink below the surface."

But the water rose to her knees and the pot would not fill, and she sang:

> "The water has risen, brother,
> And wetted my knees, brother,
> But still the lota in my hand
> Will not sink below the surface."

Then the water rose to her waist and the pot would not fill, and she sang:

> "The water has risen, brother,
> And wetted my waist, brother,
> But still the lota in my hand
> Will not sink below the surface."

Then the water reached her neck and the pot would not fill, and she sang:

> "The water has risen, brother,
> And wetted my neck, brother,
> But still the lota in my hand
> Will not sink below the surface."

At last it flowed over her head and the water-pot was filled, but the girl was drowned. The tank, however, remained brimful of sparkling water.

Now, the unhappy girl had been betrothed and her wedding day was just at hand. On the day fixed the marriage broker came to announce the approach of the bridegroom, who shortly afterwards arrived at the outskirts of the village in his palki. The seven brothers met him, and the usual dancing began.

The bridegroom's party however wished to know why the bride did not appear. The brothers put them off with various excuses, saying that the girl had gone with her friends to gather firewood or to the river to draw water. At last the bridegroom's party got tired of waiting and turned to go home in great wrath at the way in which they had been treated. On their way they passed by the tank in which the girl had been sacrificed and, growing in the middle of it, they saw a most beautiful flower. The bridegroom at once determined to possess this, and he told his drummers to pick it for him; but whenever one of them tried to pick it, the flower moved out of his reach and a voice came from the flower saying: "Take the flower, drummer, / But the branch you must not break." And when they told him what the flower sang, the bridegroom said that he would try to pick it himself; no sooner had he reached the bank than the flower of its own accord

22

floated towards him, and he pulled it up by the roots and took it with him into the palki. After they had gone a little way the palki bearers felt the palki strangely heavy; and when they looked in they found the bride also sitting in it, dressed in yellow garments, for the flower was really the girl who had been drowned.

So they joyfully took the happy couple with drumming and music to the bridegroom's house.

In a short time misfortune befell the seven brothers; they fell into the deepest poverty and were forced to earn what they could by selling leaves and sticks which they gathered in the jungle. As they went about selling these, they one day came to the village where their sister was living, and as they cried their wares through the streets they were told to go to the house where the marriage had taken place. They went there, and as they were selling their leaf plates their sister saw and recognized them; they had only ragged loincloths on, and their skins were black and cracked like a crocodile's.

At the sight their sister began to cry. Her friends asked what was the matter and she said a straw from the thatch had run into her eye, so they pulled down some of the thatch; she still went on crying and they again asked what was wrong; she said that she had knocked her foot against a stone in the ground; so they dug up the stone and threw it away. But she still went on weeping and at last confessed that the miserable-looking leaf-sellers were her brothers. Then her husband's parents told her to be comforted, and they gave the brothers oil and bade them go and bathe and oil their bodies. But the brothers were so hungry that when they got to the bathing place they drank the oil and ate the oil cake that had been given to them, and came back with their skins as rough as when they went. So then they were given more oil and some of the household went with them and made them bathe and oil themselves properly and then brought them to the house and gave them new clothes and made them a feast of meat and rice. According to the custom of the country they were made to sit down in order of age and were helped in that order; when they had all been helped and had eaten, their sister said to them, "Now brothers you come running to me for food, and yet you sacrificed me in the tank." Then they were overwhelmed with shame: they looked up at the sky but there was no escape there; they looked down at the earth; and the earth split open and they all ran into the chasm. The sister tried to catch the youngest brother by the hair and pull him out, calling, "Come back, brother, come back brother, you shall carry my baby about for me!" but his hair came off in her hand and the earth swallowed them all up. Their sister planted the hair in

23

a corner of the garden and it is said that, from that human hair, *sabai* grass originated.

Notes

1. *Bad Bonga* is the spirit believed to preside over a certain class of rice land.
2. Both the Dom and the Hadi are semi-Hinduized aborigines, whose touch is considered polluting.
3. *Eulaliopsis binata* (Retz.), previously named *Ischæmum angustifolium* (Trin.) Hack.

"Story of the Bridge"

If one wished to make a case for a possible Indic origin for the ballad of "The Walled-Up Wife," one might ponder how the ballad diffused all the way from India to the Balkans. An obvious means of such a path of diffusion would be the Gypsies, a people which originated in India but which has spread in its diaspora to Europe and beyond. In this context, a Turkish-Gypsy version of our story reported by famed Gypsiologist Francis Hindes Groome in 1899 is of considerable importance. Groome's note to the tale suggests he almost did not publish the tale because he considered it fragmentary and confused. However, he does correctly note the parallel to the Balkans versions of the ballad. Manole, for example, is the name of the central character in many Romanian versions, a name clearly cognate with the character of Manoli in this Turkish-Gypsy text.

In olden days there were twelve brothers. And the eldest brother, the carpenter Manoli, was making the long bridge. One side he makes; one side falls. The twelve brothers had one mistress, and they all had to do with her. They called her to them, "Dear bride." On her head was the tray; in her hands was a child. Whoseso wife came first, she will come to the twelve brothers. Manoli's wife, Lénga, will come to the twelve brothers. Said his wife, "Thou hast not eaten bread with me. What has befallen thee that thou eatest not bread with me? My ring has fallen into the water. Go and fetch my ring." Her husband said, "I will fetch thy ring out of the water." Up to his two breasts came the water in the depth of the bridge there. He came into the fountain, he was drowned. Beneath he became a talisman, the innermost foundation of the bridge. Manoli's eyes became the great open arch of the bridge. "God send a wind to blow, that the tray may fall from the head of her who bears it in front of Lénga." A snake crept out before Lénga, and she feared, and said, "Now have I fear at sight of the snake, and am sick. Now is it not bad for my children?" Another man seized her, and sought to drown her, Manoli's wife. She said, "Drown me not in the water. I have little

Reprinted from Francis Hindes Groome, *Gypsy Folk-Tales* (London: Hurst and Blackett, Ltd., 1899), pp. 12–13.

children." She bowed herself over the sea, where the carpenter Manoli made the bridge. Another man called Manoli's wife; with him she went on the road. There, when they went on the road, he went to the tavern, he was weary; the man went, drank the juice of the grape, got drunk. Before getting home, he killed Manoli's wife, Lénga.

I hesitated whether to give this story; it is so hopelessly corrupt, it seems such absolute nonsense. Yet it enshrines beyond question, however confusedly, the widespread and ancient belief that to ensure one's foundation one should wall up a human victim. So St. Columba buried St. Oran alive in the foundation of his monastery; in Western folklore, however, the victim is usually an infant—a bastard sometimes, in one case (near Göttingen) a deaf-mute. But in southeastern Europe it is almost always a woman—the wife of the master builder, whose name, as here, is Manoli. Reinhold Köhler has treated the subject admirably in his *Aufsätze über Märchen und Volkslieder;*[1] there one finds much to enlighten the darkness of our original. "God send a wind," etc., is the husband's prayer as he sees his wife coming towards him, and hopes to avert her doom; "My ring has fallen into the water," etc., must also be his utterance, when he finds that it is hopeless, that she has to die. The Gypsy story is probably of high antiquity, for two at least of the words in it were quite or almost meaningless to the nomade Gypsy who told it.[2] The masons of southeastern Europe are, it should be noticed, largely Gypsies; and a striking Indian parallel may be pointed out in the Santal story of "Seven Brothers and Their Sister."[3] Here seven brothers set to work to dig a tank, but find no water, so, by the advice of a *yogi,* give their only sister to the spirit of the tank. "The tank was soon full to the brim, and the girl was drowned." And then comes a curious mention of a Dom, or Indian vagrant musician, whose name is probably identical with Doum, Lom, or Rom, the Gypsy of Syria, Asia Minor, and Europe.

Notes

1. Reinhold Köhler, *Aufsätze über Märchen und Volkslieder* (Berlin, 1894), pp. 36–47.
2. Alexandre G. Paspati, *Études sur les Tchinghianés* (Constantinople: Antoine Koroméla, 1870), p. 190.
3. G. A. Campbell, *Santal Folk Tales* (Pokhuria: Santal Mission Press, 1891), pp. 106–10.

"The Song of the Bridge"

A second Turkish-Gypsy text serves to confirm the presence of the plot in Gypsy tradition. The text was reported by Gilliat-Smith in 1925 in the Journal of the Gypsy Lore Society, *where it was accompanied by a learned comparative note by Professor W. R. Halliday. The Romani (Gypsy) text, which includes many Turkish words, has not been reproduced here. Halliday's attempt to delineate a typology of the legend is noteworthy. He distinguishes between "The Bridge of Arta" found in Greek tradition and "The Building of Scutari" (= Skadar) found "among the other Balkan peoples." As a classicist, Halliday perhaps tended to favor the Greek versions by suggesting that the "most famous" texts were those of "the Greek folksong 'The Bridge of Arta.'" Folklorists from other countries certainly disputed the issue of which texts were the most "famous" or artistic. Also of interest is Halliday's peremptory dismissal of Groome"s suggestion of a possible Indic parallel to the story.*

"The Ballad of the Bridge"

1

"We have no father, we have no mother, to give us at least good counsel. How shall we make this eight years' bridge, O friends, O God?"

"What counsel shall I give you, my little ones, my young ones, my little children?

Come now and lie down in sleep. What will appear unto your lucky eyes determine in your lucky dream, O friends, O my children.

2

What will appear you will tell unto your lucky eyes."

Three brothers in their sleep determined in their lucky dreams. At one moment of the night one brother arose with a start from sleep. He arose, lit his fire, pushed the coffee pot onto the fire. He began once more to cogitate, once more he began to worry and to fret.

Reprinted from "The Song of the Bridge," *Journal of the Gypsy Lore Society* (series 3) 4 (1925): 103–14, by B. J. Gilliat-Smith, with a Note by Prof. W. R. Halliday.

3

"Come arise, O brothers, my happy ones, from your sleep. Much sweet sleep you have now slept, my little young brothers, aaah! Now I have seen a lucky dream. Let me make known to you, and tell you, my lucky dream."

4

"All hail," they say, "to thy lucky dream. Come tell us thy lucky dream."
"I will tell you, but perchance you may be angry." "We will not be angry. Come speak out thy lucky dream." "I will tell it, my little brothers. Tonight this fateful bridge desires from us a sacrifice."
The eldest brother said: "I have three little children. How shall I forgo them. Before sacrificing them, which one must I give?"
The middle brother said: "I have two little ones. Before sacrificing them, which one must I give?"
The smallest said: "I have one little one, O my friends, my masters. How shall I choose him for the sacrifice?

5

I have not yet had any pleasure in the possession of my child."
Now spoke the eldest brother: "Be not angry with me. Wives are from our hands, sons are from our loins. Of the first there are still many in the world. And perchance we too may find better ones. Whose wife brings us bread, her let us at least sacrifice, O my Lord's brothers."

6[1]

Now the roads have reddened.[2] Now they are looking who cometh.
The tray on her head; the napkin over her shoulder; a three-days-old babe is in her arms. Behold, O God, her napkin on her shoulder. Behold she comes, the beautiful bride of Minar the Čeribaši, O my friends, O God.

7

Yet grant, O God, a great squall of rain, or a great gust of wind, that her fated foot may slip, that her tray may fall from her head, that she may turn back and go to her three-days-old babe, O my friends, O God.

8

Neither rain came nor wind blew. Behold there came the fated bride of Minar the Čheribaši.
"All hail to thee, O Čheribaši Minar. All hail to you, O Master Masons. All hail to you, O my Lords. But, my friends, wherefore are you thus cogitating? Is it that you are angry with me? There was to me this day a babe of youthful days, late I washed my babe, and put to sleep, and late I brought you your bread: perchance for that you are angry?

9

And ye are cross and enraged for that? Come, friends, be seated, wash your hands, that we may eat each two mouthfuls of bread. For our day is this day and our hour is this hour. Since today our limbs áre sound, be seated that we may eat together each two mouthfuls of bread.

10

But, masters, why is your brother crying?"

"Look not at him, O bride, he is somewhat foolish. Today as he was lifting stones and planks, he let fall and lost from his hands his ring. For that the little one is crying."

"But," she said, "I have twelve brothers, all goldsmiths."

11

I will have thy ring made all of silver, and have it wrought all from the purest gold. I will have thy ring made again. Come, that we may eat together each two mouthfuls of bread."

12

"I do not want another ring. My ring remained to me from my father and my mother as a keepsake. Come, stoop down, with me, that we may search for this my ring, my friends, among these stones and these lucky planks."

"Behold, I will search with my husband for his ring. My husband, be not angry, worry not, my young husband, we will search for the lucky ring."

They arise. Here they search, there is no ring, there they search, there is no ring. They went near to the foundation of the bridge. Minar the Čheribaši descended. He planted his feet into the foundation. "O friend, beautiful one, give me your little hand. My strength is nearly spent.

13

Help me, pull me, that I may get myself out from here." "But," she said, "three nights more are my possession. I too saw in my dream that you will give me as a sacrifice to this fateful bridge.

And my twenty finger and toe nails, may the whole twenty be in your side, if you do not bring my Paul, place him in my arms, take out my breast and put it in his mouth. Thus shall my blood become lawful unto you.

14

Grant, O God, to this bridge, by thy power at both ends two cypress branches, that they may be placed as a cradle for my Paul. Further when sheep pass may they give him their udders. When rain falls may it bathe him. As many leaves as are shed, may they cover him. When the wind blows may it rock his cradle, a lullaby, my Paul, a lullaby, that my Paul may sleep."

The belief in the necessity and efficacy of "foundation sacrifice" in order to secure the stability of buildings is worldwide. Particulars about the consequent practices and their distribution together with references to the principal literature on the subject will be found in Hartland's article in Hastings' Encylopaedia of Religion and Ethics.[3]

Of this universal belief "The Song of the Bridge" is a specialized product. It is very widely distributed among the peoples of the Balkan area and this, I am sure, must be considered its home. Gypsy versions from this area are the hopelessly corrupt version from Paspati reproduced by Groome, *Gypsy Folk-Tales,* and a good Serbian-Gypsy version by Gjorgjević.[4]

Groome suggested that an Indian tale provides "a striking parallel."[5] Actually the parallel does not extend further than the building of a tank by seven brothers and the drowning of their sister (not the wife of one of them), in order that the tank may fill with water. The similarity, in fact, is derived merely from the common origin of the two stories in the belief in the necessity for foundation sacrifice, which we have noted to be worldwide. I have personally no doubt whatever that "The Song of the Bridge" is a localized form of story arising out of this widespread custom and belongs properly to the Balkan area. I am doubtful whether even the legend about the bridge at Zakho in Eastern Kurdistan[6] is a true variant. Probably the similarity is due to the coincidence of the independent invention of a similar story in connection with an identical magical belief; possibly it is really a variant, but in that case the dissimilarities would suggest that it has been brought there from the Balkan area and has suffered in transit. The bridge at Zakho demanded a life before it would stand. The firstcomer was to be sacrificed. A beautiful girl accompanied by a bitch and her puppies came in sight. In spite of the efforts of the masons, the bitch held back and the girl reached the bridge first. She was built into it alive, and only one hand with its gold bracelet remained visible outside the bridge.

The most famous of the Songs of the Bridge is, of course, the Greek folksong "The Bridge of Arta." This is well known all over Greece, and the legend is also attached to a number of other bridges in different parts of the Greek world. Politis claimed that over forty variant Greek versions were known to him.[7] A similar ballad is also widely spread among the other Balkan peoples, Albanians, Serbs, Bulgarians, Hungarians, and Romanians.[8]

Two variant types of the legend are distinguishable. I will call them "The Bridge of Arta," which is the usual form in Greek folksong, and "The Building of Scutari," which is the predominant type among the other Balkan peoples. Naturally in individual versions there is sometimes a conflation of the two types.

In "The Bridge of Arta" type a single master craftsman, usually named Manoli, and a large number of builders and apprentices fail to make the bridge stand; they are warned by a dream, a voice from the bridge, a demon from the bridge, or an archangel, to sacrifice the master craftsman's wife. The master craftsman sends the nightingale to warn his wife to delay, but the bird delivers the message in the opposite sense. The wife arrives decked in her best clothes; her husband's obvious distress is explained to her as due to his having dropped his ring. She descends to find the ring and is built into the foundation. She laments her fate, and recalls that of her two sisters, who were both similarly immured elsewhere. She curses the bridge that it may tremble like her heart and sway like her waving hair, but is induced to change her speech to a charm that it may stand like iron, as her heart has become like iron, lest her brother in foreign parts should return and pass over the bridge.

In "The Building of Scutari" there are three (the number varies) brothers who are the builders of the fortress at the orders of King Vukashin. A warning is given by a vila, dream, voice, etc., that the wife of *one of the three* must be sacrificed. They decide that they will leave the choice to fate, and that the one who comes first or brings the dinner on the morrow shall be the victim. But two of the brothers break faith and secretly warn their wives, who consequently stay at home next day and compel or induce their sister-in-law to carry out the dinner. In some versions the treachery of the brothers in breaking their oath of silence is omitted. The brother whose wife is seen approaching prays God to send a storm of wind and rain to keep her away, but in vain, the devoted wife struggles through to her doom. Her husband's grief is explained as due to the loss of a golden apple or ring; she is enticed down and is built in by the workmen. At first she thinks that they are merely joking, then, as the building reaches her girdle, she realizes the grim reality and "writhes like a snake." She finally implores them at least to leave a hole for her breast through which she may suckle her babe.

This type of ballad is associated with other buildings besides the fortress at Scutari, but only at the latter, so far as I know, is there an actual phenomenon to account for the last and characteristic episode. From the foundations at Scutari there is a place from which a chalky water drips, which is still used by mothers as a tonic for infants. This is the spot where the heroine suckled her child.

Contrary to the general view I am inclined to think "The Building of Scutari" the better and more original version than "The Bridge of Arta," the claim of which to be the parent of the legend in other

Balkan lands rests partly on the fact that it is more widely known and partly upon the quite irrelevant ground that a larger number of the modern Greek variants happen to have been collected and published.

Groome's version from Paspati is hopelessly corrupt, but belongs to the "Scutari" rather than the "Arta" type. It most resembles the Romanian version associated with the Monastery of Argeş. In this, too, the hero is Manoli, perhaps as a result of conflation with "The Bridge of Arta," and in this too the fall and death of the master craftsman follows the immuring of his wife. At the spot where he fell there is a brackish spring. Of this death of Manoli the conclusion of Paspati's version is a confused reminiscence. Similarly the mysterious snake which appears[9] must really be derived from the episode in which, when the stones reach her middle, the unfortunate victim "writhes like a snake."

The Serbian-Gypsy version recorded by Gjorgjević also belongs to "The Building of Scutari" type. Twelve brothers are warned by the emperor (= King Vukashin of the Serbian ballad) that the bridge must be completed by a certain date. They agree (the magical warning is missing) to sacrifice one of their wives, the one who first comes with the dinner. The wife of Hassan, the eldest brother, says to her sisters-in-law, "Come let us take out the dinner," puts the basin on her head, and takes her child with her. Hassan, seeing her coming, prays God to send a rainstorm and a bitter wind that the child may freeze and she turn back. The rain falls and the food is being spoiled in the basin, but the wife takes it out and struggles through with it in her hand. "Why is my Hassan so sad?" "I have lost my silver ring." "I have seven brothers, goldsmiths, who will make you another." But the eleven brothers-in-law take her off (the ruse of looking for the ring has dropped out) and wall her up. She prays them to leave her left breast and right hand free for her to suckle her child, a little room for a sheep to pass that her son may sleep, that rain may fall to wash the child and wind blow to rock his cradle. This confused ending is obviously a distortion of that represented by our version.

Mr. Gilliat-Smith's version, clearly of the "Scutari" type, now needs little comment. The dream is a form of magical warning which often occurs. The prayer for rain and wind in stanzas 6–7 differs only from the Serbian-Gypsy version in being unanswered, instead of failing in its purpose. The lost ring motif is better preserved in our version, as is also the concluding prayer.

We may perhaps notice that the problem of the brothers is developed in stanza 5 in rather an unusual and interesting way. It seems an illogical distortion (for if there are more wives to be had, there are also more children to be had, as the Egyptian deserters in Herodotus, 2.30, rather crudely pointed out) of a very old motif which occurs from a common source in the *Jatakas* and in the *Ramayana*, though as early as Herodotus (3.119) it appears in European literature as the Persian story of "Intaphernes' Wife." From Herodotus, Sophocles borrowed it for his *Antigone* 909–12.[10] A woman is given the choice of saving either husband or children or brother from execution; she chooses her brother, on the ground that she can get another husband or more children but not another brother, since her parents are dead or too old to have children.

Notes

The preceding version of the well-known "Conte du Pont," familiar to Gypsy students from the very muddled version printed by Paspati, was taken down from the old blind singer of Roustchouk, of whom a photograph appeared in the *Journal of Gypsy Lore Society*, n.s. 7 (1912 or 1913): 51.

1. In this verse there is a change in music and meter. The first lines are much quicker and almost recitative; then a wail and back to the original melody.

2. The roads have reddened with the setting sun.

3. Hartland, *Hasting's Encyclopaedia of Religion and Ethics*, 6, pp. 112–15, s.v. "Foundation."

4. Francis Hindes Groome, *Gypsy Folk-Tales* (London: Hurst and Blackett, Ltd., 1899), pp. 12–13; Gjorgjević, *Mitteilungen zur Zigeunerkunde* 2 (1906): 121–23.

5. See G. A. Campbell, *Santal Folk-Tales* (Pokhuria: Santal Mission Press, 1891), pp. 106–10; compare Cecil Henry Bompas, *Folklore of the Santal Parganas* (London: David Nutt, 1909), pp. 102–6.

6. M. Sykes, *Dar-ul-Islam* (London: Bickers, 1904), p. 160.

7. See John Cuthbert Lawson, *Modern Greek Folklore and Ancient Greek Religion* (Cambridge: Cambridge University Press, 1904), pp. 262–63; Lucy M. J. Garnett, *Greek Folk Poesy*, Vol. 1 (Guildford: Billig, 1896), pp. 70–72; Politis, Ἐκλογαί ἀπὸ τὰ τραγούδια τοῦ Ἑλληνικοῦ λαοῦ, παράρτημα τῆς Λαογραφίας, Vol. 1 (Athens, 1914), pp. 130, 287; Λαογραφία, Vol. 1 (1909), pp. 15, 630–31.

8. Reinhold Köhler, *Aufsätze über Märchen und Volkslieder* (Berlin, 1894), pp. 38–47; Auguste Dozon, *Contes Albanais* (Paris: E. Leroux, 1881), pp. 255–57; E. B. Mawr, *Roumanian Fairy Tales and Legends* (London: H. K. Lewis, 1881), pp. 97–105; W. Henry Jones and Lewis L. Kropf, *Magyar Folk-Tales* (London: E. Stock, 1889), pp. 376–77.

The references could be multiplied, but these are probably sufficient for practical purposes. In compiling this note I have had the advantage of consulting a MS collection of material by Mr. Scott Macfie. I have not been able to procure L. Sainéan, "Rites de construction d'après la poésie populaire de l'Europe orientale," *Revue de l'histoire des religions* 45 (1902): 359–96, or Dieterich's article in *Zeitschrift des Vereins für Volkskunde* (1902): 150–52.

9. Groome, *Gypsy Folk-Tales*, p. 12, three lines up from the bottom.

10. See Richard Pischel in *Hermes* 28 (1893): 465–68.

PAUL G. BREWSTER

The Foundation Sacrifice Motif in Legend, Folksong, Game, and Dance

In the nearly two hundred years of scholarly discussion of "The Walled-Up Wife," there is one theoretical approach which has prevailed. This approach, which we normally refer to as the "myth-ritual" approach, takes a literal rather than a metaphorical or symbolic reading of the text. Accordingly, a story-line which involves the sacrifice of a young woman to ensure the successful construction of a bridge, castle, or monastery was understood to refer to an actual historical custom whereby female victims were "ritually" killed as a form of "foundation sacrifice."

One serious difficulty with the myth-ritual theory is that it is not an ultimate origins explanation. In other words, if myth (or some other genre: folktale, ballad, game, etc.) derives from an actual ritual, where did that ritual come from? That issue is rarely, if ever, addressed. The critical ritual is simply stated as an axiomatic given.

Another problem with the myth-ritual theory is that one almost never finds concrete documentary evidence of the alleged ritual actually occurring. Rather it is just assumed that a particular ritual must have occurred in the far distant past.

The following essay by Paul G. Brewster, one of America's foremost authorities on traditional games, is primarily concerned with foundation sacrifice, not with "The Walled-Up Wife." However, inasmuch as Brewster devoted a substantial portion of his essay to different versions of the ballad as examples of foundation sacrifice, it was deemed worthwhile to include it in this casebook.

For a historical account of the approach, see Robert Ackerman, The Myth and Ritual School (New York: Garland, 1991). For examples of the approach, see P. Saintyves, Les contes de Perrault et les récits parallèles: Coutumes primitives et liturgies populaires (Paris: E. Nourry, 1923); and Lewis Spence, Myth and Ritual in Dance, Game, and Rhyme (London: Watts and Co., 1947). For critiques, see Joseph Fontenrose, The Ritual Theory of Myth (Berkeley: University

Reprinted from the Zeitschrift für Ethnologie 96 (1971): 71–89.

of California Press, 1966); and Robert A. Segal, "The Myth-Ritualist Theory of Religion," Journal for the Scientific Study of Religion *19 (1980): 173–85.*

One of the most widespread of superstitions is undoubtedly the belief that the immuring of a human victim in an edifice under construction ensures its permanence. So old is this belief that its origin is lost in the haze of antiquity. As we learn from the Scriptures, the practice was familiar to the Old Testament Jews. When Hiel the Bethelite wished to rebuild Jericho, "he laid the foundations thereof in Abiram, his firstborn, and set up the gates thereof in his youngest son, Segub."[1]

In ancient India the favorite sacrificial victim was a pregnant woman, and there is at Hampi a wall, sacred to women pilgrims, in memory of the time when Nachapurusa Bhistapaya buried his pregnant daughter beneath it to prevent its falling down, as it had done several times previously. It is on record that in 1872 when the Hooghly Bridge was being built across the Ganges the native population feared that to placate the river each structure would have to be founded on a layer of children's skulls.[2] The sacrifice of children is said still to occur sporadically in India, and there is in consequence an everpresent fear among the natives that their children may be kidnapped for sacrifice or for burial in the foundations of a structure being erected.

In Borneo a slave girl used to be flung into the hole for the first pole of a house and crushed to death when the pole descended. The same practice obtained in Fiji. In Siam when a new gate was being erected in the wall of a town, the builders would lie in wait and seize the first passerby, who was then buried alive beneath the gateposts.[3]

I

Traces of the foundation sacrifice abound in European legend and tradition. When Romulus founded the city of Rome, Faustulus and Quinctilius are said to have been slain and buried in a deep pit under a huge stone. In Britain the legend of Merlin relates that Vortigern could not make his fortifications stand until the foundation stone had been wetted with the blood of a child without a father.[4] The Picts are said to have bathed the foundation stones of the prehistoric "Picts' Houses" with human blood,[5] and there is also a tradition that London Bridge was "sanctified" by the blood of children.[6] Similar legends (Serbian and Montenegrin) exist about a bridge near Vishegrad and (Bulgarian) about a fort near Plovdiv.[7]

In 1615, Count Anthony Günther of Oldenburg, visiting a dyke under construction, is said to have found the workmen about to bury a child beneath it. He rescued the child and reprimanded the mother, who had sold it for the purpose.[8] When the castle of Liebenstein in Thuringia was being built, a child was purchased from the mother and walled in. As the masons worked, the little one cried, "Mother, I see thee still." Later, as the wall rose around him, he said, "Mother, I see thee a little still." As the last stone was put in place, he cried piteously, "Mother, now I see thee no more."[9] There is a similar tradition regarding the walls of Copenhagen, of which it is related that they could not stand until a little girl was built into the rampart.[10] Two brothers are said to have been entombed in the foundation of Strasburg Cathedral.[11] When the bridge of Rosporden in Brittany was being built it fell down repeatedly, and finally it was decided to immure a victim. A little boy of four was built in, with a candle in one hand and a piece of bread in the other, and when the wind howls at night he can be heard crying: "Ma chandelle est morte, ma mère, / Et de pain, il ne m'en reste guère."[12] At the building of the Celso Bridge between Caudan and Faouet in France a child was placed in a barrel and sealed into the foundation. And in Germany as recently as 1843, when a new bridge was to be built at Halle, the notion was abroad among the people that a child was wanted to be built into the foundation.[13] Similar traditions have been localized at Aberystwyth in Wales, Frankfurt in Germany, and the St. Gotthard Pass in Switzerland.

The discovery in later years of skeletons at spots where immurement was reputed to have taken place furnishes grim testimony to the veracity of such legends and traditions. A maiden is said to have been buried alive in a wall of the castle of Nieder Manderscheid. When in 1844 the wall was broken open at the point indicated by the legend, a skeleton was found embedded in it.[14] Similarly, at the demolishing of the Bridge Gate at Bremen the skeleton of a child was found.[15] There have been numerous instances of the immuring of a human being in English churches. Upon the restoration of the parish church of Wickenby in Lincolnshire, the complete skeleton of a man was found buried in the foundation of the west wall.[16] When the parish church of Holsworthy (Devon) was restored in 1885, a skeleton was found embedded in stone and mortar in one of the walls. It was noticed that a portion of the wall in which the skeleton lay was faulty and had settled. There were signs of the victim's having been buried alive and hurriedly.[17] And in the course of the restoration of a church at Brownsover in 1876, workmen found two complete skeletons under the walls. These lay in a small excavation and were covered with slabs of oak, over which the original foundation had been laid.[18]

A later development was the substitution of a model of the human victim. This was made of wax, straw, clay, bronze, silver, or almost any other substance. Substitution of the sham for the real has, of course, been common in sacrifices of all kinds down through the ages. The Romans substituted puppets for the human sacrifices to the goddess Mania and threw rush dolls into the Tiber at the atoning sacrifice held annually on the Sublician Bridge. Even earlier, the Egyptians offered an animal to their gods instead of a man, but first marked the animal with a seal bearing the image of the man bound and kneeling, with a sword at his throat.[19]

In some instances later and in others concurrently we find also the belief that the shadow of a man or a child measured and then walled up or deposited in the foundation would make the building or the bridge firm. The person whose shadow was measured and buried would die soon after. The Romanians of Transylvania believe that if the mason lays the foundation stone upon a man's shadow, the man will die within forty days, and people passing a building in course of erection are likely to hear, "Beware lest they take thy shadow."[20] The belief is current also in Greece. In a personal communication of 6 February 1956, Miss Georgia Tarsouli writes me: "In a variant [of 'The Bridge of Arta'] which I collected in the form of a legend from South Peloponnese the advice (of the river spirit) was to nail the shadow of the first passer-by. And as the man was coming, the mason with a hammer and a huge nail nailed his shadow to the foundation, and thus the building became solid but the man died soon after."[21]

There was also the actual and symbolic sacrifice of animals, whereby a fowl—usually a cock—or an animal was killed and its blood allowed to drip into the foundation pit. The practice survives in, among other places, modern Greece. Miss Tarsouli writes: "There is the custom, all over Greece, at the construction of any building to kill a black rooster over the first foundation stone. Its head is smashed with a hammer and its blood sprinkled around. The body is then given to the masons, who cook and eat it at a common meal offered by the owner of the house."[22] A dyke in Walcheren is to this day called Hontsdam because the workmen who repaired it in the twelfth century encountered quicksand and could not make the dyke firm until they had buried a live dog beneath it.[23] And in Ireland up to very recent times various animals were sacrificed on laying the foundation of a building.[24]

Although the practice of offering a human sacrifice on laying the foundation of a building was intended originally as a propitiation of the spirits of the earth, who were thought of as being disturbed, later on it sometimes passed into another conception, that the spirit of the victim would be a ghostly guardian of the building being erected. Related to the latter idea is the notion that a hero buried at the gate of a city or on the frontier of a country would protect the city from capture and the country from invasion. Thus Eurystheus,[25] in the *Heraclidae* of Euripides, before being put to death by order of Alkmena, promises the Athenians, in gratitude for their kind intercession on his behalf, forever to protect their territory against their (and his) Peloponnesian enemies; and, curiously enough, his body and severed head were actually buried separately and a good distance apart in two strategically important points. We are told that the head of Ivar, son of Ragnar Lodbrog, was buried in Northumbria to protect that district from invasion; and the head of Bran the Blessed was buried with the face toward France for the same reason.[26]

The idea of foundation sacrifice is also closely associated with the purification of the threshold. The story of the sacrifice of Odhran, or Oran, at the founding of the monastery of Hy (Iona) by St. Columba cannot be lightly dismissed in face of the generally prevalent custom of burying a living creature on such occasions. The only thing to cause wonder is that in a saint's life the account has been allowed to remain. The story is as follows: Said Columcille to his fellow monks: "It is well for us that our roots should go under ground here. It is permitted to you that some one of you should go under the earth here or under the mould of the island to consecrate it." Oran rose up readily, saying, "If I should be taken, I am ready for that." "O Oran," said Columcille, "thou shalt have the reward thereof. No prayer shall be granted to anyone at my grave unless it is first asked of thee." Then Oran went to heaven. Columba founded a church on him afterwards.[27]

In early times the sacrifice was made to placate the earth spirit or (in the case of a bridge) the spirit of the stream. Later, under the influence of Christianity, the devil came to supplant these in the popular mind. Traditionally the ruler and guardian of streams,[28] he was jealous of his prerogatives and resentful of any attempt to infringe upon them by the construction of a bridge. In most of the many folktales on this theme, the builders, dispirited at the repeated destruction of the structure by the vengeful guardian, agree to give him as his due the first living creature to cross on the bridge. Upon the confirmation of the pact they drive across a dog or some other animal, thus cheating the devil of his expected prey, a human being.[29] One such story is attached to the Devil's Bridge across the Reuss; the animal is a dog. The substitution at the completion of the Sachsenhausen Bridge at Frankfurt is a cock.[30]

II

Although the question of provenience of the numerous ballads' treating of the foundation sacrifice is not particularly germane to this paper, it may be said that most of the evidence seems to point to a Greek origin. This is the considered judgment of Entwistle, who sees in Greece the source of many European ballads.[31] Gyula Ortutay, S. Solymossy, and most other Hungarian scholars are in agreement that versions of the story came from Greece and were disseminated throughout the Balkans, Romania, and Hungary.[32] The Bulgarian scholar Arnaudov holds the same view and adds that Serbian and Romanian versions show the influence of the Bulgarian.[33] Shishmanov makes no specific mention of this particular ballad but makes a very strong case for the derivation of several others, among them all versions of the "Dead Brother" ("Constantine and Arete," "The Suffolk Miracle," etc.) in Serbia, Bulgaria, Albania, and Romania, from the Greek.[34]

The Greek ballad bears the title "The Bridge of Adana" (later identified with Arta); however, the locale is sometimes given as Hellada, Antimachia, or elsewhere. The name of the master mason, Manole, first appears in versions from Macedonia, a multilingual region whence the story spread in ballad form to Romania, where the title becomes "Meşterul Manole," to Bulgaria, which knows the ballad as "Mano maïstore," and to other parts of the Balkans. In Greece the hero is identified with a certain Manuel, an engineer whose name appears on a bridge of the seventeenth century. The diffusion from Macedonia appears to have begun sometime between 1650 and 1700.

"The Bridge of Arta"[35]

Forty-five masons and sixty apprentices
were building a bridge across the Arta river.
They built it a whole day, and at night it fell down.
The masons lament and the apprentices weep:

"Woe for our pains, alas for our labors,
To build the whole day and to see it at night fall down!"
A bird flew and sat on the other bank of the river;
it sang not as a bird, neither as a swallow,
but spoke and talked with human voice:
"If you bury not a human being, no bridge can be strong,
and it shall not be an orphan or a stranger or a passerby[36]
but the master mason's own beautiful wife."
(After much hesitation the master mason sends for his wife.)
There is she coming, along the white-shining road.
"Health and joy to you masons and to you apprentices;
what has happened to the master mason that he looks in such grief?"
"His ring fell in the first arch,
and who can go in and come out and search for the ring?"
"Do not worry [master mason?], I will go down;
I will go in and come out and search for thy ring."
She has hardly descended and gone halfway,
one helps with the mortar and the next with the lime,
and the [master mason?] himself takes and throws a huge stone.
"Woe for our fate, alas for our doom,
three sisters were we and all three illfated.
The first founded [?] the Danube bridge and another the Euphrates,
and one, the youngest, founded the bridge of Arta.
As the walnut leaves tremble, so shall tremble the bridge;
as the tree leaves fall, so shall fall the passerby."
"Sweet lady, change thy words and make another wish,
as thou hast an only brother and he may cross the bridge."
"As the wild mountains tremble, so shall tremble the bridge;
as the wild birds fall, thus shall fall the passerby,
for I have an only brother and he may cross the bridge."

In a variant of "The Bridge of Arta" (Tés Ártas tò gefúri) from the island of Corfu we find only a slight divergence from the above text.

Forty-five craftsmen and sixty apprentices:
three years they labored on the bridge of Arta.
All day long they would build it, at night it falls in ruins.
The craftsmen lament and the apprentices weep:
"Alas for our labors, our work is all in vain;
that we should build all day and it should fall at night."
And then the spirit answered from the rightmost arch:
"Unless you devote a human life, no wall is firmly founded;
And sacrifice no orphan, no foreigner, no wayfarer,
but only the beautiful lady, the master craftsman's wife."[37]

The master craftsman tries to warn his wife not to approach the bridge, but the nightingale, which serves as messenger, misunderstands and instead urges her to hasten to the bridge. The conclusion follows that of the first text.

In a version published by Passow[38] the master mason lies down for a nap on Easter Sunday. In a dream he is told that the foundation will never be firm unless a human being be buried in it and that his own wife is to be the victim. He sends laborers to bid her dress in her finest and come quickly. When she arrives, he tells her that he has lost his ring in the foundation, and she volunteers to search for it. As she descends, the workmen heap lime and mortar upon her, and the husband strikes her with his mallet. As in the other two texts, the ballad ends with the wife's curse upon the bridge. Here, however, the curse is not lifted.

In Romanian versions of the ballad the structure being erected is the monastery of Curtea din Argeş or, as in some Transylvanian forms, a bridge on the Danube near the fortified city of Barcan (Banat). Southern Carpathian texts invariably give Manole as the name of the master mason, while in other areas he is Petre, Siminic, or Miclaus. The decision that the first wife to bring her husband's lunch is to be immured is made by the workers.

Incidentally, Transylvanian texts contain several episodes unknown to Greek tradition and foreign even to the Wallachian-Moldavian: the searching by Negru Voda of the "deserted" walls intended as the foundation of the future monastery, the encountering of the shepherd boy (or the young swineherd), Negru Voda's punishment of the masons and their flight down the roof, etc.

"Meşterul Manole"[39]

The ballad begins with the search of Negru Voda (the black voivode) and his ten companions for a site suitable for the constructing of a monastery. Of the ten companions, nine are master masons and Manole is their chief. They meet a flute-playing young shepherd whom the Negru Voda asks about the location of certain deserted walls in the vicinity. The shepherd directs them to the spot, and the Negru Voda instructs his masons to build the monastery there. They are to work with haste day and night. If the edifice meets the expectations of the Negru Voda, they are to be given wealth and the rank of boyars; if not, they are to be buried alive in the foundation.

The masons hurriedly
Stretch out their tapes,
Take their measurements,
And dig deeply into the soil;
Soon they build,
Build a wall.

But all the day's labor
In the night crumbles;
The second day the same;
The third, the same;
The fourth, the same.

Their efforts are in vain,
Because the work of the day
In the night collapses.

The prince, exasperated,
Reproaches them;
Then in his anger
Again threatens
To wall them all up
In the foundations.

The poor masons
Renew their work
And, trembling, labor
All through a summer day
From dawn till dark.

Then Manole
Leaves his tools,
Goes to bed and goes to sleep
And has a strange dream,

Then suddenly rises
And says these words:
"You, my companions,
You nine master masons
Do you know what dream
I have had while asleep?

A voice from Heaven
Told me clearly
That all our works
Will collapse
Until we together
Swear here
To seal up in the wall
The first woman,
Wife or sister,
Who appears
Tomorrow at dawn
Carrying a living thing
For one among you.

If you wish the boon
Of completing the building
Of this holy monastery,
Monument of glory,
Let us swear all together
To keep the secret;
Let us swear to immolate,
To wall up in the wall
The first woman,
Wife or sister,
Who appears
Tomorrow at dawn."

Manole awakens early and immediately begins to climb up the lofty scaffolding, from which he can see far into the distance. He sees his young wife coming along the road, bearing flowers and also food and wine. He falls to his knees, clasps his hands, and prays God for a flood which will make her turn back. God answers his prayer, but she continues to come on. Manole then prays for a great wind. This also is granted. But although the force of the wind uproots trees and overturns mountains, the wife continues to approach.

And now the masons,
Nine master masons
Feel at the sight
A shudder of joy,
While Manole,
Grief in his soul,
Takes her in his arms,
Climbs upon the wall,
Puts her down there—alas!
And speaks to her thus:
"Stay there, my proud love,
Remain there without fear,
Because we want to play a joke,
To pretend to wall you up."

The woman believes him
And laughs goodnaturedly,
While Manole,
Faithful to his dream,
Sighs and begins
To build the wall.

The wall rises
And covers his wife
Up to her ankles,
Up to her knees.

But she, poor thing,
Has stopped laughing
And, seized with fright,
Laments thus:
"Dear Manole, Manole!

Enough of this game,
Because it is fatal.

Dear Manole, Manole,
O, Master Manole!

The wall squeezes me
And breaks my body."

Manole keeps silent
And continues building.

The wall continues to rise to her hips and to her breast. At this point she weeps bitterly and announces that she is about to become a mother.

> The wall presses upon me
> And kills my child;
> My breasts hurt and weep
> Tears of milk.

The wall has now risen to her head and she can hardly be seen. Her groans are barely audible.

> Negru Voda comes
> To pray
> At the holy monastery,
> Glorious monument,
> Without equal in the world.

He asks the master masons if they could ever build a monastery bigger and more beautiful. When they answer boastfully that they can, he throws down the ladder and the scaffolding and leaves them on the roof to perish. They make themselves wings from little boards and attempt to fly through the air.

They fall, and, upon touching the earth, turn into stones. As

Manole is about to leap into the air, he hears issuing from the wall a
feeble voice complaining.

"Dear Manole, Manole
O, Master Manole!
The cold wall weighs upon me,
And breaks my body,
And my breasts are drained
And my life spent."

At these touching words
Manole pales;
His spirit is troubled.
His vision becomes clouded;

He sees everything turning round—
Sky, earth, clouds;
And from the top of the roof
He falls suddenly.[40]

On the spot where he falls
Gushes forth a fountain,
A fountain of clear water,
Bitter and salty,
Water mixed with tears,
With bitter tears!

A Bulgarian version, familiar in the vicinity of Sofia and apparently
typical, has the usual beginning:

Skillful Manoil is building bridges.
He builds them daily, they collapse at night.
Two hundred helpers, three hundred apprentices
For weeks and months have been losing the fight.

Manoil then proposes that, all else having failed, they resort to
magic. The three hundred apprentices and the two hundred helpers
approve the desperate measure; the first wife to arrive with her husband's lunch on Monday is the one destined to be buried alive in the
foundation of the bridge. Each of the workers except Manoil, the hon-
est master builder, tells his wife not to bring his lunch. In an effort
to save his wife, Manoil instructs her to do many extra chores before
bringing his lunch—to bathe the twins, Peter and Pavel, to go to the
mill, to paint the fence, and so on—and then not to hurry in the
morning. As Marika, the wife, passes through the village she calls to
her neighbors to come with her as they do every day, but one by one
they give the same reply, that they will overtake her later.

The elements themselves try to come to Marika's rescue by hin-
dering her progress. As soon as she is out in the fields, a dust storm
sweeps down upon her, filling her husband's lunch with dust and
sand. She returns home, prepares another lunch, and sets forth again.
Now it begins to rain so hard that water, waist deep, covers the road.
But nothing can stop Marika. When Manoil sees her coming, he begins to weep. "Why are you weeping?" asks his wife. He explains
that he has dropped his engagement ring into the foundation of the

45

bridge. Marika goes down to look for the golden ring, and then the others inform her of the hopelessness of her situation. She asks plaintively:

> "Manoil, haven't I been a good wife to you?
> Manoil, didn't I do all you wanted?
> Why do you bury me in this cold ground?
> What will you do about our little children?
> What will you tell them when they cry and ask for me?"

She then begs to be allowed to go and kiss her children goodbye, but the workers feverishly build around her. When the cruel task is completed and the workers have gone home, the master builder, heartbroken, remains to mourn his lost wife and grieve over the future of his two motherless children.[41]

There are in Bulgaria many variants of this tragic story, but all have preserved the fundamental conception that it was necessary to make a human sacrifice in order that a structure might be saved from repeated destruction.

Hungarian folklorists and other Hungarian scholars have devoted a great deal of research to this ballad, partly in an effort to disprove the Romanian claim that the Hungarian form is merely a translation of "Meşterul Manole." The Hungarian ballad, "Kömüves Kelemenné," was first published by Kriza in 1863; since that date twenty-five or more additional versions have been recovered.

"Kömüves Kelemenné"

Twelve masons are charged with the building of the fort of Deva. The walls always collapse. Finally the leader decides that the body of the first wife to visit the spot must be put into the lime. Unknown to him, his own wife is on her way. The coachman warns her not to continue (having had a premonitory dream). Kelemen wishes obstacles to come into her way and thus prevent her coming, but she arrives safely. She is permitted to go home and bid farewell to her friends and her little son, then goes back to meet her fate. The little boy looks everywhere for his mother. He finally wanders to Deva, where he learns what has happened and falls into the ditch and dies.

Three Albanian texts of this ballad have been published; doubtless others remain to be collected.[42] All those published concern the construction of a bridge, *Ura e Sejt* (the Holy Bridge).

"Rozafati"[43]

Three Christian brothers construct a fortress.[44] Thirty masons are working, but the work of the day is destroyed by night. A saint tells them that the wife of one of them must be immured. The brothers agree to keep secret the words of the saint; however, the two elder brothers break their promise and tell their wives. The mother of the brothers calls the daughters-in-law in turn to take food to the fortress. The youngest wife says that she cannot go because her son is small and cries when left alone. The wives of the two elder brothers are excused from going. The youngest wife (wife of the youngest brother) brings the food. The youngest brother tells her frankly what her fate is to be. She accepts her lot without question. However, she begs that, when immured, her breast be exposed and holes left for her eyes, hands, and feet. The ballad ends with the mother's wish: "Let the fortress be strengthened and my son become a king and enjoy it."

Some of the Albanian variants have obviously arisen in a Moslem environment.[45] While in "Rozafati" the three brothers are Christian, in another text, "The Song of the Fortress of Shkadra in Old Times," they are simply three brothers. In the former the person who passes by and advises the brothers as to what must be done in order that the structure may last is a "saint," while in the other he is simply "an old man." The second variant referred to here contains only one additional motif, the dream of the youngest wife that she will be immured.

"Židanje Skadra" (The Building of Scutari)[46]

In Yugoslav versions of the ballad the three brothers are Vukashin, Uglyesha, and Goyko. With fifteen score of masons they have labored for three years to build Skadar on the Boyana River. Each night the walls are toppled by a vila. At the beginning of the fourth year the vila advises King Vukashin.

"Plague not thyself, Vukashin, and squander not thy gear! King, thou canst not for the fortress the strong foundation lay, Much less raise up the wall thereof, until upon a day Come news of Stoya and Stoyan, for like names have the twain; Sister they are and brother. Into the wall amain Shalt thou wall them. And the fortress shall be stablished in the land."

Vukashin sends Desimir in search of the two, giving him six packs of money. After three years Desimir returns unsuccessful. Rado the builder drives his men even harder but to no avail. The vila now orders that the first wife to bring her husband's dinner on the following day be immured. The brothers swear not to tell their wives but two of them break their oath. The queen, their mother, asks each of the wives in turn to take the dinner.

"Hear and good health to thee, sister!
My head beginneth to ache;
I cannot conquer it. Prithee the
meal to the masons take."

"Good health to thee, queen," she
answered, "my sister that is so dear!
I cannot master this aching arm.
Speak thou to our sister here."

She went to the youngest sister,
and unto her said she:
"O thou young wife of Goyko, do
thou harken now to me!

It is this—good health to thee,
sister!—my head beginneth to ache;

I cannot conquer the pain. Do
thou the meal to the masons take."

Goyko's young wife gave answer:
"I would do it gladly, O queen;
But all unbathed is my little child,
and the linen not washed clean."

Answered the queen: "With the
dinner to the masons do thou go.

Let our sister bathe thy baby; I will
whiten the linen like snow."

Then the young wife of Goyko
thereto would say no more;
Forthwith unto the masons their
mid-day meal she bore.

When she meets Goyko, he is weeping. At her insistence on knowing the reason he answers allegorically that he has dropped an apple of gold into the Boyana. She tries to comfort him. He turns aside, and the others lead her to the wall. She thinks it all a jest until the wall reaches her girdle. Then she pleads that they use a slave girl in her stead.

"Let me not, my dearest lord, be
walled up in the hold,
But send unto my mother, that hath
a treasure of gold,

And purchase thou a slave girl
with her money in that hour,
And wall the slave girl into
the foundations of the tower."

Realizing that there is no escape, she begs that her breasts be left exposed so that the baby, Yovo, can be brought to suckle her and that a window be made so that she can see him when he is brought and taken away. Rado the builder grants her request. For seven days she suckles the baby. At the end of that time she is unable to speak but her milk continues to flow for a year. And it still flows!

> Yea, even today the white milk flows,
> for a miracle most high,
> And a healing draught for women
> whereof the breasts are dry!

It will be noted that, although the victim tries (by pleas and the offer of a substitute) to escape her fate, there is never on her part any doubt as to the efficacy of the immurement.

What is at least an analogue, if not an exact parallel to the foundation-sacrifice theme as treated in the ballads above, is an episode in the Armenian national epic *Sassna Dzurer* (Daredevils of Sassoun).[47] Although in prose, it is interspersed with verse and may in earlier times have been composed entirely of the latter. The episode in question runs as follows:

Meherr builds a huge monastery called Marouta's High Mother of God, which is destroyed by Misra Melik, king of Egypt. Meherr's son, David, determines to rebuild it. His uncle, Ohan, whose voice is so loud that it can be heard from seven cities and who has to wrap himself in seven buffalo hides and fasten a plow-chain around his chest when he shouts, lest he burst, calls for workers.

Hear me, hear me, Sassoun's firelight
Is lit again, we shall rebuild
Marouta's High Mother of God.
Take up your tools and come in haste
To start today without delay.
Oh I am calling, let them come
He who loves God let him come.
We need stone cutters, by the
  thousand.
Gravel carriers, water carriers
By the hundred, by the thousand.
Oh I am calling, let them come
He who loves God let him come.
We need masons, plasterers
By the hundred, by the thousand.
We need wood carvers, masters
  and men
By the hundred, by the thousand.
Oh I am calling, let them come
He who loves God let him come.

The new monastery is built in seven days. On the night of the seventh day Marouta's High Mother of God appears to David in a dream, saying to him: "David, draw your dagger and lay it under the foundation stone. Consecrate the new church at a great mass, and I shall rise upon the foundation." When David awakes next morning, the monastery has disappeared—stones, plaster, wood, everything. He tells the others his dream and they hasten to build the monastery once again. This time David lays his dagger under the foundation stone, Marouta's High Mother of God rises upon it, and the monastery stands firm.[48]

III

The classic example of the foundation-sacrifice theme in the games of children is, of course, the very old but still popular "London Bridge." This game has been the subject of numerous learned articles, some of the authors supporting the theory that it preserves a record of actual human sacrifice, others ridiculing the whole idea, maintaining that to accept it would be placing far too much credence in the persistence of racial memory. One of the more familiar of the song texts is the following:

London Bridge is broken down,
Dance over my lady Lee;
London Bridge is broken down,
With the gay lady.
How shall we mend it up again?
We will mend it up with gravel
    and sand,
But gravel and sand will wash away.

We will mend it up with iron and steel,
But iron and steel will bend and break.
We will mend it up with silver
    and gold;
Silver and gold will be stolen away.
We will put a man to watch all night;
Suppose the man should fall asleep?
We will put a pipe into his mouth.[49]

In other versions it is suggested that the bridge be guarded by a cock and a dog, which will give warning of the approach of a trespasser. However, no amount of watching is of any avail.

It is unfortunate that the ominous conclusion has almost entirely disappeared from English (and American) tradition, having been replaced usually by a tug-of-war, a feature often found in other games as well. Perhaps the most unmistakable hint of the original situation occurs in a similar arch game, "Here's the Robbers Coming Through," apparently a derivative of "London Bridge."

> Here's the robbers passing by,
> passing by, passing by;
> Here's the robbers passing by,
> My fair Lady!
> What did the robbers do to you?
> They stole my watch and stole my chain.

The chorus at the end of each verse, accompanied by the chopping action of the swiftly descending arched arms, is

> Chip Chop
> Chip Chop
> The last man's head is OFF![50]

A text of "Brö, Brö Brille," the Scandinavian equivalent, has the closing line "The one who comes last will be put in a black pot."[51] The endings of some German versions, too, are suggestive.

> Kriegt Alle durch, kriegt Alle durch,
> Den letzten wollen wir fangen.
> Was gibst du mir zum Pfande?
> Den hintesten, den du kriegen kannst.[52]

It is in the more primitive forms such as the above that the true significance of the game is to be seen. Particularly to be noted are the following points: (1) the edifice is destroyed or ruined at night; (2) every kind of material—wood, stone, and even gold—is tried in vain; and (3) neither the vigilance of the watchman nor the presence of the cock and the dog avails to protect the structure from the attacks of the offended spirit or spirits. There seems little room for doubt that the child caught and held prisoner at the end of the line represents the earlier price paid for allowing the bridge to stand. Somewhat later, when the thoughts of men turned more and more toward the Final Judgment, the game entered a new phase. Now the question was not regarding the sacrifice of the victim but whether the prisoner should belong to the devils or to the angels, represented as waging perpetual warfare and contending particularly for the possession of departed souls.

Analogous to the German versions quoted above are the French "Le Pont-Levis," "La porte du Gloria," and "Olive Beavé," although the last of these has been contaminated by amalgamation with other games. "Le Pont-Levis" has the stanza

> Trois fois passera,
> La dernière, la dernière;
> Trois fois passera,
> La dernière y restera.[53]

One of the lines of "Olive Beavé" is also suggestive, though occurring in another context: "Je la donne, si tu l'attrape."[54]

The second stage of development, that in which all the players are caught by the descending arms and divided into two lines according to their preferences, is well represented by the Italian "La Porta," in which the gates are those of the Inferno and of Paradise. The two keepers are St. Paul and St. Peter, and the choice made by each of the other players is between water and wine. As the two lines separate and move away in opposite directions, those bound for the Inferno shriek and cry, while those going to Paradise sing gaily. In German versions, the leaders are often devil and angel, king and emperor, or sun and moon.[55]

In comparatively recent times the religious allusions disappeared from the game, and the captive, now accused merely of theft, was represented as being locked up in jail.

> You've stole my watch and kept my keys,
> Kept my keys, kept my keys;
> You've stole my watch and kept my keys,
> My fair lady!
> Off to prison she must go!
> Take the key and lock her up!

It is noteworthy that the prisoner who is caught so opportunely is haled off to prison despite the fact that she has committed only petty larceny (stolen watch and chain or stolen watch and lost the key). Significant, too, is the fact that an excessive price ("three hundred" to "ten hundred" pounds) must be paid to secure his freedom. Nothing could indicate more clearly that his fate has already been determined and that it is through sacrifice that the river spirit is to be appeased.

Present-day versions of the game bear little resemblance to those of an earlier time, usually terminating with a tug-of-war between the two groups of players. Arch games of the latter type are to be found in many areas: Europe, French West Africa, Haiti, Java, Burma, and among the Dogon, Chaga, Wadschagga, and other African tribes.

Many conjectures have been made as to the origin and the age of our game. Because of the fact that in some British versions there appears the refrain "Dance over my lady Lee!" there has been an attempt to connect this name with the family Leigh (seat Stoneleigh). There is a tradition that human victims were immured in the foundations of a bridge in Stoneleigh Park. Those who accept this theory point out also that Sir Thomas Leigh was lord mayor of London in 1558. However, the game is undoubtedly much older than this. According to Zingerle *(Das deutsche Kinderspiel im Mittelalter)*, the game was known in the Middle Ages to Meister Altswert, Fischart, and Geiler von Keiserberg. Rabelais mentions it as one of the games of Gargantua. And Newell considers it to be the same as the "Coda Romana," played by Florentine children as early as 1328. It may be recalled that London Bridge, erected by Isemberg, a Frenchman brought to England by King John, was actually broken down in the reign of Henry. The reason is interesting. The king had granted the bridge revenues to his queen, Eleanor of Provence, who squandered them instead of expending them on the maintenance of the bridge. The collapse occurred sometime in the thirteenth century.[56] While this appears to be the earliest date assigned in English tradition, it does not necessarily follow that the game does not antedate it in other parts of the world.

IV

Admittedly, proof of the existence of the foundation-sacrifice theme in the dance rests upon rather tenuous evidence. However, the widespread use of the arch figure strongly suggests that it may once have had a much greater significance than it has today.[57] In other words, the same process may have been operative here that we have already seen in the case of "London Bridge," in which the conclusion of the game has lost its former sinister character and degenerated into a mere tug-of-war. The phenomenon is not unknown in balladry where a supernatural element or anything else more or less fantastic and hence not intelligible (or perhaps not pleasing) to the later singer is replaced by something more prosaic.[58]

Perhaps the best example of a dance in which the foundation-sacrifice theme is definitely present is the Slovenian "Rojna Vrsta." The dancers form a line, men and women holding hands. The line winds into "snails" and out again, alternating with a closed circle. Finally the serpentine line runs through the "door" or the "bridge." In the "door" form, the whole line of dancers runs under the clasped and upraised hands of the end couple. In the "bridge" form, the dancers break into two groups, one of which stands with linked and lifted hands, creating the "bridge." Those of the other group ask permission to cross the "bridge." Permission is granted on condition that "a black-eyed maiden" be sacrificed. A little girl filling the description is sent first under the "bridge"; then the rest of the dancers follow. When they have crossed the bridge three times, the dancers disperse.[59]

In Yugoslavia during the Easter season young girls perform a dance known as "Kros, krosnjice," in which there is a bridge motif. One couple after another of the dancers (each couple separately) passes, singing, underneath an "arcade" of uplifted arms of the other participants. The "Visnjica" and the "Kroz vlakale" of other districts belong to the same type and are also danced only at Eastertime.[60] My informant is careful, however, to write that here the passing under the arch seems to be merely a pattern and without ritual or other significance, except that it may perhaps symbolize the Resurrection. She points out further that there is a widespread belief among the Yugoslavs that passing through or under something (trees, stones, etc.) brings health, happiness, and regeneration.[61] There too, however, seem to be traces of a ritual sacrifice in the Slovenian dance "Most,"[62] and in Croatia there are dances called "Subi most" (Dry Bridge) and "Pot most" (Under the Bridge), but these latter names appear to refer only to the evolutions of the dancers.

The arch figure is, of course, prominent in the dances of many widely separated parts of the world. The United States, for example, has the "Virginia Reel" and a Western favorite, "Inside Arch and Outside Under"; England, the "Sir Roger de Coverley"; Spain, "Los Seises"; Ireland, the "Bridge of Athlone" and the "Gates of Derry." It appears also in the Basque "Ezpata Dantza" and elsewhere.

V

It will have been noted that, with the sole exception of Oran's, the immurements (or inhumations) described above have been involuntary. There might be added here the self-immolation of the legendary Marcus Curtius (fourth century B.C.), who, when an earthquake opened a chasm in the Forum, leaped in full armor on horseback into it, thus fulfilling a soothsayer's pronouncement that the fissure could be closed only by the sacrifice of Rome's chief treasure, which Curtius interpreted as meaning a brave man. Somewhat similar in nature is a story related of the Slav folk hero Joe Magarac, a worker in the Monongahela Valley steel mills who made rails by squeezing the hot steel through his fingers, four rails from each hand. Finally he had made so many rails that the mills had to shut down from Thursday night to Monday morning. On Monday morning the smelter boss found Joe sitting in a big ladle with the hot steel boiling up around his neck. Having heard the big boss say that he wanted the best steel possible to build a new mill, Joe had sacrificed himself to improve its quality.

Despite the antiquity of the foundation sacrifice, the theme occasionally appears even yet in the second half of the twentieth century. In Victoria Holt's *The Legend of the Seventh Virgin* (New York, 1965) six novices and a nun break their vow of chastity. The former are expelled from the convent. To show their defiance, they dance in a meadow nearby and are turned into stones. The nun, who had corrupted them, is immured in the convent wall.[63] In Seabury Quinn's short story "The Doom of the House of Phipps"[64] there is an allusion to the old belief in immurement as a protection of a building, though in this instance this method of disposal of the victim's body is chosen simply for better concealment:

> "By Abraham and Isaac, and by the Joshua whose name I bear, I'll lay the hearthstone of my house according to the ancient rites!" my brother swore. "My house shall have to guard it that which none other in the colony can boast."
>
> And then they digged a great hole in the earth before the fireplace, and laid her bound therein, and rolled the hearth-slab forward to cement it over her.

Notes

1. 1 Kings 16:34.
2. Opie and Opie, *The Oxford Dictionary of Nursery Rhymes*, pp. 270–76.
3. G. L. Gomme, *Folklore Relics of Early Village Life*, p. 28.
4. Nennius, *Historia Britonum*, pp. 39–42.
5. Tylor, *Primitive Culture*, 1: 104; Leslie, *Early Races of Scotland*, 1: 149.
6. Spence, *Myth and Ritual in Dance, Game and Rhyme*, pp. 87–88.
7. Petrovich, *Hero Tales and Legends of the Serbians*, p. 25. The legend is sometimes localized also at the Kadı-Köprı (Turk., "the bridge of the judge") on the river Struma.

A similar story comes from Japan. When Horiō Yoshiharu became daimyo of Izumo he arranged to build a bridge over the turbulent river at Matsue. Many labored to carry out his wishes, but the work did not prosper. Countless large stones were flung into the rushing water with the idea of making a solid base on which to construct the pillars, but many of the stones were washed away, and as soon as the bridge took tangible form it was wrecked by the fierce torrent. It was believed that the spirits of the flood were angry, and in order to appease them it was deemed necessary to offer a human sacrifice. A man was accordingly buried alive below the central pillar, where the water was most turbulent. When this had been done, the work prospered and the bridge remained intact for three hundred years (Davis, *Myths and Legends of Japan*, pp. 342–44).

8. Baring-Gould, *Strange Survivals*, p. 15.
9. Tylor, *Primitive Culture*, 1: 105.
10. Baring-Gould, *Strange Survivals*, p. 14.
11. Waterman, *The Story of Superstition*, p. 9.
12. Sébillot, *Le folk-lore de France*, 4: 89–90. At the building of the castle of Henneberg a mason sold his child to be built into the wall. When the last stone was put in place, the child screamed. The father, horror-stricken at what he had done, fell from a ladder and broke his neck (Elworthy, *The Evil Eye*, p. 80).
13. Opie and Opie, *Oxford Dictionary of Nursery Rhymes*, p. 275.

14. Ibid.
15. Baring-Gould, *Strange Survivals*, pp. 15, 36.
16. Ibid.
17. Elworthy, *The Evil Eye*, p. 79.
18. G. L. Gomme, *Folklore Relics of Early Village Life*, p. 35.
19. Elworthy, *The Evil Eye*, p. 82.
20. Krappe, *The Science of Folklore*, p. 74.
21. See also Rodd, *Customs and Lore of Modern Greece*, p. 168; Trumbull, *The Threshold Covenant*, p. 47; Schmidt, *Das Volksleben der Neugriechen*, p. 196.

The importance attaching to a person's shadow, examples of which appear in the superstitions of many peoples (for example, the reluctance to having a photograph taken lest the camera catch the shadow/soul and take it away), is so familiar as to need no comment here. It may be noted, however, that in some areas the Devil is popularly believed to lack a shadow. An old Ozark mountaineer who claimed to have encountered the Devil on a path described him as "just an ordinary feller." When asked how he knew then that it was the Devil, he replied, "He didn't throw no shadder!" (Vance Randolph, *Ozark Superstitions*, p. 276).

In a number of recent stories of the weird, the shadow is the malignant agent of a living person, performing evil deeds which the latter could not execute in human form. See, for example, A. Merritt's *Creep, Shadow, Creep.*

The name of the individual was also of the utmost importance, Rhys writes (*Nineteenth Century*, October 1891, p. 566): "The whole Aryan family believed at one time, not only that his name was a part of the man, but that it was the part of him which is termed the soul, the breath of life, or whatever you may choose to define it as being." It was for this reason that early man was so fearful of its being learned by another, who might use the knowledge to injure him. Hence nicknames and the giving of multiple names, of which one is known only to the father and the mother. Related to the idea that possession of the name of another gives one power over him are the numerous stories (e.g., "Rumpelstiltskin") in which the guessing of the name of a dwarf or a supernatural being results in the guesser's escape or in his acquiring a treasure.

The Pythagoreans taught that the actions and the success of mankind were dependent not only upon fate and genius but also upon their respective names, a theory persisting among present-day numerologists. The Greeks believed, for example, that Achilles defeated Hector because the numeral letters in the former's name amounted to a greater sum than those in the name of the latter (Rapaport, *The Folklore of the Jews*, p. 88).

In old Russia, where in some provinces an animal was killed and buried on the spot where the first log or the first stone was to be placed and where, in other provinces, the builders simply called out the name of some bird or beast, believing that it would then rapidly die, it is significant that the peasants were very polite to the builders on the latter occasion, because their own names might be maliciously called out instead by the workmen if they were annoyed or angered (Ralston, *Songs of the Russian People*, pp. 126–27). For analogous beliefs among other Slavic peoples, see Tihomir R. Djordjević, *Ile oci u verovanju fužnih Slovena* (The evil eye in beliefs of the southern Slavs), pp. 61–62.

22. Personal communication, 6 February 1956.

23. Baring-Gould, *Strange Survivals*, p. 16.

24. Krappe, *The Science of Folklore*, p. 74.

25. Eurystheus was the uncle of Hercules and setter of the twelve tasks.

26. Guest, *Mabinogion*, p. 383.

27. Tylor, *Primitive Culture*, 1: 94. The same story is given in Eleanor Hull, *Folklore of the British Isles*, pp. 207–8.

28. However his power ends at midstream. Cf. Robert Burns's poem "Tam o' Shanter."

29. Elworthy, p. 81.

30. Bett, *The Games of Children*, p. 112.

31. *European Balladry*, chap. 3: "Balkan Ballads."

32. Ortutay, *Szekely népballadak*; "Kómüves Kelemenné," *Ethnographia* (1923). L. Vargas, on the other hand, advances the theory that the original form was created by the Hungarians prior to their arrival in Europe (*Forschungen zur Geschichte der Volksballade im Mittelalter: Die Herkunft der ungarischen Ballade von der eingemauerien Frau* [Budapest, 1960]), a view which G. Megas (βιβλιογραφια) shows to be untenable.

33. Arnaudov, *Vgradena nevesta: Ocerki po bälgarski folklor*, pp. 509, 576.

34. Shishmanov, *Legendes religieuses Bulgares*.

35. Politis, *Eklogaì apò tà tragoúdia tou hellenikon laou*, No. 89, sent me by Georgia Tarsouli on 6 February 1956. She writes that this sixteenth-century bridge in Epirus is still standing. It is sometimes localized at the Peneius River or the Spercheius.

36. At one period these (and prostitutes and deformed or sickly individuals) were chosen as victims. Later it came to be felt that the spirits would be better pleased with the sacrifice of the strong or the beautiful.

37. Passow, *Tragoúdia romaíika: Popularia carmina Graeciae recentioris*, pp. 388–90.

38. Ibid., No. 512.

39. From the collection of the Institute of Ethnography and Folklore of Bucharest, through the courtesy of Professor Mihai Pop.

40. Arnaudov, *Vgradena nevesta*, pp. 569–73. A Bulgarian fragment, *Mano malstore*, says that Manuel built a tower and climbed to the top; there he was dazzled by the glitter of the ornaments of the widow Gjurgja's daughter and fell.

41. Summary kindly furnished by Dr. Linda Dégh, of Budapest.

42. Skendi, *Albanian and South Slavic Oral Epic Poetry* (*MAFLS*, 44), p. 312. These have been published in Elezović, "Tri arnautske varijante motiva o zazidjivanju nevestre," pp. 391–98.

43. Skendi, *Albanian and South Slavic Oral Epic Poetry*, pp. 312ff.

44. Usually it is a bridge, not a fortress.
45. On this point see Hörmann Kosta, *Narodne pjesme Muslimana u Bosni i Hercegovini* (Popular songs of Moslems in Bosnia and Hercegovina). 1: No. 3.
46. Noyes and Bacon, *Heroic Ballads of Servia*, pp. 15–23 ("The Building of Skadar"); and Subotic, *Yugoslav Popular Ballads*, pp. 40–47. The foundation-sacrifice theme appears also in the Yugoslav legend "Zidanje Skadra na Bojani," a version of which appears in *Bosanka Vila* 14, 2 (1899): 28. There are also numerous legends of women or girls being walled up as a punishment; see *Bosanka Vila* 2, 4 (1887): 61; 8 (1893): 290–91, 13, 6 (1878): 93.
47. Known also as *Sassna pahlevanner* (Sassoun's strongmen); *Sassountsi Davit* (David of Sassoun); *Davit yev Meherr* (David and Meherr); *Sanasar yev Baltasar* (Sanasar and Baltasar); *Chochante doun* (House of the great).
48. Surmelian, *Daredevils of Sassoun*, pp. 143–47. In this episode the dagger may be interpreted symbolically as a substitute for David, or the idea may have been that its effectiveness lay in the fact that as his constant companion it was imbued with his personality. As an interesting sidelight it may be pointed out that J. Rendel Harris suggested many years ago that the coins and documents deposited at the laying of a cornerstone in much later times are "ransom money for the *person* that ought to be there" (*Folk-Lore* 15: 441).
49. Opie and Opie, *The Oxford Dictionary of Nursery Rhymes*, pp. 272–73.
50. Daiken, *Children's Games Throughout the Year*, p. 99.
51. Ibid.
52. Opie and Opie, *The Oxford Dictionary of Nursery Rhymes*, pp. 274–75.
53. Bett, *The Games of Children*, pp. 101–2.
54. Ibid.
55. Choices are widely varied: silver or gold, rose or cabbage, diamond necklace or gold pin, etc. Among some African tribes (e.g., the Chaga and the Wadschaga) the game does not end with the usual tug-of-war. Instead, the last player uncaught approaches the "door-keepers" carrying a *Dracaena* leaf (which makes a request irresistible) and asks for a child to carry firewood, another to bring water, etc. In this way he effects the release of all the others and the game begins anew.
56. The first bridge, a wooden one, across the Thames was built at Southwark in 994. The first stone bridge (which required twelve years to complete) was constructed in 1196. The latter was partly destroyed by fire in 1200, completely destroyed by the Great Fire of 1666, and again in 1673.
57. Where the arch figure does not form a part of the dance pattern, dancers sometimes carry over their heads half-hoops decorated with flowers. These flowered arches are a feature of the Mexican "Dansa de los arcos" and of certain Spanish dances.
58. This is true, for example, in the English "James Harris," in which the seducer was originally an incarnate evil spirit who, after luring his victim aboard ship, reveals his demonic nature by displaying a cloven hoof. In later versions the supernatural element has completely disappeared and the seducer is merely an unscrupulous homewrecker.

59. *Journal of the International Folk Music Council* 4 (1952): 5.

60. Letter of 17 June 1955 from Ljubica and Danica Yanković. According to Miss Tarsouli, of Athens, there is in one of the Greek provinces a dance called "Kayapa" (arch, arcade, bridge), danced only on Easter Monday by young girls. In the course of this dance the girls perform all the episodes described in the ballad.

61. For numerous examples, see the article by Djordjević in *Ethnologija* 1 (1940): 318ff.; and Sima Trojanović in *Srpski Ethnograiski sbornik Srpske Akademija nenka* 45 (1930).

This belief, particularly as it regards the curing of certain ailments (e.g., hernia and rickets) is very widespread. For Scandinavian examples, see Carl-Herman Tillhagen, *Folklig Läkekonst* pp. 292–98, and particularly the exceptionally fine photograph on p. 293. More information on Yugoslav practices is available in Phyllis Kemp, *Healing Ritual: Studies in the Technique and Tradition of the Southern Slavs*, pp. 143–44.

62. See *Slovenske narodslovne studije*, Vol. 2, which contains three pertinent articles: Marolt's "Most" (Bridge), pp. 47–56; "Crnomaljsko kolo-most," pp. 56–73; and Boris Orel's "Mitos o Mostu," pp. 74–91.

63. An attempt, not entirely successful, to prove that such charges against the Church are unfounded has been made in Thurston, *The Immuring of Nuns*, pp. 125ff.

64. Quinn, *The Phantom Fighter*, pp. 242–43.

References

Argenti, P., and H. J. Rose. *The Folk-Lore of Chios*. 2 vols. Cambridge, 1949.

Arnaudov, *Vgradena nevestia: Ocerki po bălgarski folklor*. Sophia, 1934.

Arwidsson, A. I. *Svenska fornsånger*. Stockholm, 1834–42.

Baring-Gould, S. *Strange Survivals*. London: Methuen, 1892.

Barton, F. R. "Children's Games in British New Guinea." *Journal of the Royal Anthropological Institute* 38 (1908): 276–77.

Baud-Bovy, S. *Chansons populaires du Dodécanèse*. Athens, 1935.

Béart, Ch. *Jeux et jouets de l'ouest africain*. 2 vols. Dakar, 1955.

Bett, Henry. *The Games of Children*. London: Methuen, 1929.

Cocchiara, G. "Il ponte di Arta e i sacrifici di costruzione." *Annali del Museo Pitrè* 1 (1950): 38–81.

Costermans, B. J. "Spelen bij de Mamvu en Logo in de gewesten Watsa-Faradje." *Zaïre* 2, 5 (Mai 1948).

Daiken, Leslei. *Children's Games Throughout the Year*. London, 1949.

Davis, F. Hadland. *Myths and Legends of Japan*. Boston: Nickerson, n.d.

Dawkins, R. M. *Modern Greek in Asia Minor*. Cambridge, 1916.

Dennis, R. B. "Games and Children's Play." *Journal of the Burma Research Society* (Rangoon, n. d.): 29–31.

Dieterich, K. "Die Volksdichtung der Balkanländer." *Zeitschrift des Vereins für Volkskunde* 4 (1902): 150–52.

Djordjević, Tihomir. R. *Ile oci u verovanju fužnih Slovena.* Beograd, 1938.

Doke, C. M. "Games, Plays and Dances of the Khomani Bushmen." *Bantu Studies* 10 (1936): 463.

Dozon, A. *Contes albanais.* Paris, 1881.

Elezović, C. "Tri arnautske varijante motiva o zazidjivanju nevestre." *Zbornik A. Belić* (1937): 391–98.

Eliade, Mircea. *Commentarii la legenda Mesteruliu Manole.* Bucharest, 1943.

Ellis, W. *Polynesian Researches.* London, 1832–36.

Elworthy, Frederick Thomas. *The Evil Eye.* New York, 1958.

Entwistle, William J. *European Balladry.* Oxford: Clarendon Press, 1939.

ERE = Encyclopedia of Religion and Ethics (ed. J. Hastings). New York and Edinburgh, 1926, 2: 848a-57a; 4: 109b-15b.

Frazer, J. G. *The Golden Bough,* Vol. 2: *Taboo and the Perils of the Soul.* New York, 1935.

Garnett, Lucy M. J., and J. S. Stuart-Glennie. *Greek Folk Poesy.* 2 vols. London, 1896.

Georgeakis, G., and L. Pineau. *Le folk-lore de Lesbos.* Paris, 1894.

Gomme, Alice Bertha. *The Traditional Games of England, Scotland and Ireland.* 2 vols. London, 1894–98.

Gomme, G. L. *Folklore Relics of Early Village Life.* London, 1883.

Groome, F. H. *Gypsy Folk-Tales.* London, 1899.

Guest, Lady Charlotte. *The Mabinogion.* London: J. M. Dent, 1902.

Gutmann, Bruno. "Kinderspiele bei den Wadschagga." *Globus* 15, 95 (1909).

Halliday, W. R. *Indo-European Folk Tales and Greek Legend.* Cambridge, 1933.

Harris, J. Rendel. "Notes from Armenia in Illustration of *The Golden Bough.*" *Folklore* 15 (1904): 427–46.

Hoffmann-Krayer, E., and H. Bächtold-Stäubli. *Handwörterbuch des deutschen Aberglaubens.* Berlin-Leipzig, 1927–42.

Holkot, Robert. "Super Sapientiam Salamonis." *Ethnographia* 22 (1911): 177.

Hull, Eleanor. *Folklore of the British Isles.* London: Methuen, 1928.

Journal of the International Folk Music Council 4 (1952): 5.

Karadžić, Vuk S. *Srpske narodne pjesme.* Beograd, 1895. 2: 25.

Kemp, Phyllis. *Healing Ritual: Studies in the Technique and Tradition of the Southern Slavs.* London, 1935.

Köhler, Reinhold. "Eingemauerte Menschen." *Aufsätze über Märchen und Volkslieder.* Berlin, 1894.

Kosta, Hörmann. *Narodne pjesme Muslimana u Bosni i Hercegovini* (Popular songs of moslems in Bosnia and Hercegovina). Sarajevo: J. Kusan, 1933.

Krappe, A. H. *Balor with the Evil Eye.* New York, 1927.

Krappe, A. H. *The Science of Folklore.* New York: Barnes and Noble, 1930.

Kremenliev, Boris. *Bulgarian-Macedonian Folk Music.* Berkeley, 1952.

Lawson, J. C. *Modern Greek Folklore and Ancient Greek Religion.* Cambridge, 1910.

Lelékos, N. *Enidórpion.* Athens, 1888.

Leslie, Forbes. *The Early Races of Scotland and Their Monuments.* Edinburgh: Edmunston and Douglas, 1866.

Lexikon für Theologie und Kirche. Freiburg, 1958.

Liebrecht, F. *Zur Volkskunde.* Heilbronn, 1879.

Mannhardt, Wilhelm. "Das Bruckenspiel." *Zeitschrift für deutsche Mythologie und Sittenkunde* 4 (1859): 302–9.

Marolt, Franc. "Crnomaljsko kolo-most." *Slovenske narodslovne studije,* Vol. 2, 56–73. Ljubljana, 1936.

Marolt, Franc. "Most." *Slovenske narodslovne studije,* Vol. 2, 47–56. Ljubljana, 1936.

Marolt, Franc. "Tri obredja iz Bela Krojna." In *Glazbena Matica.* Ljubljana, 1936.

Merritt, A. *Creep, Shadow, Creep.* New York: Avon Book Company, 1943.

Miladinov, D., and K. Miladinov. *Bălgarski narodni pjesni.* 2nd ed. Sofia, 1891.

Nennius, *Historia Britonum.* London, 1838.

Newell, William Wells. *Games and Songs of American Children.* 3rd ed. New York and London, 1911.

Noyes, G. R., and L. Bacon. *Heroic Ballads of Servia.* Boston, 1913.

Opie, Peter, and Iona Opie. *The Oxford Dictionary of Nursery Rhymes.* Oxford, 1951.

Orel, Boris. "Mitos o Mostu." *Slovenske narodslovne studije,* Vol. 2, 74–91. Ljubljana, 1936.

Ortutay, Gyula. *Szekely népballadak.* Budapest, 1935.

Overbeck, Hans. *Javaansche meisjesspelen en kinderliedjes.* Jogjakarta, 1958.

Passow, A. *Tragoúdia romaíika: Popularia carmina Graeciae recentioris.* Leipzig, 1860.

Petrovitch, W. M. *Hero Tales and Legends of the Serbians.* London: G. G. Harrap, 1914.

Politis, N. G. *Eklogaì apò tà tragoúdia tou hellenikon laou.* Athens, 1932.

Politis, N. G. "Cola pesce in Grecia." *Archivio per lo studio delle tradizioni popolari* 22 (1903): 212–17.

Quinn, Seabury. *The Phantom Fighter.* Sauk City, Wisc., 1966.

Ralston, W. R. S. *Songs of the Russian People.* London, 1872.

Randolph, Vance. *Ozark Superstitions.* New York: Columbia University Press, 1947.

Rapaport, Angelo S. *The Folklore of the Jews.* London, 1937.

Raum, Otto Friedrich. *Chaga Childhood: A Description of Indigenous Education in an East African Tribe.* London, 1940.

Rhys, John. "Welsh Fairies." *Nineteenth Century* 30 (1891): 564–74.

Rodd, Rennell. *The Customs and Lore of Modern Greece.* London, 1892.

Rouse, W. H. D. "Folklore from the Southern Sporades." *Folk-Lore* 10 (1899): 182–85.

Sainéan, L. "Les rites de la construction d'après la poésie populaire de l'Europe orientale." *Revue de l'histoire des religions* 45 (1902): 359–96.

Schmidt, B. *Das Volksleben der Neugriechen und das hellenische Altertum.* Leipzig, 1871.

Sébillot, Paul. *Le folk-lore de France.* 4 vols. Paris, 1904–1907.

Shishmanov, L. *Legendes religieuses Bulgares.* Paris, 1896.

Sioula, I. A. "Demode asmata Nigrites tes Makedonias." *Laografia* 5 (1916): 577–84.

Skendi, S. *Albanian and South Slavic Oral Epic Poetry.* Philadelphia, 1954.

Solymossy, Sándor. "Kómüves Kelemenné." *Ethnographia* (1923).

Spence, Lewis. *Myth and Ritual in Dance, Game and Rhyme.* London, 1947.

Starkie, Walter. *Don Gypsy.* New York, 1937.

Stefanović, S. "Die Legende vom Bau der Burg Skutari: Ein Beitrag zur interbalkanischen und vergleichenden Sagenforschung." *Revue internationale des etudes balkaniques* 1 (1934): 188–210.

Stefanović, S. "Legenda e židanju zkadra." *Studije o naradnoi poezije.* Beograd, 1933.

Strekelj, Karel. *Slovenska narodne pesmi.* Ljubljana, 1904–1905, Vols. 2–3.

Subotic, D. *Yugoslav Popular Ballads: Their Origin and Development.* Cambridge, 1932.

Surmelian, Leon. *Daredevils of Sassoun.* Denver, 1964.

Taipi, Kasem R. *Zana popullore.* N. p., 1933.

Talos, I. "Balada mesterului Manole si variantele ei transilvanene." *Revista de folclor* 7, 1–2 (1962): 22–57.

Theros, A. *Ta tragoúdia ton hellenon.* 2 vols. Athens, 1951–1952.

Thurston, E. *Omens and Superstitions of Southern India.* London, 1912.

Thurston, Herbert. *The Immuring of Nuns.* London: Publications of the Catholic Truth Society, 1898.

Tillhagen, Carl-Herman. *Folklig Läkekonst.* Stockholm, 1958.

Tomasseo, N. *Canti popolari Corsi, Illirici, Greci, Toscani.* Venice, 1842.

Trumbull, H. Clay. *The Threshold Covenant.* New York: Scribner's Sons, 1896.

Tucker, A. N. "Children's Games and Songs in the Southern Sudan." *Journal of the Royal Anthropological Institute* 63 (1933): 180–81.

Tylor, E. B. *Primitive Culture,* 1: 94ff. London, 1872.

Waterman, Philip. *The Story of Superstition.* New York and London, 1929.

Yanković, Ljubica, and Danica Yanković. *Narodne Igre.* Vol. 2 (1937), pp. 35, 45, 92, 156; Vol. 5 (1949), pp. 25, 26, 122, 173, 356.

Zingerle, Ignaz V. *Das deutsche Kinderspiel im Mittelalter.* Innsbruck, 1873.

The Greek Ballad
"The Bridge of Arta" as Myth

Much of the scholarship devoted to "The Walled-Up Wife" ballad falls under the rubric of nationalistic folklore study. Accordingly, Serbian folklorists have investigated "The Building of Skadar," Hungarian folklorists have considered "Clement Mason," Romanian folklorists have pondered "Meşterul Manole," Greek folklorists "The Bridge of Arta," and so forth. Sometimes scholars take international comparative outlooks; sometimes they tend to treat the ballad solely in terms of national texts.

If an item of folklore is found in more than one society, which is usually the case, then it is always risky to discuss that item as though it were unique and peculiar to only one society. In the following essay, written by an expert on modern Greek folklore, we find an ingenious interpretation of "The Bridge of Arta" in the light of an element of classical Greek mythology. It should be noted that modern Greek folklore specialists have a strong penchant for seeking to prove that modern Greek folklore represents survivals from classical Greece.

For discussions of folkloristics in Greece, see Alke Kyriakidou-Nestoros, "The Theory of Folklore in Greece: Laographia *in Its Contemporary Perspective,"* East European Quarterly *5 (1972): 487–504;* Michael Herzfeld, Ours Once More: Folklore, Ideology, and the Making of Modern Greece *(Austin: University of Texas Press, 1982); and Loring M. Danforth, "The Ideological Context of the Search for Continuities in Greek Culture,"* Journal of Modern Greek Studies *2 (1984): 53–85. For the most comprehensive examination of Greek versions, 333 of them, see Georgios A. Megas,* Die Ballade von der Arta-Brücke: Eine vergleichende Untersuchung *(Thessalonika: Institute for Balkan Studies, 1976).*

"The Bridge of Arta" is one of the best known of all Greek narrative songs, and versions of it have been collected from all parts of the

Reprinted from Roderick Beaton, *Folk Poetry of Modern Greece* (Cambridge: © Cambridge University Press, 1980; reprinted with the permission of Cambridge University Press), pp. 120–24.

Greek-speaking world, as well as from Bulgaria, Albania, Serbia, Romania, and Hungary. As a result of the song's popularity and wide distribution it has been a subject for studies of "diffusion" for close on a hundred years. Scholars have been unable to reach agreement, however, on the song's country of origin (although the majority opinion favors Greece) or, if the song *is* indigenous to Greece, on which of the regional variants is closest to the original.[1]

The broad outlines of the story are these. A master builder, with a varying number of craftsmen and apprentices, is engaged on a building. In all the Greek versions this is a bridge, although elsewhere in the Balkans it may be a castle or a monastery. What the masons build by day, however, falls down by night, and the master builder is in despair until it is revealed to him by a supernatural agent that the bridge will not stand firm unless a human sacrifice is built into the foundations. In most of the Greek versions it is spelled out to him that the sacrifice must be his own wife, although the selection of the victim (always the master builder's wife) may be made in a number of ways. The master builder sends for his wife, who, to his chagrin, comes all too quickly to the site. In most of the Greek versions the wife is tricked into descending into the foundations, usually on the pretext of recovering a ring which the master builder has accidentally dropped, and once she is there the masons begin to immure her. As she is being walled up the woman vainly appeals to her husband's sense of pity, then curses the bridge, often lamenting the fact that she is the last of three sisters to die in this way. The master builder reminds her that she has a brother or son still living who will one day have to cross the bridge and so persuades her to revoke her curse and bless the bridge instead.

No less than sixteen "historical-geographical" studies of this ballad are summarized and discussed by Megas (1971), whose own approach shows little advance upon that of his predecessors. The essential weakness in all these arguments is the assumption that certain variants of the song must be derived from others (according to varying sets of criteria) and that, depending on the criteria selected, the evolution of the song through a series of variant-types can be traced. The truth is, however, that every oral variant is of equal validity, and has an equal claim to be regarded as "original" (cf. Lord 1960, pp. 99–123). The song does not evolve according to a mysterious Darwinian principle, beyond the control of individual singers, but is created anew every time it is sung, the resulting version being determined by the capabilities of each singer and his free artistic choice within the narrow structural conventions of his tradition.

Once these premises are granted, the question "Which is the original version?" loses most of its meaning, to be replaced by the question "What is the myth expressed?" Since it is in the nature of myth to undergo certain transformations between one culture and another, there is no reason to insist that the myth expressed is precisely the same in all the languages and cultures in which the song is found. There may be significant, and consistent, differences between the myth as expressed by the Bulgarian, Hungarian, and Greek ballads, and this would be a proof not of historical diffusion but of cultural adaptation. This is perhaps why "The Bridge of Arta" so often seems native to the region and people whose versions are best known to each commentator.

In regard to only the Greek versions of the ballad, there are two important features which give a clue to the nature of the myth expressed. The first is the name given to the bridge in different versions. The most common of these is the Bridge of Arta, although other local names are sometimes substituted, such as the Bridge of Adana in Cappadocia and of Larisa in Thessaly, and the improbable location "on the shore" in the islands of Evia and the Sporades. Otherwise the bridge is not geographically located but instead is given a mythical significance. The next most common name after "The Bridge of Arta" is the mythical "Bridge of Hair" (τῆς Τρίχας τὸ γιοφύρι), and there may be a similar mythical intent in the Cypriot and Asia Minor versions, which place the bridge "Down at the edge of the world" (Megas 1971, pp. 92–93).[2]

Scholars following the methods of the "historical-geographical" school have devoted much attention to the real monuments mentioned in the song: according to Baud-Bovy the Bridge of Adana is the oldest monument referred to, and therefore the song must have originated in Cappadocia with the building of that bridge in the reign of the emperor Justinian (Baud-Bovy 1936, p. 170), while Megas on statistical grounds attaches the song to the Bridge of Arta, although that bridge was almost certainly not built until some centuries after the time when he believes the song originated.[3]

Such theories are credible only if one believes that the song relates a historical fact associated with the building of one of these bridges. But the ease with which the song evidently attaches itself to any local monument of sufficient importance (by far the greatest number of "Arta" variants come from the Greek mainland, although not from Arta itself) is shown by the predominance of unusually imposing monuments in the song (the Bridges of Arta and Adana in Greek versions, the castle of Shkodër [Skutari] in Albanian, etc.) and by the large number of such monuments with which it has become associated throughout the Balkans. Since the song is not historical there is no need to believe that any of the actual monuments named is an essential part of the myth.

With "The Bridge of Hair" we are on quite different ground. In our attempt to isolate the mythical core of the song, we are justified in rewriting the name of any *real* bridge as "Once upon a time a bridge . . ." The name Arta or Adana or Larisa would be introduced by singers in order to add verisimilitude and a degree of local immediacy to a fictional story, just as many realist novelists have introduced historical events and even characters into their fictions in order to strengthen the illusion of reality for their readers. But rewritten in the same way, *"tis Tríhas to yofýri"* becomes "once upon a time a bridge of *hair* . . ." Since this is the only *mythical* description of the bridge, much greater importance must be attached to "The Bridge of Hair" than might have been expected from a statistical count of its occurrences (17.41 percent according to Megas, as against 33 percent for "Arta"), and this is further borne out by its exceptionally wide distribution.[4]

The mythical significance of "The Bridge of Hair" is not hard to find. In Greek popular usage the phrase is recorded as meaning figuratively any exceedingly long-drawn-out task, but the usage "He crossed the bridge of hair," meaning that someone has successfully negotiated great difficulties or danger (Politis 1901, pp. 621–22), suggests that no distinction is to be drawn between "The Bridge of Hair" (τῆς Τρίχας τὸ γιαφύρι) and "The Hair Bridge" (τὸ Τρίχινο γεφύρι).[5] The latter, according to a popular belief attested in many parts of Greece, connects the world of the living with that of the dead: "In the underworld the souls have to cross a bridge, the Hair Bridge. This is as slender as a hair and is most unsteady. Whatever soul is unable to cross falls into the river which runs beneath and is lost." (Politis 1904, 1: 612, No. 983).

And in a Thracian popular tradition this bridge is actually called the Bridge of Hair as it is in the song: "In the mouth of the dead man they would put a coin for him to give to the angel and cross the bridge. Whoever had been a just man would easily cross the Bridge of Hair (τῆς Τρίχας τὸ γιοφύρι) and whoever was a sinner would fall into the Touna" (*Thrakiká* 11 [1939]: 197). The reference to the river Touna, or Danube, which is frequently mentioned in versions of the song, further strengthens the link between this tradition and "The Bridge of Arta."

It is possible that this belief and the myth on which the song is based are connected with the Islamic *Sirat*, which is described in the Ma'rifetnāme as "narrow as the edge of a sword" (Gill and Kramers 1953, p. 81) and in the Mulla 'Alī Qārī as "finer than a hair and sharper than a sword" (Hughes 1885, p. 595). According to the Islamic sources this bridge connects the earth with Paradise, and while the righteous cross it in a moment, the souls of the guilty fall off it into Hell, which gapes below. This belief was presumably known to the Turks, and it would be interesting to know whether there are Turkish songs or popular accounts in any way comparable to the Greek.[6]

But the belief and its attendant myths are by no means confined to Islamic culture. The idea that the other world is connected to this by a bridge supernaturally difficult to cross is found in Celtic, Icelandic, Indian, Indonesian, Melanesian, Eskimo, and American Indian traditions (Thompson 1955–58, F 152). Against this background it would be quite reasonable to suppose that the song "The Bridge of Arta" is connected in some way with myths concerning the passage from life to death.

The second main feature which supports this analysis of the song is found in those versions where the master builder's wife is persuaded to go down into the foundations of the bridge, generally on the pretext of recovering a ring. At this point the wife may call to her husband above to say that she has found nothing, or he may reveal the ruse, telling her that he has the ring and never lost it; but by far the most telling are those versions in which the wife, searching for the ring in the foundations of the arch, comes upon the apparently severed hand of a man or monster, or discovers snakes and vipers knotted together. This description, when it occurs, is too consistent to be gratuitous, and it may be supposed that those singers who included or added it did so with a definite purpose. Descriptions of severed limbs and in particular the formulaic evocation of snakes and vipers are a sure indication that the world of the dead is being described. These images make sense only if the bridge represents a crossing from this world to the next. By including these details the singers were able to emphasize the supernatural character of the bridge and incidentally, in doing so, to heighten the dramatic effect: even before she is killed by the masons throwing down rocks and lime on top of her, we know that the master builder's wife has already entered Hades, from which there is no return.

According to Megas this whole episode of the ring is an intrusion from another song (in fact a series of songs or widely diverging variants) in which a young man is enticed by a beautiful woman to go down a well and recover a ring for her; but the woman turns out to be a spirit and refuses to hold the rope for him to ascend. In many of these songs too, the hero becomes aware of his fate by the discovery of knotted snakes at the bottom of the well (Megas 1971, pp. 113–19). There is no reason, however, to believe that this theme was ever restricted to a single form and to the context of the "haunted well," and it is perfectly in accord with the structural principles of the tradition that the theme, with the roles of the protagonists inverted, should form an equally integral part of songs which tell the story of the Bridge of Hair.

A final feature which tends to confirm this approach to the song is the reason for which the dying wife is persuaded to revoke the curse which she has put upon the bridge, and which often includes a specific wish that travellers who attempt to cross the bridge should fall off. In a number of versions the master builder prevails upon her to take back this curse and bless the bridge instead, by reminding her that she has a brother or a son who will one day cross it. If the bridge is the perilous hair bridge which the souls of the living must cross after death, then it is easy to see why this argument might have such force.

Notes

1. The instinct to claim national ownership of ballads is not confined to scholars whose work is otherwise of a high standard, such as Vargyas and Megas. An apparently "official" claim to Albanian ownership of "The Bridge of Arta" ballads attacks simultaneously on two fronts—first showing the alleged primacy of the Shkodër (Skutari) versions and then, to reinforce the point, claiming that even if this were not so and Arta were the "original" location of the ballad, the region round Arta has belonged culturally to the Albanians (or Illyrians) since prehistoric times (Sako 1966).

2. In Cypriot versions which begin thus or with a vaguer indication ("Down at the five rivers, down at the five roads") the bridge is often called the Bridge of Hair at the *end* of the song (Papadopoullos 1975, pp. 28, 176; Megas 1971, p. 81, summary of a text from Athens Academy Archive). These instances have not been included in Megas' statistical summary.

3. I have been unable to find any reliable information about the building of the present bridge outside the town of Arta. According to the *Megáli Ellinikí Enkyklopaídia* it was built either in 1602 or 1606, but the source of the author's information (Karamanos 1928) seems to be a folk tradition (Politis 1904, 2: 774–75; Megas 1971, p. 91).

4. Baud-Bovy thought that "The Bridge of Hair" was the most frequent but disregarded its importance on the grounds that "ce nom, lui non plus, ne

doit pas être primitif" (1936, p. 169). The suggestion was taken up again by K. Romaios, who correctly saw the song as essentially mythical in nature but made the mistake of assigning its *origin* to a specific local ritual, the Rousalia (Romaios 1952). In fact, as Megas has shown, "Arta" occurs considerably more frequently in the recorded variants of the song, although this need not diminish the importance of "The Bridge of Hair."

As to the distribution of "The Bridge of Hair," this is found in Epiros, the Peloponnese, the Cyclades, Thrace, Asia Minor and offshore islands, the Dodecanese, Pontos, Cappadocia (Megas 1971, p. 93), and Cyprus (see note 3). It is not found in Crete, although the opening of this Cretan version conveys a similar sense:

Κάτω 'ς τὸ μαῦρου ποταμὸ καμάρα θεμελιόνουν,
Καμάρα θενὰ χτίσουνε μὴν πνίγουντ' οἱ διαβάταις
(Jeannaraki 1876, p. 209)

Down at the black [unhappy] river they are digging the foundations for an arch,
They're going to build an arch so that travellers won't drown.

To save travellers from drowning is an improbable reason for building a bridge, unless it is in fact the Bridge of Hair, which serves precisely that purpose.

5. The hybrid form τριχογιόφυρο (hairbridge) is also found in one version of the song from the Peloponnese (Megas 1971, p. 92).

6. That the popular belief about the hair bridge had a Turkish origin was first suggested by B. Schmidt (1871, p. 240) and rejected out of hand by N. G. Politis as "most improbable" (1901, p. 623).

References

Baud-Bovy, S. 1936. *La chanson populaire grecque du Dodécanèse*, Vol. 1: *Les textes*. Paris.

Gill, H. A. R., and J. H. Kramers. 1953. *Shorter Encyclopaedia of Islam*. Leiden and London.

Hughes, T. P. 1885. *A Dictionary of Islam*. London.

Jeannaraki, A., 1876. Ἄσματα κρητικὰ μετὰ διστίχων καὶ παροιμίων. Leipzig.

Karamanos, Καραμάνος, K. M. 1928. "Ἄρτα - λαογραφία." In Μεγάλη Ἑλληνικὴ Ἐγκυκλοπαίδεια, Vol. 5, 680–81. 2nd ed., Athens.

Lord, A. B. 1960. *The Singer of Tales*. Cambridge, Mass.

Megas, G. A. 1971. "Τὸ τραγούδι τοῦ γεφυρίου τῆς Ἄρτας: Συγκριτικὴ μελέτη." *Laografía* 27: 25–212.

Papadopoullos, Παπαδόπουλλος, Θ. 1975. Δημώδη κυπριακὰ ἄσματα, ἐξ ἀνεκδότων συλλογῶν τοῦ ΙΘ´ αἰῶνος. Publications of the Cyprus Research Centre, 5. Nicosia.

Politis, N. G. 1901. Μελέται περὶ τοῦ βίου καὶ τῆς γλώσσης τοῦ ἑλληνικοῦ λαοῦ—Παροιμίαι, Τόμ. Γ'. Athens; photographic reprint, Erganis, Athens, 1965.

Politis, N. G. 1904. Μελέται περὶ τοῦ βίου καὶ τῆς γλώσσης τοῦ ἑλληνικοῦ λαοῦ—Παραδόσεις. 2 vols. Athens; photographic reprint, Erganis, Athens, 1965.

Romaios, Ρωμαῖος, K. 1952. "Δημοτικὰ τραγούδια Σέρβων καὶ Βουλγάρων δανεισμένα ἀπὸ ἑλληνικὰ πρότυπα." Arheíon tou Thrakikoú Laografikoú ke Glossikoú Thisavrou 17: 307–65.

Sako, Z. 1966. "Eléments balkaniques communs dans le rite de la ballade de l'emmurement." Studia albanica (3e année) 2: 207–13.

Schmidt, B. 1871. Das Volksleben der Neugriechen. Leipzig.

Thompson, S. 1955–58. Motif-Index of Folk-Literature. 6 vols. Revised and enlarged ed., Copenhagen and Bloomington, Indiana.

Vargyas, L. 1967. Researches into the Medieval History of Folk Ballad. Budapest.

"Master Manole and the
Monastery of Argeş"

It may come as something of a surprise for the reader to learn that one of the most celebrated essays written about "The Walled-Up Wife" was penned by Mircea Eliade (1907–1986), who was arguably the leading scholar of myth, ritual, and religion in the twentieth century. Born in Romania, Eliade maintained an interest in his native folklore all his life. Although his focus is clearly on the Romanian versions of the legend/ballad, his mastery of the comparative folklore literature is amply demonstrated in his erudite footnotes. Eliade's approach includes a healthy dose of "myth-ritual," but is also infused with some hints of Jungian archetypal influence. For Eliade, "The wife who consents to be immolated so that an edifice may rise on her own body indubitably represents the scenario of a primordial myth—primordial in the sense that it reports a spiritual creation very much earlier than the protohistorical and historical periods of the peoples of southeastern Europe." In Eliade's view, the ballad is thus a survival *from prehistoric times, survival of a myth tied to a foundation or construction sacrifice. The ballad accordingly cuts through eons of time, linking the present inextricably with the past. For Eliade then, "contemporary" folklore can be "contemporary" and an "archaic" survival simultaneously.*

For an entrée into Eliade's voluminous writings, see Douglas Allen and Dennis Doeing, Mircea Eliade: An Annotated Bibliography *(New York: Garland, 1980). For scholarship devoted to the Romanian version since Eliade, see Ion Taloş,* Meşterul Manole: Contributie la studiul unei teme de folclor european *(Bucharest: Editura Minerva, 1973); and his later essay, "Die eingemauerte Frau: Neuere Forschungsarbeiten über die südosteuropäische Bauopfer-Ballade,"* Jahrbuch für Volksliedforschung 34 (1989): 105–16.

Reprinted from Mircea Eliade, *Zalmoxis: The Vanishing God* (Chicago: University of Chicago Press; © 1972 by the University of Chicago), pp. 164–90.

Folk Poetry and Religious Folklore

In a book published in 1943, *Comentarii la Legenda Meşterului Manole* (Bucharest, Ed. Publicom, 144 pp.), we attempted a first exegesis of the spiritual universe revealed by the famous Romanian ballad of "Master Manole and the Monastery of Argeş." Another study, *Manole and Construction Rites*, will pursue and develop the investigation on a larger scale, embracing matters of interest to Romanianists and Balkanologists, folklorists, and historians of religions. Various reasons having so far deferred its publication, we propose, in the following pages, to indicate its general outlines and to record some of its findings.

As a subject of study, the legend of the Monastery of Argeş can be approached from different, but complementary, points of view. If we leave aside the literary imitations, translations, and adaptations of the ballad collected and published by Alecsandri—all of which belong to literary history and comparative literature—and confine our investigation strictly to the various productions that belong to folklore, several approaches suggest themselves. The first problem (1) is one of esthetics: the literary value of the various recorded versions and their possible comparison with similar folk creations of the Balkan Peninsula and Danubian Europe; (2) next comes the historical problem, with its several aspects: *(a)* the dissemination of the motif in the folklore of southeastern and Danubian Europe; *(b)* the possible borrowings and mutual influences within these cultural areas; *(c)* identification of the "center of origin" of the region in which the ballad came into existence as a poetic entity. Besides these two points of view, which are chiefly of interest to specialists in Romanian and Balkan folklore and *Stilkritik*, we must also take into account: (3) the point of view of the general folklorist, who undertakes to collect and compare similar legends and beliefs among other European peoples, even when they have not given rise to autonomous poetic creations; (4) the point of view of the ethnologist, who considers the whole corpus of construction rites, documented practically everywhere in the world, and attempts to find their place in the various cultural structures; and finally (5), the point of view of the historian of religions, who, while using the conclusions of the folklorists and ethnologists, sets himself to rediscover the existential situation that gave rise to the ideology and rites of construction, and tries, above all, to make the theoretical universe based upon such a situation intelligible.

The researches of L. Şăineanu, M. Arnaudov, P. Skok, P. Caraman, D. Caracostea, G. Cocchiara, and D. Găzdaru have adequately advanced the study of Romanian and Balkan ballads; the details of the investigation and the relevant bibliographies will be found in their several studies.[1] For our purpose it will suffice to cite the basic document: "Mânăstirea Argeşului" (first published by Vasile Alecsandri in his *Balade adunate şi îndreptate* [Iaşi, 1852]), of which an English prose translation follows:

"*The Ballad of Master Manole and the Monastery of Argeş*"

I

Down the Argeş, through a lovely valley, comes the Black Prince with ten companions—nine great masters, apprentices, and masons, and the tenth, Master Manole, who surpasses them all. They are going together to choose a site for a monastery worthy to be remembered. And as they went along they met a poor shepherd, playing his flute. As soon as he saw him, the prince spoke to him:

"Little shepherd, playing your flute as you lead your flock upstream, or lead your flock downstream, have you never, as you passed, seen an abandoned wall, left unfinished among pillars and hazels?"

"Yes, Lord, as I passed I have seen an abandoned wall, left unfinished. When my dogs see it, they rush to it, howling dismally."

Hearing him, the prince is glad and quickly sets off again to find the wall, with nine masons, nine great masters, and the tenth, Manole, who surpasses them all.

"There it stands, my wall. Here I have chosen the place for my monastery. So you, great masters, apprentices, and masons, make ready now to fall to work, raising and building a high monastery, unequalled on earth. I will give you gold, I will make you noblemen. Otherwise, I will have you walled in, walled in alive, in the foundations."

II

The masters hurried, stretched out their measures, measured the ground, dug wide trenches, worked without stopping, and raised the wall. But, work as they would, all the work they did fell during the night. And it was the same on the second day, and the third day the same, and again on the fourth day. They worked in vain. The prince was amazed and chided them, he scowled and threatened them: "I will bury you alive in the foundations!"

The great masters, apprentices, and masons trembled as they worked, worked as they trembled, through long summer days, from dawn to dark. But Manole, meanwhile, stopped and worked no more; he lay down to sleep and dreamed a dream. When he woke he spoke to them thus:

"Nine great masters, apprentices, and masons, do you know what I dreamed while I lay sleeping? From the sky I heard someone speaking to me thus: 'All that is built will fall at night until we decide, all of us together, to wall in the wife or the sister who at dawn tomorrow will be the first to come bringing food to her husband or her brother.' So if you want to finish this holy monastery, worthy to be remembered, we must all promise and swear to keep the secret; and the wife or sister who tomorrow at dawn will be the first to arrive, her we will sacrifice and wall in."

III

It is dawn, and Manole springs up. And he climbs the hoarding of branches and, higher still, up on the scaffold; and he looked across the field and searched the road. Alas, what did he see? Who was coming? It was his young wife, the flower of the fields! Nearer she came; she was bringing him food to eat, wine to drink. As soon as he saw her, his heart bounded. He fell to his knees and prayed, weeping:

"O Lord, pour down on the mountains a foaming rain that will change the streams to torrents! Make the waters rise to stop my sweetheart, make them stop her in the valley and turn her back!"

The Lord took pity on him and heard his prayer. He gathers the clouds, darkening the sky. And suddenly there falls a foaming rain that flows in streams and swells the torrents. But however hard the rain fell, it did not stop his sweetheart. On she walked, nearer and nearer. Manole sees her, and crosses himself again:

"O Lord, make a wind blow, blow over the earth! Let it strip the pines and bend the sycamores and throw down the mountains and make my sweetheart turn and go back to the valley!"

And the Lord took pity on him and made a wind blow, a wind over the earth, that bent the sycamores and stripped the pines and threw down the mountains. But Ana does not turn back. Doubtfully she walked along the road, nearer and nearer, and then—alas for her!—she was there.

IV

The great masters, apprentices, and masons were glad when they saw her. But Manole sadly embraces his sweetheart, takes her in his arms, and climbs the scaffold. He set her on the wall and said to her, jestingly:

"Fear nothing, my dear one, for we are going to wall you in up here, but it is only in jest."

Ana trusted him and laughed and blushed. And Manole sighed and began to raise the wall. The wall grew and buried her, up to the ankles, then to the calves. And she—poor thing!—stopped laughing and said:

"Manole, Manole, stop your jesting now, for the jest is not good, Manole, Manole, Master Manole! The wall presses me too hard and breaks my little body!"

But Manole did not answer her and went on working, the wall rose

74

ever higher, burying her, up to the ankles, up to the calves, up to the ribs, up to the breasts. But she—poor thing!—went on weeping and speaking to him:

"Manole, Manole, Master Manole, the wall presses me too hard and crushes my breasts and breaks my child."

Manole, in a fury, worked on. And the wall rose and covered her, up to the sides, up to the breasts, up to the lips, up to the eyes. And so the poor thing was seen no more; but they heard her still, speaking from the wall:

"Manole, Manole, the wall presses me too hard, and my life is failing!"

V

Down the Argeş, through a lovely valley, comes the Black Prince to say his prayers in the monastery, the rich building, the monastery so high, unequalled on earth. The prince looked at it and was glad and spoke to them thus:

"You, my masters, ten great masons, tell me the truth, with your hands on your hearts, if you can build me another monastery—one in my memory, far more shining and far more beautiful!"

And the great masters, apprentices, and masons, sitting on the wood-work high on the roof, were proud and glad, and they answered him:

"Such great masters as we, masons and apprentices—there are none others on this earth. Know then, that, whenever you please, we can build another monastery, far more shining and far more beautiful."

The prince listens and ponders. Then he orders the scaffold torn down, the ladders taken away, and the masons, the ten great masters, left to rot there on the woodwork high on the roof. The masters ponder, and they make themselves wings that fly, wings of light shingles. They spread them then and jump off into space. But they fall, and where they strike the ground their bodies are shattered. And poor Manole, Master Manole, even as he jumps he hears a voice coming out of the wall, a stifled voice, a most dear voice, sobbing and saying:

"Manole, Manole, Master Manole, the wall presses me too hard and crushes my weeping breast and breaks my child and my life is failing."

He hears it so close to him that he is bewildered. His eyes darkened, the world was spinning, the clouds came back, and from the woodwork high on the roof, he fell, dead; and where he was shattered a clear fountain sprang up, a trickle of water, salt with his tears.[2]

Some Balkan Ballads

In the Neo-Greek ballads the construction that collapses every night is the Bridge of Arta. The variant from Corcyra, used by Sainéan, shows us forty master masons and sixty journeymen working in vain for three years. A genie *(stoicheion)* finally reveals to them that the bridge cannot be finished except at a price: the wife of the chief master mason must be sacrificed. On hearing this, he faints. When he returns to his senses he writes his wife a message ordering her to dress slowly and come to him on the scaffold, but still so slowly that she will not arrive until late, about noon. He gives his message to a bird; but the bird tells his wife to hurry. Finding him sad and downcast, she asks him why; the master mason tells her that he has lost his wedding ring under the bridge, and she goes down to look for it. It is then that the masons immolate her. The wife dies bemoaning her fate. They were three sisters, she laments, and all three died in the same tragic way: the eldest under the bridge over the Danube, the second under the walls of the city of Avlona, and now she, the youngest, under the Arta Bridge. She ends with imprecations: may he tremble as her heart is trembling now, and may those who cross the bridge fall from it as her hair is now falling from her head.[3] In another variant the voice of an archangel announces that the master mason's wife must be immured.[4] In the version from Zakynthos the architect receives the revelation in a dream; as she dies, his wife laments that one of her sisters was immolated in the foundations of a church, another in the walls of a monastery, and she, the third, under the Arta Bridge.[5] In a variant from Trebizond the master mason hears a voice asking him: "What will you give me to keep the wall from falling again?" He answers: "Mother and daughter I can have no longer, but wife I can, and perhaps I shall find a better one."[6] There are still more cruel variants, such as the one from Thrace, in which, when the wife goes down to look for the wedding ring, the master mason calls to her: "I have it here, but you will never leave there!"[7] However, we do not intend to examine all the Neo-Greek versions, of which there are many.[8]

In the Macedo-Romanian version, "Cântilu a pontulu di Narta," the heroes are three brothers, all master masons. A bird reveals to the eldest that he must immure the wife of the youngest. This version contains a notable detail that is lacking in both the Daco-Romanian type and the Neo-Greek variants: the victim begs that her bosom be left uncovered so that she can continue to suckle her infant.[9] This detail also appears in a variant from Herzegovina[10] (the Gypsy woman immured under the Mostar Bridge), in a Bosnian version[11] (about the city of Tešang), and in nearly all the Serbian and Bulgarian forms. These tell the following story: For ten years Master Manole, with his two brothers, has been working on the fortified city of Smilen without being able to finish it. A dream reveals to him that he must sacrifice the first wife who comes to the scaffold the next day. The three brothers swear to one another that they will not tell their wives, but only Manole keeps his oath. When his wife arrives and finds him in tears because, he says, he has lost his wedding ring, she goes down to look for it and is immured. She asks that her breast be left uncovered so that she can suckle her infant, and soon afterward a fountain of milk begins to flow from the wall.[12] A variant from Trevensko ends with Manole reflecting: "That is why it is not good to swear an oath, for a man is often mistaken."[13]

The Serbo-Croatian ballads, recorded by Vuk Stefanović Karadžić at the beginning of the nineteenth century and published in his authoritative collection of popular songs, tell of three princely brothers who are building the city of Scutari. A fairy (vila) destroys all their day's work during the night. She reveals to one of the brothers, Vukašin, that the city cannot be built unless they are able to find and immure the twins Stojan and Stojana.[14] For three years an emissary, Dišimir, travels over the world without finding them. Vukašin goes back to work, but still fruitlessly. This time the vila reveals to them that, instead of the mythical twins, they can immure the wife of one of the brothers. The rest of the story follows the familiar pattern: The three brothers swear to one another that they will let their wives suspect nothing, but only the youngest, Gojćo, keeps his word, and his faithful wife ends by being immured. She begs them to leave "a little window for her breast" so that she can suckle her infant, and another window in front of her eyes so that she can see the house.[15] The ballad of the city of Scutari is also known in Albania.[16]

Finally, the Hungarian versions present twelve master masons building the city of Deva. Their leader, Clemens, decides to sacrifice the first wife who comes with food for them the next day. There are no supernatural elements (genie, fairy, archangel, dream), nor do the master masons take an oath. When the wife arrives, Clemens tells her what her fate is to be and begins to immure her. The infant cries, and the mother consoles it: "There will always be kind ladies to suckle it and kind youths to rock it."[17]

The Exegeses: Folklorists, Historians of Literature, *Stilkritiker*

Every national type of ballad comprises an original structuring of its various dramatic, psychological, and literary elements. A comparative study must analyze them meticulously, not only from the point of view of the life of the narrative, but also on the plane of stylistics and literary quality. It is obviously risky—not to say presumptuous—to pronounce upon the artistic value of each national type; such a judgment would presuppose not only a thorough knowledge of Hungarian, Romanian, and all the Balkan languages, but also a profound familiarity with their folk literatures and their individual esthetics. Even so, certain general conclusions emerge from the mere treatment of the ballad material. Sainéan summarized the results of his comparative studies as follows:

> From the point of view of beauty and comparative originality, the Serbian and Romanian versions take first place; the Bulgarian songs, because of their loose form, give the impression of being detached fragments; the Albanian traditions are pale imitations of the Greek or Serbian ballads, and the Macedo-Romanian song is an almost literal reproduction of one of the Neo-Greek versions; the Magyar variants seem to echo the Romanian ballad, while the Neo-Greek versions, because of certain characteristic features, seem to occupy a place apart in this group of poetic productions.[18]

In making this classification, Sainéan was thinking as much of the genesis and dissemination of the ballads as of their respective literary values. The opinions of scholars differ most in regard to their genesis. Politis, Arnaudov, Caraman, and, most recently, Cocchiara agree—though for different reasons—in locating the place of origin in Greece. Arnaudov would derive the Albanian, Bulgarian, and Macedo-Romanian ballads from the Greek type; the Serbian type from the Albanian and Bulgarian forms; the Romanian type from the Bulgarians; and the Hungarian type from the Romanians.[19] Yet Caracostea remarks that Arnaudov also speaks of polygenesis, which would militate against the rigidity of the schema he advances. On the other hand, Arnaudov himself had noted the small circulation of the ballad in northern Bulgaria. But we should expect the opposite phenomenon if that region is really the bridge by which the ballad passed into Romania.[20] However this may be, it is certain that circulation took place in both directions. D. Găzdaru found the name Curtea, an echo of "Curtea de Argeş," in a Bulgarian variant, which implies that the Romanian form passed south of the Danube.[21]

Skok came to very different conclusions. In his view, the Macedo-Romanian masons played an essential part in the creation and dissemination of the ballad. The Croatian scholar observes that in all the Romanian variants the masons are regarded as beings outside the common run of mankind ("Manole is a genie who communicates with the divinity"); in addition, their trade itself condemns masons to sacrifice their families; hence their tragic fate. The poetic elaboration of this motif, Skok holds, is inconceivable except in a masonic milieu. Now the trade of mason was practiced throughout the Balkan Peninsula by Macedo-Romanians, among whom masons are called *goge;* the Macedo-Romanians had so thoroughly identified themselves with masons that the Macedo-Romanian word *goga* became, for the Serbs and Albanians, synonymous with *mason.*[22]

However we may judge Skok's general thesis, he was the first to call due attention to the capital role of masons in the thematization of the ritual of constructions. Down to the last century the master masons preserved "trade secrets" that are unquestionably archaic. As we shall soon see, the work of building is bound up with a ritual and a symbolism that come down to us from a very distant past. Every craft, but especially the crafts of the mason and the blacksmith, was imbued with a ritual meaning and a symbology that were accessible only to "initiates." This astonishing conservatism is partly explained by the profound echo that the different modalities of "making," "constructing," "building" have always awakened in the depths of the human soul. A whole mythology of "making" still survives, in many forms and variously disguised, in human behavior.[23]

According to Skok, the name Manole itself suffices to prove the Romanian origin of the ballad.[24] Caraman, on the contrary, comes to the conclusion that this anthroponym belongs specifically to the Neo-Greek onomastic vocabulary and that it passed into Romanian with Greek phonetics.[25] The name Manole, he avers, is the symbol of the architect in Greece.[26] On the other hand, in the Serbo-Croatian versions the master mason, Rado, is called Neimaru or Neimare; and the substantive *maimare* occurs in the Macedo-Romanian and Bulgarian ballads. This word, Caraman remarks, represents Turkish *mimar,* "architect," which, by a frequent process in folk etymology, the Macedo-Romanians assimilated to Romanian *mai mare, mai marlu,* "greater."[27] In our opinion this fact at least partly confirms Skok's hypothesis concerning the role of the Macedo-Romanians in the dissemination of the ballad.

Caraman accepts Politis' thesis, though for different reasons: in the Romanian scholar's view, the archaism and thematic simplicity of the Neo-Greek ballads shows that the soil of Greece was the site of the passage from construction *ritual* to the *literary* folk creation. For Caraman, again, the perfection of the Romanian and Serbian forms is further proof that the Romanians and Serbs did not "invent" the ballad, that they only elaborated it and exploited all its artistic possibilities. Cocchiara rejects this last argument: for him, there can be no question of a literary evolution, for each song originates with its author; what is more, he seems not to be convinced of the literary superiority of the Romanian forms.[28]

It is to be regretted that the eminent Italian folklorist did not know Caracostea's comparative and stylistic study. In some penetrating pages Caracostea has rightly brought out the artistic qualities of the Romanian versions. For him, it is in its Romanian form that the legend fulfilled its esthetic destiny, whatever its "origin" and however frequently its southeastern European variants may occur. Caracostea rightly emphasizes the ritual nature of the beginning of the ballad "Curtea de Argeş:" the search for a propitious site to build the monastery,[29] whereas in all the other forms the action begins with the mysterious collapse of the walls during the night. The late lamented critic also shows that in the Romanian form Manole always remains at the center of the action, whereas in the Serbian ballad, for example, the accent falls on the wife and her mother love. In the Romanian ballad the woman accepts her ritual immolation with resignation and even serenity; in other versions from southeastern Europe the wife laments and curses her fate. The ballad of "The Monastery of Argeş" has a continuation, which, contrary to the view of certain folklorists, is not an excrescence: Manole's winged flight and his tragic death. Death in some sort restores to him the wife he has just sacrificed.

But stylistic analysis of the ballads does not exhaust their rich content. An entire study could—and should—be made on the structure of the imaginary universes revealed by the various poetic creations. It is significant that the "construction" varies: it can be a bridge (Greece, Bulgaria, Macedo-Romanians), a city (Yugoslavia, Bulgaria, Albania, Hungary), or a monastery (Romania). To be sure, the choice is in great part explained by the real existence of such works of architecture: the folk imagination was struck in one place by the presence of a bridge, in another by the building of a monastery,[30] in yet another by a city wall. But once these "real objects" have been transfigured into images, they no longer belong to the immediate universe, possess a utilitarian function. Freed from the concrete context, the images recover their specific dimensions and their primordial symbolism. But a ballad, like any other creation on the imaginary plane, no longer deals with "real objects" but with images, archetypes, symbols. Hence it would be of the utmost interest to study the different universes of our ballads from this point of view. Such a study would proceed to elucidate all the symbolic meanings of the

Bridge (initiatory ordeal, perilous passage from one mode of being to another: from death to life, from ignorance to illumination, from immaturity to maturity, etc.); it would then elucidate the cosmological structure of the "City," at once *imago mundi* and "Center of the World," the sacred site where communication between Heaven, Earth, and the Underworld is possible; finally it would dwell on all the cosmological and paradisal symbolism of the Monastery, at the same time image of the Cosmos and of the Heavenly Jerusalem, of the Universe in its visible totality and of Paradise.

We must add at once that such an exegesis of images and symbols is validated today both by the history of religions and by depth psychology. In other words, the analysis of an image and the interpretation of its symbolism can deliberately disregard what consciousness of its symbolism the individual or the society that serves as the vehicle for the image may or may not possess. A symbol delivers its message and fulfills its function even when its meaning is not apprehended by *consciousness*.[31] This makes it all the more remarkable that the symbolism of the church-monastery was still perceived and culturally valorized by eastern European Christendom, the heir of Byzantium.[32] In other words, until the most recent times the people of the Balkano-Danubian area were conscious that a church or monastery represented both the Cosmos and the Heavenly Jerusalem or Paradise: there was a conscious cognition of the architectonic and iconographic symbolism present in the sacred buildings, and this cognition was effected both through religious experience (liturgy) and through the traditional culture (theology). More precisely, there was a historically recent religious re-evaluation and revivification (Christianity) of an archaic symbolism: for the sanctuary as *imago mundi* and Center of the World is already present in the Paleo-Oriental cultures (Mesopotamia, Egypt, India, China, etc.).[33]

Construction Rites: Morphology and History

The archaism of the images and symbols present in the ballads is abundantly confirmed by the practices and beliefs concerning constructional sacrifices. We know that such beliefs are found almost everywhere in Europe, though they did not give rise to a folk literature comparable to that of southeastern Europe. There is no need to rehearse them here. Since the days of Jacob Grimm, and more especially of Felix Liebrecht,[34] investigators have collected a considerable number of legends, superstitions, and customs more or less directly based upon the rituals of construction. A far-reaching series of investigations had begun to appear in the *Revue des traditions populaires* from 1890; Paul Sébillot, G. L. Gomme, R. Andree, E. Westermarck, and others published variously oriented contributions, while Paul Sartori brought together a very rich documentation in 1898.[35] All this material was used and supplemented by us in 1943, and by Cocchiara in the study that he published in 1950.[36] At this point we will only state that the motif of a construction whose completion demands a human sacrifice is documented in Scandinavia and among the Finns, the Letts, and the Estonians,[37] among the Russians and the Ukrainians,[38] among the Germans,[39] in France,[40] in England,[41] in Spain.[42] A celebrated episode is the one reported by the Armorican monk Nennius (second half of the tenth century) in his *Historia Britonum* (chap. 18): when the fort that King Gorthigern was building fell every night, the druids advised him to pour the blood of a "fatherless" child over it, and the king did so.[43] According to the *Life of Saint Columba*, written by Saint Adamnan, a similar sacrifice was offered by Columba (Colmcille) when he built the church of Hy.[44]

It must be made clear that such beliefs and legends were dependent upon a ritual scenario: whether a human effigy or the "shade" of a victim was involved, or one of the countless forms of sacrifice by substitution (immolation of an animal on the foundations or upon first entering the house) was considered sufficient, a blood sacrifice always assured the solidity and long life of a building. This is not the place to discuss the problem of sacrifice by substitution, some aspects of which are still obscure.[45] Suffice it to say that the discovery of skeletons in the foundations of sanctuaries and palaces in the ancient Near East, in prehistoric Italy, and elsewhere puts the reality of such sacrifices beyond doubt.[46] The presence of effigies or symbols in the foundations further testifies to the various practices by which victims were substituted.

In the form of attenuated ritual, of legend, or of vague beliefs, constructional sacrifices are found almost all over the world. A considerable number of facts has been collected in modern India, where the belief certainly had a ritual reality in ancient times.[47] Similar sacrifices are found in the Central American cultures,[48] but also in Oceania and Polynesia,[49] in Indochina,[50] in China,[51] and in Japan.[52] Special mention must be made of the sacrifice at the founding of a village among the Mande people of the Sudan—a complex ritual, fully studied by Frobenius, the symbolism of which is not without resemblances to the symbolism implicit in the foundation of Rome.[53] Obviously, in each instance individual studies must determine to what extent the immolation of victims is documented ritually and to what extent it survives only as legend or superstition.

A large volume would be required for an adequate exposition and discussion of the many forms this type of sacrifice has assumed down the ages and in different cultural contexts. To put it briefly, we will only say that, in the last analysis, all these forms depend upon a common ideology, which could be summarized as follows: to last, a construction (house, technical accomplishment, but also a spiritual undertaking) must be animated, that is, must receive both life and a soul. The "transference" of the soul is possible only by means of a sacrifice, in other words, by a violent death. We may even say that the victim continues its existence after death, no longer in its physical body but in the new body—the construction—which it has "animated" by its immolation; we may even speak of an "architectonic body" substituted for a body of flesh.[54] The ritual transference of life by means of a sacrifice is not confined to constructions (temples, cities, bridges, houses) and utilitarian objects;[55] human victims are also immolated to assure the success of an undertaking,[56] or even the historical longevity of a spiritual enterprise.[57]

Blood Sacrifices and Cosmogonic Myths

The exemplary model for all these forms of sacrifice is very probably a cosmogonic myth, that is, the myth that explains the Creation by the killing of a primordial Giant (of the type of Ymir, Purusa, P'an-ku): his organs produce the various cosmic regions. This motif was disseminated over an immense area; it occurs with the greatest frequency in eastern Asia.[58] In general, the cosmogonic myth has been shown to be the model for all myths and rites related to a "making," a "work," a "creation." The mythical motif of a "birth" brought about by an immolation is found in countless contexts: it is not only the Cosmos that is born as the result of the immolation of a Primordial Being and from his own substance; the same is true of food plants, human races, or different social classes.[59] Best known of all are the Indonesian and Oceanian myths that relate the voluntary immolation of a Woman or Maiden in order that the different species of food plants may spring from her body.[60]

It is in this mythical horizon that we must seek the spiritual source of our construction rites. If we remember, too, that the traditional societies saw the human dwelling as an *imago mundi*, it becomes still clearer that every work of foundation symbolically reproduced the

83

cosmogony. The cosmic meaning of the dwelling was reinforced by the symbolism of the Center; for, as is beginning to be better seen today, every house—*a fortiori* every palace, temple, city—was believed to be at the Center of the World.[61] In some recent studies we have shown that the homologation house-Cosmos (in many variants: the tent assimilated to the celestial vault, the central pole to the *axis mundi*, etc.) is one of the distinguishing characteristics of the nomadic hunting and pastoral cultures of America, northern and central Asia, and Africa.[62] But the idea of a Center through which the *axis mundi* passes and which, in consequence, makes communication between Sky and Earth possible is also found at a still earlier stage of culture. The Achilpa of Australia always carry a sacred pole with them on their wanderings and decide what direction they shall take by the direction toward which it leans. Their myth relates that the divine being Numbakula, after "cosmicizing" the territory of the future Achilpa, creating their ancestor, and founding their institutions, disappeared in the following way: he made the sacred pole from the trunk of a gum tree, anointed it with blood, and climbed up it into the sky. The sacred pole represents the cosmic axis, and settling in a territory is equivalent to a "cosmicization" from a center of radiation. In other words, despite their being constantly on the move, the Achilpa never leave the "Center of the World": they are always "centered" and in communication with the Sky into which Numbakula vanished.[63]

We can, then, distinguish two conceptions in regard to the religious function of the human dwelling: (1) the earlier, documented among hunting peoples and nomadic pastoralists, consecrates the dwelling and, in general, the inhabited territory by assimilating them to the Cosmos through the symbolism of the "Center of the World"; (2) the other, and more recent, conception (it first appears in the societies of the paleocultivators, the *Urpflanzer*) is characterized, as we have seen, by repetition of the cosmogonic myth: because the world (or food plants, men, etc.) arose from the primordial sacrifice of a Divine Being, every construction demands the immolation of a victim. We should note that, in the spiritual horizon concomitant with this conception, the actual substance of the victim[64] is transformed into the beings or objects that issue from it after its death by violence. In one myth the mountains are the bones of the Primordial Giant, the clouds his brain, and so on; in another the coconut is the actual flesh of the Maiden Hainuwele. On the plane of construction rites the immolated being, as we have seen, acquires a new body: the building that it has made a "living," hence enduring, thing by its violent death. In all these myths death by violence is creative.

From the viewpoint of cultural history, it is in the conception of the paleocultivators that we must situate the blood rites integral to construction. A. E. Jensen came to a similar conclusion, chiefly on the evidence of the rites that accompany the building of the "men's house" *(dárimo)* among the Kiwai.[65] According to Landtmann, the ceremony is conducted as follows: When it is decided to build a *dárimo*, the village chooses an elderly couple and informs their eldest son of the choice; he rarely refuses: he daubs his face with mud and begins to mourn for his old parents, for it is the common belief that they will not outlive the completion of the building. The old man receives the name "father of the *dárimo*," and his old wife that of "burning woman." It is they who play the principal part in the building of the cult house. The work comprises the erection of a central pillar, anointing it with the blood of an enemy, and, above all, the sacrifice of a prisoner, for a new cult house is not fit for use before such a sacrifice.[66] The myth that provides the basis and the justification for this ritual relates how the divinity who was immolated *in illo tempore* became the first of the dead: the *dárimo*, the cult house, is the terrestrial reproduction of the beyond. According to Jensen, the Kiwai rite represents the archetype of the *Bauopfer* [construction sacrifice], and all the other forms of constructional sacrifice found throughout the world are connected with the same exemplary model. We consider it difficult to follow him so far. Rather, we believe that the Kiwai rite represents an already specialized variant of the original scenario, which included only the following moments: immolation of a divine being, followed by a "creation," that is, his metamorphosis into a substance or a form that did not exist before. The Kiwai sequence— especially the immolation of the divinity, his transformation into the realm of the dead, and the reproduction of the latter in the cult house—already presents an amplification of the original schema.

Archaism and Survival

Whatever may be concluded as to the Kiwai version, constructional blood sacrifices very probably belong, as historico-cultural phenomena, to the spiritual world of the paleocultivators. Does this mean that wherever we find such rites we have vestiges transmitted without a break from those distant times? No. Nor does it mean that the presence of the *Bauopfer* in any given culture necessarily implies that the culture belongs entirely to the plane of the paleocultivators. In a number of cases, rites or myths have passed from one people to another and from one historical epoch to another without entailing a transmission of the original culture implied by such rites and myths. In our view there is something of greater importance than the chronological precisions that can be arrived at concerning such beliefs; it is the fact that certain cultures or certain peoples have chosen or preserved some particular vision of the world, whereas others have rejected it or very soon forgotten it. We mean that establishing the origins, the age, and the historical vicissitudes of a belief or a cultural complex suffices neither for an understanding of them as spiritual phenomena nor to make their history intelligible. Two other problems, which we consider just as important, immediately arise: *(a)* What is the real meaning of all these beliefs and all these cultural complexes? *(b)* For what reason has some particular people preserved, elaborated, and enriched them? These are difficult questions, to which it is not always possible to give a satisfactory answer, but which must not be forgotten when one undertakes to write even the most elementary page of a history of the spirit.

To return to our Balkano-Danubian ballads: the archaism of their motifs and images stands out still more clearly after all that we have said. The wife who consents to be immolated so that an edifice may rise on her own body indubitably represents the scenario of a primordial myth—primordial in the sense that it reports a spiritual creation very much earlier than the protohistorical and historical periods of the peoples of southeastern Europe. It is still too early to attempt to determine how and by what means this mythico-ritual scenario managed to survive in southeastern Europe. Yet we are in possession of several facts that can explain the archaism of these creations of Balkano-Danubian folk poetry. They are these: (1) The Balkano-Danubian countries are the only ones in which the constructional sacrifice has given rise to remarkable folk literary creations; (2) The scarcity of similar legends among the Russians, the Poles, and the Ukrainians seems to exclude the hypothesis of a Slavic origin for this literary motif; (3) The Romanians and all the Balkan peoples preserve a common substratum, inherited from the Thracians (and which, furthermore, is the principal unifying element for the entire Balkan Peninsula); (4) Other cultural elements common to all the Balkan peoples seem still more ancient than the Geto-Thracian heritage, presenting, as they do, a pre-Indo-European aspect;[67] (5) Finally, we must bear in mind that the Thracians and the Cimmerians shared in a protohistorical culture whose successive irradiations crossed central Asia and instigated the appearance of new cultural aspects on the shores of the China Sea and at Dongson.[68]

We must not let ourselves be led astray by the "contemporaneousness" of folklore: it very often happens that beliefs and customs still alive in certain eminently conservative parts of Europe (among which Romania and the Balkans must always be reckoned) reveal strata of culture more archaic than the one represented, for example, by the "classic" Greek and Roman mythologies. The fact is especially evident in regard to everything to do with the customs and magico-religious behavior of hunters and herders. But even among the agriculturalists of contemporary central Europe it has been possible to show to what an extent considerable fragments of prehistoric myths and rituals have been preserved.[69] Systematic research in the field of Romanian and Balkan paleoethnology is still to be undertaken; but it is already established that a certain number of pre-Indo-European cultural elements have been better preserved there than anywhere else in Europe (perhaps with the exception of Ireland and the Pyrenees).

It is not always possible to reconstruct all the phases through which a religious concept passed before it crystallized into folk artistic creations. Then too, as we have already said, it is not here that the chief interest of the investigation lies. It is far more important to arrive at a thorough understanding of the original spiritual universe in which such primordial religious conceptions arose—for they are conceptions that, despite the numerous religious re-evaluations they have undergone (of which the last, Christianity, was also the most radical), have nevertheless survived, at least in the form of "superstitions," of folk beliefs imbued with extremely ancient images and symbols. The fidelity of a people to one or another mythical scenario, to one or another exemplary image, tells us far more about its deeper soul than many of its historical accomplishments. It is not without significance for an understanding of the southeastern European peoples that they alone created the masterpieces of their oral literatures on the basis of so archaic a ritual scenario. D. Caracostea thought he could prove that, among all these productions of the folk, the Romanian ballad of Master Manole was artistically the most accomplished. Even if certain Balkanologists and folklorists are not of his opinion, the fact remains—and it is important—that the ballad of the constructional sacrifice is reckoned a masterpiece in no other Balkan literature. Now it is agreed that the high point of Romanian folk poetry is represented by the ballad of Master Manole and by the "Mioritza." It is significant that these two creations of the Romanian poetic genius have as their dramatic motif a "violent death" serenely accepted. Whether or not this conception derives directly from the famous Getic "joy in death" could be discussed forever. The fact remains that Romanian poetic folklore never succeeded in surpassing these two masterpieces whose seed is the idea of creative death and of death serenely accepted.

Notes

1. Lazăr Şăineanu, *Studii folklorice* (Bucharest, 1896); L. Sainéan [Şăineanu], "Les rites de construction d'après la poésie populaire de l'Europe Orientale," *Revue de l'histoire des religions* 45 (1902): 359–96; M. Arnaudov, "Văgradena nevěsta," *Sbornik za narodni umotvorenija i narodopis* 34 (1920): 245–512; Petar Skok, "Iz balkanske komparativne literature: Rumunske paralele 'zidanju Skadra,'" in *Glasnik Skopskog naučnog društva* (Skoplje, 1929), pp. 220–42; P. Caraman, "Consideratii critice asupra genezii şi răspândirii baladei Meşterului Manole în Balcani," *Buletinul Institutului de filologie română "Alexandru Philippide"* 1 (Iaşi, 1934): 62–102; Giuseppe Morici, "La vitima dell'edifizio," in *Annali del R. Istituto superiore orientale di Napoli* 9 (1937): 177–216; D. Caracostea, "Material sud-est european şi formă românească," *Revista Fundaţiilor regale* (December 1942): 619–66 (see now *Poezia traditională română* 2: [Bucharest, 1969], 2: 185–223); G. Cocchiara, "Il Ponte di Arta e i sacrifici di costruzione," in *Annali del Museo Pitrè* 1 (Palermo, 1950): 38–81; D. Găzdaru, "Legenda Meşterului Manole," in *Arhiva* (Iaşi, 1932), pp. 88–92; Găzdaru, "Contribuţia Românilor la progresul cultural al Slavilor" 3, in *Cuget românesc*, An. 2. No. 3 (Buenos Aires, 1952): 155–59. To shorten the notes, we will in most cases merely give references to the bibliographies contained in our *Comentarii* and in Cocchiara's well-documented study. The learned Italian folklorist seems not to have known our book, though he mentions it (p. 71 n. 118); otherwise he would have taken into account the researches of Găzdaru, Arnaudov, and Caracostea, whose findings we used.

2. Now see Vasile Alecsandri, *Poezii populare ale Românilor* (Bucharest: Ediţie îngrijită de Gh. Vrabie, 1965), 1: 250–60, 2: 159–64 (notes and variants); A. Amzulescu, *Balade populare româneşti* (Bucharest, 1964), 3: 7–58. Cf. also Ion Taloş, "Balada Meşterului Manole şi variantele ei transilvănene," *Revista de folclor* 7 (1962): 22–56; p. 41, bibliography of the variants recorded in Romania and among the Romanians in Yugoslavia; M. Pop, "Nouvelles variantes roumaines du chant du Maître Manole," *Romanoslavica* 9 (1963): 427–55; O. Papadima, "Neagoe Basarab, Meşterul Manole şi vânzătorii de umbre," *Revista de folclor* 7 (1962): 68–78, reprinted in O. Papadima, *Literatura populară română* (Bucharest, 1968), pp. 605–18; G. Vrabie, *Balada populară română* (Bucharest, 1966), pp. 69–108; Lorenzo Renzi, *Canti tradizionali romeni* (Florence, 1969), pp. 75–86 (stylistic and esthetic analysis of the ballad). The folk traditions having to do with construction have been well ana-

lyzed recently by Ion Taloş, "Bausagen in Rumänien," *Fabula* 10 (1969): 196–211).

3. Translations of texts and bibliographical references in Sainéan, "Les rites de construction," pp. 362–63; Arnaudov, "Văgradena nevěsta," pp. 389ff.; Caracostea, "Material sud-est european," pp. 628ff.; Cocchiara, "Il Ponte di Arta," pp. 38–39. Cf. also Eliade, *Comentarii la Legenda Meşterului Manole* (Bucharest, Ed. Publicom, 1943), p. 30.

4. Eliade, *Comentarii,* p. 30; Cocchiara, "Il Ponte di Arta," p. 39.

5. Sainéan, "Les rites de construction," pp. 364–65; Cocchiara, "Il Ponte di Arta," p. 40.

6. Caracostea, "Material sud-est european," p. 629; Eliade, *Comentarii,* p. 31.

7. Caracostea, "Material sud-est european," p. 629; Eliade, *Comentarii,* p. 31.

8. More than forty, according to N. G. Politis' researches; cf. Cocchiara, "Il Ponte di Arta," p. 38 n. 3. But Gheorghios Megas recently stated that he knew 264 variants; cf. Megas in *Laografia* 18 (1959–61): 561–77. The number of Neo-Greek versions and their archaism is impressive, and these elements must be taken into account in any systematic study of the genesis of the ballad. As we shall see, Cocchiara, following Politis and other scholars, is convinced that the true *humus* of the legend is in Greece, and he cites, among other reasons, the fact that the constructional sacrifice is still currently practiced in Greece, in the form of the "flight of the shade" ("Il Ponte di Arta," p. 31). The argument is not conclusive, for as Cocchiara himself remarks (pp. 46–47) the practice is extremely widespread throughout the Balkan Peninsula and in Romania. Similar beliefs and legends are also documented in Armenia (cf. H. D. Siruni, "Legenda fetiţei zidite," *Ani. Anuarul de cultură armeană* [Bucharest, 1941], pp. 243–46) and in the Caucasus (see below, n. 28).

9. It was Kurt Schladenbach who first studied "Die aromunische Ballade von der Artabrucke," in *Jahresbericht des Instituts für rumänische Sprache* 1 (Leipzig, 1894), pp. 79–121. The article escaped the perspicacity of Cocchiara ("Il Ponte di Arta," pp. 42–43), who, however, uses the excellent text published by V. Petrescu, *Mostre de dialectul macedo-român* (Bucharest, 1880), 2: 84–88 and the variants recorded by P. Papahagi, *Basme aromâne* (Bucharest, 1905), pp. 70 and 555.

10. Cf. Eliade, *Comentarii,* p. 31 (citing Paul Sébillot, *Les travaux publics et les mines dans les traditions et les superstitions de tous les pays* [Paris, 1894], p. 93, and *La revue des traditions populaires* 7 [1892]: 691).

11. Eliade, *Comentarii,* p. 31, following Friedrich S. Krauss, "Das Opfer bei den Südslaven," *Mitteilungen der anthropologischen Gesellschaft in Wien* 17 (1887): 16–21; F. S. Krauss, *Volksglaube und religiöser Brauch der Südslaven* (Münster, 1890), pp. 158ff.

12. Translations and commentaries in A. Strauss, *Bulgarische Volkslieder* (Vienna, 1895), pp. 407–8; Caracostea, "Material sud-est european," pp. 632ff., following Arnaudov; Eliade, *Comentarii,* pp. 31–32; Cocchiara, "Il Ponte di

Arta," pp. 43–44. A similar song of the Bulgarian Gypsies has been analyzed by W. R. Halliday, "Song of the Bridge," *Journal of the Gypsy-Lore Society,* 3d series, 4 (1925): 110–14.

13. Arnaudov, quoted by Caracostea, "Material sud-est european," pp. 632–33.

14. On the etymological symbolism of these names (*stojati,* "to stand upright") see our *Comentarii,* p. 33.

15. Cf. texts and bibliographies in Eliade, *Comentarii,* pp. 32–34; Cocchiara, "Il Ponte di Arta," pp. 46–48. The variants are recorded in the article by S. Stefanović, "Die Legende vom Bau der Burg Skutari," *Revue internationale des études balkaniques* 1 (1934): 188ff.

16. Cf. Cocchiara, "Il Ponte di Arta," pp. 49–50.

17. Cf. Sainéan, "Les rites de construction," pp. 392ff.; Arnaudov, "Văgradena nevěsta," pp. 413ff.; Caracostea, "Material sud-est european," pp. 640ff.; Eliade, *Comentarii,* p. 34. Now see Lajos Vargyas, *Researches into the Medieval History of Folk Ballad* (Budapest: Akadémiai Kiado, 1967), pp. 173–233: "The Origin of the Walled-Up Wife."

18. Sainéan, "Les rites de construction," pp. 360–61.

19. Arnaudov, summarized by Caracostea, "Material sud-est european," p. 630 n.; Eliade, *Comentarii,* p. 28.

20. Caracostea, "Material sud-est european," p. 630 n.; Eliade, *Comentarii,* p. 29.

21. D. Găzdaru, "Legenda Meşterului Manole," in *Arhiva* (1932), pp. 88–92; Găzdaru, *Contribuţia Românilor la progresul cultural al Slavilor* (1952), especially pp. 157–59.

22. Skok, "Iz balkanaske komparativne literature," p. 241; Caracostea, "Material sud-est european," p. 624; Eliade, *Comentarii,* p. 29; Găzdaru, *Contribuţia Românilor,* p. 159.

23. On this problem see my book *Forgerons et Alchimistes* (Paris: Flammarion, 1956). See also my "The Forge and the Crucible: A Postscript," *History of Religions* 8 (1968): 74–88.

24. Skok, "Iz balkanaske komparativne literature," pp. 225 and 245; Caracostea, "Material sud-est european," p. 625 n.; Cocchiara, "Il Ponte di Arta," p. 52.

25. Caraman, "Consideratii critice," pp. 95ff.; Cocchiara, "Il Ponte di Arta," p. 52.

26. Caraman, "Consideratii critice," p. 94.

27. Ibid., p. 95; Cocchiara, "Il Ponte di Arta," p. 53 n. 46.

28. Cocchiara, "Il Ponte di Arta," p. 51. A new hypothesis has recently been advanced by Lajos Vargyas: according to him, the origin of the ballad is to be sought in the Caucasus, where it is documented among the Georgians (it is also found among the Mordvinians); the Magyars, who in the seventh and eighth centuries nomadized between the Caucasus and the Don, brought the ballad to Europe and transmitted it to the Bulgarians; the other Balkan peoples acquired it from the Bulgarians; cf. L. Vargyas, "Die Herkunft der un-

garischen Ballade von der eingemauerten Frau," *Acta Ethnographica* (Budapest, 1960), and English translation, "The Origin of the Walled-Up Wife," cited above, n. 17. The hypothesis is not convincing (see the critiques by G. A. Megas in *Laografia* 18 [1959–61]: 561–77; by G. Hadzis in *Ethnographia* 71 [1960]: 558–79; and by Adrian Fochi in *Limbă şi Literatură* 12 [1966]: 373–418). As Ion Taloş observes, Vargyas does not explain the complete absence of the ballad from Hungary (for of the thirty-six Hungarian variants, one was recorded in Czechoslovakia and thirty-five in Transylvania). In addition, the transmission of the ballad to the Bulgarians is not proven; cf. Taloş, "Balada Meşterului Manole şi variantele ei transilvănene," pp. 51–52.

29. In a note published in *Revista Fundaţiilor regale* (April 1944): 213–15, Maria Golescu commented on the theme of "abandoned and unfinished walls," in light of the fact that the Romanian voivodes and boyars were accustomed to restore ruined churches and finish those whose construction had been interrupted for many years as the result of historical vicissitudes. The author refers especially to Ion Donat, *Fundaţiile religioase ale Olteniei* 1 (Craiova, 1937), pp. 22ff., 37ff. Now see Ion Taloş, "Bausagen in Rumänien," *Fabula* 10 (1969): 196–211, especially pp. 204ff. Cf. also D. Strömbäck, "Die Wahl des Kirchenbauplatzes in der Sage und im Volksglauben mit besonderer Rücksicht auf Schweden," in *Humaniora* (Locust Valley, N.Y., 1960), pp. 37ff.

30. It is worth noting the importance of "Curtea de Argeş" and the legends crystallized around "Negru Vodă" for what could be termed the historical mythology of the Romanians.

31. This methodological problem is too important to be decided in a few lines. See my *Images et symboles* (Paris: Gallimard, 1952) and my studies: "Symbolisme du 'vol magique,'" *Numen* 3 (1956): 1–13, reprinted in *Mythes, rêves et mystères* (Paris, 1957), pp. 133–48, and "Centre du monde, temple, maison," in *Le symbolisme cosmique des monuments religieux*, ed. G. Tucci (Rome, 1957), pp. 57–82.

32. On all this see Hans Sedlmayr, *Die Entstehung der Kathedrale* (Zürich, 1950), pp. 118ff. and passim.

33. See my books: *Traité d'histoire des religions* (Paris: Payot, 1949; 2d ed. 1952), pp. 315ff.; *Le mythe de l'éternel retour* (Paris: Gallimard, 1949), pp. 21ff.; *Images et symboles*, pp. 47ff.; and the study cited above, "Centre du monde, temple, maison."

34. Cf. Felix Liebrecht, *Zur Volkskunde: Alte und neue Aufsätze* (Heilbronn, 1879), pp. 284–96 ("Die vergrabenen Menschen").

35. Paul Sartori, "Ueber das Bauopfer," *Zeitschrift für Ethnologie* 30 (1898): 1–54. See also K. Klusemann, *Das Bauopfer* (Graz-Hamburg, 1919); L. D. Burdick, *Foundation Rites, with Some Kindred Ceremonies* (New York: Abbey Press, n.d.), a learned but chaotic work; the author is unaware of Sartori's investigations; Inger Margrette Boberg, *Baumeistersagen*, FFC, No. 151 (Helsinki, 1955); cf. the articles "Bauopfer" and "Einmauern" in Hans Bächtold-Staubli and Eduard Hoffman-Krayer, eds., *Handwörterbuch des deutschen Aberglaubens*, 10 vols. (Berlin, 1927–1942).

36. In the following notes we shall confine ourselves to citing the bibliographies contained in the studies by Sartori and Cocchiara and in our book, *Comentarii*. When the occasion arises we will cite certain works not recorded in the Italian folklorist's study.

37. Finns: Sartori, "Ueber das Bauopfer," p. 13; Eliade, *Comentarii*, p. 38; Cocchiara, "Il Ponte di Arta," p. 55 n. 53. Letts: Andrejs Johansons, "Das Bauopfer der Letten" (*Arv* 18–19 [1962–63], reprinted in *Der Schirmherr des Hofes im Volksglauben der Letten* [Stockholm, 1964], pp. 55–75); Estonians: Oskar Loorits, *Grundzüge des estnischen Volksglaubens* 2, 1 (Lund, 1951), p. 136; for the dissemination of the motif see the map, p. 137.

38. Valeriu St. Ciobanu, *Jertfa zidirii la Ucraineni şi Ruşi* (Chişinău, 1930); D. Zelenin, *Russische (Ostslavische) Volkskunde* (Berlin, 1927), p. 287; Eliade, *Comentarii*, p. 38; Cocchiara, "Il Ponte di Arta," p. 55 n. 51.

39. Sartori, "Ueber das Bauopfer"; Jan de Vries, "De sage van het ingemetselde kind," *Nederlandsch Tijdschrift voor volkskunde* 32 (1927): 1–13; Cocchiara, "Il Ponte di Arta," p. 55 and n. 55.

40. Eliade *Comentarii*, p. 39; Cocchiara, "Il Ponte di Arta," p. 60.

41. Cocchiari, "Il Ponte di Arta," pp. 58ff.

42. A. Popescu-Telega, *Asemănări şi analogii în folklorul român şi iberic* (Craiova, 1927), pp. 12ff.; Eliade, *Comentarii*, p. 40; Cocchiara, "Il Ponte di Arta," p. 60 n. 77.

43. Bibliography in Cocchiari, "Il Ponte di Arta," p. 56 nn. 57–58; add A. H. Krappe, "Un épisode de l'historia Britonum," in *Revue celtique* (1924), pp. 181–88; cf. also Eliade, *Comentarii*, p. 40. The motif of the fatherless child is an independent folklore theme.

44. Cocchiara, "Il Ponte di Arta," p. 57 and n. 60.

45. See, for the present, Eliade, *Comentarii*, pp. 58ff.

46. Eliade, *Comentarii*, p. 42 and n. 20; Cocchiara, "Il Ponte di Arta," pp. 67–68, 70–71. See also B. Nyberg, *Kind und Erde* (Helsinki, 1931), pp. 185–87; Loorits, *Grundzüge des estnischen Volksglaubens*, p. 136.

47. M. Winternitz, "Einige Bemerkungen über das Bauopfer bei den Indern," *Mitteilungen der Anthropologischen Gesellschaft in Wien* 17 (1887): [37]–[40]; cf. also M. Haberlandt, "Ueber das Bauopfer," ibid., [42]–[44]; fundamental Buddhist text, *Jātaka*, no. 481 (4: 246); cf. Paul Mus, *Barabudur* 1 (Paris-Hanoï, 1935), pp. 202ff.; Eliade, *Comentarii*, p. 43.

48. Eliade, *Comentarii*, p. 42.

49. Ibid., p. 42 and n. 17; Cocchiara, "Il Ponte di Arta," p. 66.

50. Cocchiara, "Il Ponte di Arta," p. 62 n. 86.

51. W. Eberhard, "Chinesischer Bauzauber: Untersuchungen an chinesischen Volksmärchen," *Zeitschrift für Ethnologie* 71 (1939): 87–99, especially pp. 98–99. In folklore, W. Eberhard, *Typen chinesischen Volksmärchen*, FFC, No. 120 (Helsinki, 1937), p. 146, and *Folktales of China* (Chicago, 1965), pp. 135–37, 231. On present-day sacrifices cf. J. J. Matignon, *La Chine hermétique* (Paris, 1930), p. 244.

52. Cocchiara, "Il Ponte di Arta," p. 62; see also Masao Oka, summarized by Alois Closs, "Das Versenkungsopfer," *Wiener Beiträge zur Kulturgeschichte und Linguistik* 9 (1952): 66–107 and especially p. 89.

53. L. Frobenius, *Kulturgeschichte Afrikas* (Leipzig, 1933), pp. 177–80; Cocchiara, "Il Ponte di Arta," pp. 64–65. Cf. also my *Traité d'histoire des religions*, pp. 321ff., and Cocchiara, "Il Ponte di Arta," pp. 71ff.

54. Morphologically, this "transference of life" has its place in the well-known series of religious monuments "animated" by relics or by representations of vital organs: eyes, mouth, etc. See Paul Mus, "La tombe vivante," in *La terre et la vie* 7 (1937): 117–27. An Indian boat is made "alive" by drawing two eyes on it; cf. J. Hornell, "Indian Boat Designs," in *Memoirs of the Asiatic Society of Bengal* (Calcutta, 1920).

55. According to the *T'ao chouo*, for several years potters "had tried in vain to complete the firing of a great jar decorated with dragons, ordered by the emperor. One of them sacrificed himself and jumped into the aperture in the chimney of the kiln; he died, but the jar was made"; cf. Max Kaltenmark, *Le Lie-sien tchouan, traduit et annoté* (Peking, 1953), p. 45. For metallurgical sacrifices see my study, "Symbolisme et rituels métallurgiques babyloniens," in *Studien zur analytischen Psychologie C. G. Jung* (Zürich, 1955), 2: 42–46, and especially my book *Forgerons et alchimistes*.

56. When Xerxes sailed for Greece he had nine boys and nine girls buried alive in order to assure his victory. And Themistocles, in obedience to an oracle, had three young prisoners sacrificed on the eve of the Battle of Salamis (Plutarch, Vita Themistocles 13).

57. Saint Peter was accused of having sacrificed an infant one year old, *puer anniculus*, to assure Christianity a duration of 365 years. The fact that Saint Augustine felt it necessary to answer such a calumny shows that in the fourth century of our era the pagan world still believed in the efficacy of this magical technique; cf. J. Hubaux, "L'enfant d'un an," *Collection Latomus*, Vol. 2: *Hommages à Joseph Bidez et à Franz Cumont* (Brussels, 1949), pp. 143–58.

58. Cf. Alfred Kuhn, *Berichte über den Weltanfang bei den Indochinesen* (Leipzig, 1935); A. W. Macdonald, "A propos de Prajâpati," *Journal asiatique* 240 (1952): 323–38.

59. See the works cited in the preceding note and the references given in my study, "La Mandragore et les mythes de la 'naissance miraculeuse,'" in *Zalmoxis* (Bucharest, 1942), 3: 3–48.

60. See A. E. Jensen, *Hainuwele* (Frankfurt am M., 1939), p. 59; Jensen, *Das religiöse Weltbild einer frühen Kultur* (Stuttgart, 1948), pp. 33ff. and passim. Cf. also Eliade, *Aspects du mythe* (Paris, 1963), pp. 129ff.

61. For the symbolism of the Center of the World see my works cited in n. 33 above.

62. Cf. Eliade, *Le chamanisme et les techniques archaïques de l'extase* (Paris: Payot, 1951), pp. 236ff. (2d ed., 1968, pp. 211ff.; English translation, pp. 260ff.); Eliade, "Centre du monde, temple, maison," passim.

63. This mythico-ritual complex has recently been studied by Ernesto de Martino, "Angoscia territoriale e riscatto culturale nel mito Achilpa delle origini," *Studi e materiali di Storia delle religioni* 23 (1951–52): 51–66.

64. For our purpose it is of no consequence whether there is a voluntary sacrifice (type: Hainuwele) or an immolation (type: Ymir, P'an-ku, etc.).

65. Jensen, *Das religiöse Weltbild einer frühen Kultur*, p. 58; Jensen, *Mythos und Kult bei Naturvölkern* (Wiesbaden, 1951), pp. 210ff.

66. Gunnar Landtman, *The Kiwai Papuans of British New Guinea* (London, 1927), pp. 10ff., 17ff.

67. This is especially true of religious symbolism, dances, and musical instruments. Cf. Dr. Jaap Kunst, "Cultural Relations between the Balkans and Indonesia," in *Koninklijk Instituut voor de Tropen*, Medeling, No. 107 (Amsterdam, 1954).

68. Cf. Robert Heine-Geldern, "Das Tocharerproblem und die pontische Wanderung," *Saeculum* 2 (1951): 225–55; Heine-Geldern, "Die asiatische Herkunft der südamerikanischen Metalltechnik," *Paideuma* 5, 7–8, (April 1954): 347–423, especially pp. 350ff.

69. Cf., for example, Leopold Schmidt, *Gestaltheiligkeit im bäuerlichen Arbeitsmythos: Studien zu den Ernteschnittgeräten und ihrer Stellung im europäischen Volksglauben und Volksbrauch* (Vienna, 1952).

SHARON KING

Beyond the Pale: Boundaries in the "Monastirea Argeşului"

Now that the reader is well acquainted with the Romanian versions of "The Walled-Up Wife," he or she may be better able to appreciate a literary analysis of one aspect of the ballad. Inasmuch as the whole point of this casebook is to encourage students of folklore to undertake diverse theoretical approaches to ballads, folktales, legends, and other folkloristic genres, the following thematic reading of the ballad may prove useful.

Sharon King was trained in comparative literature at the University of California at Los Angeles. She is a specialist in poetry and the theater.

———

The ancient ballad of "Master Manole and the Monastery of Argeş," known in variants all over southeastern Europe, is eminently a tale of construction, a story which plumbs the depths of the art of building and the building of art. In terms of its themes of ritual sacrifice, of Masonic mysteries, the poem has been scrupulously analyzed by comparative folklorists Mircea Eliade, Ion Taloş, Gheorghe Vrabie, and many others. Yet few have examined the process of the monastery's construction as the text itself, in its most well-known Romanian variant, puts it forth—a construction ceaselessly defined and delimited in space, in time, in nature, in human feeling. In this very brief analysis I shall examine the various boundaries and how they function within the ballad text. For I believe the poem is fundamentally about boundaries—boundaries both literal and symbolic, limits held to or limits surpassed—and it vividly portrays the consequences of going beyond these bounds.

As the ballad begins, the Black Prince passes by with his retinue of nine master masons, and a tenth, Manole, who is repeatedly said to surpass them all ("Manole, zece, care-i şi întrece.")[1] Artistic skill thus

This essay is appearing for the first time in this volume.

becomes the poem's first barrier, a metaphysical one, which Manole alone can cross. The prince urges them on to an old wall, unfinished and abandoned, at which dogs are said to bark and howl wildly. This wall, which the prince hails as his own ("Iată zidul meu"), represents both physical barrier, which the world of nature and instinct dare not approach, and terminus, the end of the prince's quest. For it is here that he orders his craftsmen to erect a high monastery, "unlike any other that has ever been" (cum n-a mai fost altă). The artifact he would have them build will thus embody the breaking of a boundary—the exceeding of the normal limits of human capacity—while paradoxically representing a very real physical, even mortal, obstacle to the master masons: the prince heartlessly threatens to wall them alive into the foundations should they fail to complete this task he has assigned them. The irony is mordant: the masons will literally be fixed forever at their own level of artisanship unless they can go beyond it.

And so they desperately endeavor to go beyond it, hurriedly stretching out ropes, measuring the building area, furiously digging ditches, working without cease at these tasks of boundary-making that are the necessary preludes to building. Yet Nature, or perhaps that which goes beyond it, the Supernatural, seems to rebel against this grim construct, born of ambition and hubris, and imposes its own limits: night after night the monastery collapses, and all the masons' frantic work, done as the prince menaces them, is in vain. Manole now shuns the work and, lying down, has a dream: a voice from the sky tells him the monastery shall not be finished until they decide to wall up within the building the first sister or wife to come to them. This vision crystallizes the prince's threat, eternalizing a boundary past which some human being might never go again; at the same time, as a mode of sacrifice, it exceeds all bounds for cruelty and barbarity, as the masons' reactions make clear. Yet if they are to finish their work, crossing the limit of endlessly building into eternally built, moving from the realm of futile accomplishing into fixed accomplishment, they must swear to this future sacrifice, further binding themselves ("să ne legăm") into the limits of secrecy. This they do, and this oath represents yet another boundary, one never within the ballad broken, though broken by the telling of the ballad.

The morning after this fateful vow, Manole climbs the scaffolding so as to have the first glimpse of she who is to be their sacrificial victim. As the fate of ballads would have it, of course, it is his own beloved wife, Ana, he sees coming across the fields from afar. And Manole falls to his knees and begs God to send waters to fill the river to overflowing ("să îmflă şiroaie," let the streams or rivulets be inflated), that is, to overthrow their limits, exceed their natural boundaries, so as to turn his wife back from her course. God hears, and the waters do come, but in vain, for they form no barrier for Ana, and she struggles ever forward to her husband. Again Manole pleads for God to send another supernatural barrier, this time an unearthly wind that will bend and strip the trees, a wind that will overturn the mountains. Yet nothing within or without Nature's boundaries will sway her from her path, will cause her to turn away from the ones she loves. Her love and devotion cannot be contained; they exceed all measure, outdo even the forces of the Divine and the Supernatural. And once more the irony is superb, for her extraordinary power for love and faithfulness is at once the greatest force within the poem, and the cause of hero and heroine's downfall.

Manole, broken, amidst the relieved cheering of his companions, greets Ana gravely as she traverses the boundary from her role as heroine to that of victim. Ever mindful of the oath that constrains him, he sets her on the wall, teasing her that they shall wall her up in jest ("Că vrem să glumim / Şi să te zidim," We want to play a joke / And wall you up). And thus in fulfillment of the dream, Manole begins his macabre task, almost mechanically, with only a sigh to show his emotion as she laughs at the joke, never suspecting, never doubting the one she loves. And the text narrates dispassionately the passive rising of the wall, as it crosses ever upward, covering her ankles, her calves, her thighs ("Zidul se suia / Şi o cuprindea / Pîn' la gleznişoare / Pîn' la pulpişoare"). Ana is progressively becoming the living embodiment of a boundary while she grows ever more physically fixed and contained within the monastery wall, as if the love that could not be confined by God or nature shall now be imprisoned by art and human ambition.

And then suddenly the tone of the ballad alters, deepens tragically; Ana's steadfast belief finally breaks down, and she no longer laughs but cries in terror:

> Nici că mai ridea
> Ci merea zicea: "Manoli, Manoli,
> Meştere Manoli! Agiungă-ţi de şagă,
> Că nu-i bună, dragă."

> No longer did she laugh,
> But kept on saying: "M, M,
> Master M, Stop playing the joke,
> Because it's not a good one, darling."

At some point while the wall went up it crossed an invisible line between joke and horror. The joke is now no longer funny; the game has surpassed the bounds of humor. Thus she begs Manole to stop, to step back within safe confines, but of course it is too late. And the wall rises higher and higher, surrounding her body amidst her pitiful pleas for him to stop:

> Zidul rău mă strînge
> Trupușoru-mi frînge! . . .
> Copilașu-mi plînge
> . . . Viața mi se stinge!"

> "The bad wall presses me
> It is breaking my body
> It is making my child weep
> My life is going out."

The physical barrier now encompassing her makes her excruciatingly aware of her own frail mortality, the material boundary that is the human body. And finally she is completely encompassed, smothered in the bricks' embrace, the babe inside her crushed as well, as if a final symbol of the life that is restricted and stifled by the exigencies of art.

For by this sacrifice the monastery can finally be completed, crossing the boundary of time present into time immemorial; by this incredible act of denying his human impulses and feelings, Manole, who was said to be the greatest artisan, becomes it, moving into the realm of fame that was his to possess. His dream is fulfilled, and the masons' work can be achieved, this, the building that surpasses all limits, the high monastery "such as never before had been." Yet the prince, though pleased, remains unsatisfied, and demands of his master craftsmen whether they could in fact build a monastery even more beautiful and bright than the one just finished. Their vanity piqued, the masons respond affirmatively, vowing that they could indeed surpass this their best creation:

> "Ca noi, meșteri mari
> Calfe și zidari
> Alții nici că sînt
> Pe acest pămînt!
> Află că noi știm
> Oricînd să zidim
> Altă monastire
> Pentru pomenire

Mult mai luminoasă
Şi mult mai frumoasă."

"We, great masters,
Journeymen and masons
No others like us
On this earth
Behold, we are able
Anytime to build
Another monastery
For holy worship
Much more bright
And more beautiful."

They are peerless on earth, they affirm, so far do they exceed all in talent. But their excellence, their surpassing the bounds of normal skill, like Cordelia's truth, is in fact their only reward: once they have proclaimed it, the prince coldly orders the scaffolding removed from their master creation and leaves them there to die and rot upon it. One may well conjecture that this act is symbolic of the limitation he would impose upon them and the construction that belongs to him; the artisans shall never be permitted to exceed the talent poured out upon this masterpiece of blood and stone; the building is truly to be their first and last great work, a boundary beyond which, in art or in life, they shall never again go. But these craftsmen do not resign themselves to biding within the wall of space hanging about them; after some reflection, they attempt to escape the confines set upon them. Nor do they seek release merely from the monastery wall; they also would have done with their physical, human limitations, for they form shingles into wings and jump from the walls, thus attempting to fly to freedom. But like Icarus, their flight is doomed to failure, and they fall to their deaths, emblems of their fatal, overweening pride.

Manole's fate is different. As he prepares to leap from the wall to join his companions, once more he hears the panting voice of his Ana emanating from the wall, still proclaiming the misery of her immuration at the hands of him whom she loved best. The symbolism seems chillingly clear: just as her love and fidelity knew no bounds, so her horror at his cruelty and treachery, howsoever unwilling, can never be dammed up, in life or in death. The body may have been walled up, but the voice cannot be silenced; its power to proclaim identity and protest the unfair demise also obeys no earthly limits. Yet this is not the only possible interpretation; the voice coming from the wall might also be Manole's Telltale Heart, the echo of the artisan's overwhelming guilt, a guilt so keen that it breaks the boundaries of the subconscious and appears to him as part of the objective world. Whatever the voice might represent, however, its effect is real: his eyes bathed in tears, he gives up ("se pierdea," loses himself); the world spins about him, clouds whirl, and he falls to his death. Where he falls, a spring arises, calm and shallow, running with salty tears.

> Iar unde cădea
> Ce se mai făcea?
> O fîntîna lină
> Cu apă puțină
> Cu apă sărată
> Cu lacrimi udată!

No greater contrast could there be to the waters he had called down from heaven to spill over their banks and prevent Ana from coming to him, waters which her boundless love was still able to overcome. His love is regret, bitterness, a quiet well of eternal brooding and suffering, never exceeding its banks but turning in upon itself forever.

Although I shall not attempt to elicit a definitive attitude, a "moral," if you will, to this ballad, I do wish to suggest several themes the text seems to point to, signposts that establish possible boundaries of meaning about the meaning of these boundaries I've been discussing. First of all, the ballad of "The Monastery of Argeş" is a descriptive tale, not a proscriptive one; there is no way one can interpret the crossing or surpassing of boundaries as unequivocally bad or good, decisively to be eschewed or to be sought after. Rather, going beyond the normal limits—of artistic construction, of human talent or passion—is depicted simply as an occurrence, carrying with it consequences possibly admirable, or tragic, or both. Manole fulfills his destiny of being the greatest artisan, but only at the cost of losing his wife. Ana's love overcomes all obstacles set before it, only to bring her face to face with death. And she dies immured, but the work of art can be completed and survives. What this ballad deals with, then, is the very complex interrelation between human ambition or will and human endeavor, an interaction fraught with shadings of intense horror as well as superb artistry. For surely another theme—perhaps the primary one—of this ballad is the conception of art: what its limits and limitations are, and what they should be. The ballad seems to value and applaud the artistic creation of the monastery, for all the enigmatic malevolence of the prince and the ruthlessness of the sacrifice. But ultimately, it makes clear, there is a high price to be paid for such great art. The ballad of "Master Manole and the Monastery of Argeş" makes no attempt to conceal the dire consequences awaiting those who dare to go beyond the pale, where no one has gone before.

Note

1. All references from the ballad are taken from the bilingual edition *Romanian Popular Ballads*, ed. Leon Leviţchi (Bucharest: Minerva, 1980), pp. 404–29.

References

Comisel, Emilia. *The Rumanian Popular Ballad*. Studia Memoriae Belae Bartok Sacra. Budapest: Academiai Kiado, 1959.

Eliade, Mircea. "Master Manole and the Monastery of Argeş." In *Zalmoxis, the Vanishing God*, trans. Willard R. Trask. Chicago: University of Chicago Press, 1972; rpt. 1986.

Leviţchi, Leon, ed. *Romanian Popular Ballads*. Bucharest: Minerva, 1980.

Taloş, Ion. *Meşterul Manole* Bucharest: Minerva, 1973.

Vrabie, Gheorghe. "Jertfa Zidirii sau Mesterul Manole." In *Eposul Popular Românes*. Bucharest: Albatros, 1983.

ŞERBAN ANGHELESCU

The Wall and the Water:
Marginalia to "Master Manole"

*As there are competing folkloristic approaches, so also are there com-
peting literary analyses. The following brief essay examines an op-
positional theme of mobility versus immobility rather than "boundaries." To the extent that the greatness of a work of art, whether folk
or sophisticated high culture, is indicated by the variety of interpretations it inspires, the quality of "The Walled-Up Wife" as verbal art
is attested by the diversity of readings it has engendered.*

A famous text will always have a reading ceremony associated with it.
The neophyte and latest interpreter will aggregate himself to an imaginary society comprising notorious names of predecessors that have
cultivated the same object and looked at the text with reverence. The
latest comer will venerate his forefather-readers; he will classify and
place them in a hierarchy; in a word he will model and fashion out a
small society, a club of specialists. Moreover, as he walks straight
into mythology, the newcomer will probably consider himself a hero
shedding light on long-forgotten, centuries old meanings, one saving
from temporary death an originary truth latent under successive lay-
ers of interpretation. It is our hope that we shall manage to keep detached from the fascination of these imaginary devouring spaces.

What we suggest in this study is an interpretation of *one* variant of
the ballad, which we have chosen for the high recurrence of a fundamental opposition further set forth and accounted for. Our main interest will be to detect the mobility-immobility play, given that this
play lies at the basis of the whole text pattern, in our acceptation.

We shall not take into account either ethnographic documents re-
lating to building rituals or the so-called mythical and symbolic
horizon of the ballad. To our mind this is a legitimate approach, as
every identification reading will include the text in a preexisting

Reprinted from the *Cahiers roumains d'etudes littéraires* 4 (1984): 79–83.

world and relatively easily find a family for it, rather than discover the way in which the text modifies and makes preceding or contemporary cultural objects liable to a new evaluation.

There has been unanimous agreement as to admitting that the aim of both the prince and the masons is that of a monastery being built, which will become "a cloister divine." The whole ballad is consequently estimated as pointing to the hard work necessary for the initially announced project to be turned into fact, i.e. the raising of a religious edifice, while a close reading will show that the main question is the raising of a wall. The wall discovered after long wanderings becomes obsessive; it is the wall that will be raised and will collapse, the wall on which Manole lies down and has a dream, the wall that will rise and gird the victim in, that will grow hard, hold the woman tight, cover her, make her milk and tears flow; the wall is manifest of the tension holding between solid form and fluid existence. In the last instance, this is a spectacular and complicated process of balancing apparently irreducible antagonisms, and the work it implies is in the gravest and most exact sense abstract. We believe that such work symbolizes the building of patterns of the real and therefore clearly exceeds the common expectations related to a folklore text

From the very beginning an old incomplete wall is being looked for, without any explanation being provided for it; the wall has long been abandoned and rises somewhere on a waterbank. The site of the future monastery is therefore a fragment, a hard reminiscence to find out, hidden as it appears in aquatic vegetation; it is an abandoned, frustrated thing, like an old guilt or trauma that the masons' work is to remedy, or like the much despised stone that is thrown away only finally to turn into the foundation stone. The wall is a thrilling thing, though: it keeps moving at night and bringing to nought its daily ascent:

> Those craftsmen amain
> Started work again,
> Straight they stood the wall,
> Hard they raised it all,
> For three years did toil
> Their work not to spoil,
> But whate'er they wrought
> At night came to nought.

The double movement—up and down—assertion and denial, an exasperating and terrifying pulsation for the masons, we consider an expression of unexpected mobility, of the flowing of a substance that is immobile par excellence. We can notice a clear-cut disjunction between the diurnal movement of the hands engaged in the mysterious toil that sets things straight, hardens and raises them, and the autonomous nocturnal movements of the wall resulting in a fall, collapse, and return to the original point. Stupefying and intolerable is the life of the wall which must be constrained to stand, and must be "killed." We do not know anything about the relation extending between the old wall and the new one. We shall therefore establish a possible articulation among the three terms: the running water, the old wall, the new wall. The new wall turns fluid; the old one, monstrous and infirm, is, by virtue of its association with the nocturnal movement, conducive to the image of a ghost. As is known, a human life that comes to an abrupt end entails, in the popular belief, the instability of the deceased man, the transgression of the spatial limits imposed through the funeral ritual, and the nocturnal contact with the world of the living. One of the defense methods used on such occasions is that of immobilizing the transgressor by thrusting a pole into his heart.

As the diurnal movement—the masons' work—proves useless, the solution lies in putting an end to manual toil and discovering the inner, cerebral movement. Manole's method is submission to the object, listening to its voice at the time that suits it. The inadequate dynamism of the subject is therefore given up:

> So, my bonnie, lo
> This Manole saw,
> Wretched and pensive
> Painful sighs did give.
> Though strain hard they would
> Their toil was no good.
> Wide awake he lay
> At the break of day
> Work he hardly could
> All day long he stood
> By some thought beset
> From morn to sunset
> When his work he broke
> Home he did not walk
> Kept he by the wall
> When the night did fall,
> By the wall he kneeled,
> Down to lie he seemed
> And a dream he dreamed
> As asleep he lay

In his dream he'd say
That in vain they toiled
And their work was spoiled
Unless they did raise
At the cloister base
A wall to gird in
A young wife serene.

There follows the masons' swearing: "Took they the oath fine, /
By bread and by brine, / By th'icons divine." The oath is to entail
supreme stability to a union necessary for the wall to be firmly
raised, but the nine masons break the oath, and that means moving
away from sacred bonds and giving away the secret, which will result in the collapse of the oath-taking, as of the wall-making.

When they homeward trod
Swore they on the road
Their homes to reach
Their wives for to teach
How to keep away
From the site by day:
Mark ye not to come
At the rising sun
Through fog and through clay
Early on Thursday
On the path winding
Fresh food for to bring!

Manolc himself, awe-stricken at the thought of Caplea, his own
wife's fate, indirectly breaks the sacred alliance by conjuring God to
turn her off her way:

"Grow, O Lord, green heath
On the road beneath,
Grow a thicket wild
With brambles behind:
My spouse for to scare
Make her come not dare,
Make her waste the meat,
Take back to her feet,
And beat her retreat."

While the wall once raised keeps collapsing implacably, Caplea
embodies the opposite process. Her irrepressible heading for the wall

is symbolic of victory in the building process. The mason's wife is repeatedly pushed back homewards, while she keeps turning up, unlike the wall, which, though permanently raised, keeps coming back to nought. Seen from this angle, Caplea's progress may be interpreted as prefiguring the ultimate ascent of the wall. The woman stands for *the* food carrier: she brings victuals and suckles her baby, therefore sustains and grows life. She prepares the food and feeds on her own substance—milk; eventually she will become the complete food of the work initiated by the male brotherhood, when she is swallowed by the wall. The gradual girding in of the founding victim reveals the essential tension holding between constraint, condensation, fixity and the apparently dominated and defeated flow of tears and milk. "'Manole, Manole! / Good Master Manole, / The wall weighs like lead / Tears my teats now shed, / My babe tears has shed.'" Let us emphasize the alternation of positions occupied by the actants in the mobile-immobile opposition.

While the mason master implored his wife's permanence in the protecting space of the household and conjured obstacles to rise in front of her dynamic energy, as she is being built in, Caplea implores the cessation of the wall-raising and her return home, but Manole, firm and determined, accepts the victorious movement of the wall:

> Stood Manole sad,
> Not a word he said,
> Bitter tears he shed,
> His masons bricks laid,
> Then wall for to raise
> The shrine on to base.
> Built they the wall stout,
> Manole called out:
> "Get me bricks and lime,
> Raise the wall I pine,
> 'Tis a work divine!"

The wall embodies the union of opposites, of the mobile and the immobile, which have so far been antagonistic. A "melting groan" can still be heard from the completed monastery as a last expression of the afore-maintained tension between fluid and stone. The wall, and in the last instance the monastery, is a fully stable vessel concluding the flow of tears, groans, and milk, and circumscribing the open living body, almost as a clear will putting limits to movement without abolishing it. The wall sets the body under the rule of discipline and shape. All this has been done through suffering.

There is, though, within the episode of the building in, the peaceful situation of the immobile caught in a vast fluid movement. The baby will be salved by snowfalls, washed by rains and rocked by winds. Here the fluid integrates, feeds, and defends whom we suppose to be unmoved:

> "And your little child,
> My sweet baby mild,
> Be our Lord's new child;
> Left home on its bed,
> Unswaddled, naked,
> The fairs it will mind,
> The fairs meek and kind,
> Bending o'er the sill
> Give it suck they will;
> Snow, if thou should fall,
> Ye, snow, salve it all;
> And, rain, should ye rain,
> Wash it with your main;
> Winds, if ye do blow,
> Rock it to and fro,
> Rock it fro and to,
> Make it grow anew!"

This is a unique, fixed, unsplit point, a mere center. The acts by which the prince consecrates the edifice at the beginning and in the end operate a clear cut in the ambiguous and contradictory adventure of the wall-raising. Prince Negru secures the unique quality of the work, as his own authority will not admit of any equivalent.

> "Ye have wrought so nicely,
> Made a shrine so stately,
> Such a cloister fair
> For words and for prayer,
> Such a shrine of worth
> Peerless on this earth."

Manole's answer is dictated by an inner ballad law. The master proclaims the possibility of movement, of multiplicity and progress. He contests the existence of the limit and of the center because of a dominant anxiety—exhaustion—ruling him. Unlike all the other masons, the master, who "excels masons young and old / His heart like ice cold," is defined from the very beginning by an inherent oxymoron, one consubstantial with his personality, by virtue of oppo-

107

sites (mobile/immobile, warm/cold) coinciding. Warm like blood, milk, and tears; cold like stone.

The great master's adventure is longer and more complex than his wife's, as his resources and possibilities of movement are vaster: he is a house builder, she is merely a house dweller; he girds and builds in his wife, but cannot dwell in himself. The master is, therefore, the house-fed spring flowing afar, feeding on his wife's tears. The masons are doomed to die, by abandonment on the shrine roof upon the prince's order. They are condemned to asceticism, one that foreruns and makes their flight possible. Thirsty, hungry, and beaten by wind and rain, the masons take Manole's advice and tie wings to their bodies. The answer given to their mortal fixity is the hypermobility of their flight. The nine masons turn into stones as soon as they touch the ground. Their wings, following Manole's teaching, are tied, therefore superficially attached to their bodies. Manole hammers steel rivets through his wings into his own flesh; he thus fixes himself for the first time, as in self-sacrifice, to give up movement. His self-riveting will release his blood, the source of his liberty:

> Manole stood up
> And a shingle plucked,
> Carved it out again,
> With his might and main,
> Hammered rivets keen
> Of iron and steel
> Through his flesh with thirst
> And his blood out burst,
> Yet he did not mind,
> For 'twas God's command.

The answer to female tears and milk is given by male blood and tears, if we consider Manole's weeping while he was building his wife in. Manole's last metamorphosis reconciles and ultimately purifies water and stone. The spring rising in stone rounds off the circle initiated by the river and the abandoned wall and frees the built-in tears, as a way out beyond the strict border of wall-building. Thus comes to an end the adventure of the two ways of being in the world, that of the mobile and of the immobile. A love and death story.

"Kulh" (The Waterway): A Basketmaker's Ballad from Kangra, Northwest India

One of the genuine difficulties impeding the analysis of folklore texts stems from the lack of context. In the nineteenth century and to some extent in the twentieth century as well, folklorists were content to record texts without regard to contexts. Hence as a result, we have books and books full of folklore texts with little or no idea about when and where or for what reason or purpose they were performed. The incompleteness of folklore recording is signalled by the fact that so many early collections of folksongs provide words only, without any indication of the music. What is clearly needed in folkloristics is faithful recordings of actual performances with as much attention to context as possible. As an example of the possibilities of such ideals, we present a text of our story recorded in the 1990s in northwest India by a trained anthropological folklorist who was in fact collecting from her "home" area. The richness of ethnographic detail is in marked contrast with most of the other texts of this ballad available in print.

Kirin Narayan is a professor of anthropology at the University of Wisconsin–Madison. Those who would like to read more of her folklore fieldwork results should see her prize-winning Storytellers, Saints, and Scoundrels: Folk Narrative in Hindu Religious Teaching *(Philadelphia: University of Pennsylvania Press, 1989).*

In Kangra, Himachal Pradesh, ballads known as *dholru* are traditionally performed during the lunar month of Chaitra (March-April). The caste of Dumna, whose traditional occupation is that of basketmaker, working with bamboo, is responsible for singing these ballads in the courtyards of upper-ranking castes in their prescribed service area. Going from house to house in groups of three—two women and a man with a drum—the Dumnas sing a ballad or two that the host

This paper appears for the first time in this volume.

may sometimes specially request. Each *dholru* ballad ends with an allusion to the month of Chaitra. It is considered inauspicious to use the name of the month during the month of Chaitra before one has heard a basketmaker sing it. In return for singing, and so removing the inauspiciousness attached to this month, the Dumnas are given grain or cash.

"*Kulh,*" or "The Waterway," is one of the most famous *dholru* ballads. Waterways are the main form of irrigation for Kangra's contoured terraces, guiding waters that melt in the peaks above into farmers' fields. This ballad is associated in local legend with the waterway flowing through the town of Charhi (also known as Charhi Garoh), near Dharamsala. There is a temple here, believed to have been built by the brother of the sacrificed woman. Each year, a ritual gathering associated with the beginning of the planting of rice is held at this temple; water is taken to certain villages, and the repair of the waterway is communally undertaken. Dumnas, however, do not perform in the village of Charhi.

Rajputs of various rankings are the dominant castes of Kangra, with extensive landholdings and social power. In the ballad of "The Waterway," Rajputs of the lordly Rana caste are the central characters. Many Rajput values and social arrangements are evident in this song: male honor, female seclusion, village exogamy, and the expectation that household services will be provided by other lesser-ranking castes.

I was in Kangra in March 1991. However, in the village where I was living, the local basketmakers no longer performed. These basketmakers had discarded their traditional occupations, and were employed in building roads, as domestic servants, and in running vegetable stalls; I was told that they considered such public performances for payment to be demeaning. I was thus unable to tape these *dholru* ballads in the live context. However, I was intrigued, for in the course of taping upper-caste women's songs, many women singers would make reference to different *dholru*. Though not low-ranking basketmakers themselves, many accomplished upper-caste singers knew these ballads too. As one enthusiastic woman of the Rana caste, Judhya Devi, said, speaking the Pahari dialect, "I'm interested in all kinds of songs! I listen everywhere I go . . . I've learned all the *dholrus* too, by sitting down with the Dumnas and listening to their songs. I can hear a song once and it goes and sits inside me . . ." Similarly, Urmila Devi, a woman of the Sud trader caste, sang *dholru* herself and could also recall her mother singing this ballad of "The Waterway" as she sat at her spinning wheel many decades ago.

Dropping off a commission of bamboo baskets for my mother (who lives in Kangra), Jounfi Ram, a small, twinkling man of the basket-maker caste from a nearby village, learned of my interest in songs. He did not sing himself, he said, but he could bring some of his relatives to sing before my recorder. In July, he arranged for his wife, niece, and nephew-in-law to visit. Like him, they were people of unusually small stature, dark and angular. At first, they were ill at ease being received inside the house, and being given tea as though they were guests. I only understood later that basketmakers are seen to be impure to most higher castes, who would not mingle with them so easily. Apart from removing the inauspiciousness of the month of Chaitra, basketmakers also perform as drummers at mortuary rites, and so are associated with death.[1]

Over the course of several hours, Dharmu, Samna Devi, and Soma Devi sang eight different *dholru* as Jounfi Ram looked on. Each ballad had a different melody, and the male and female voices alternated and blended to the beat of the drum. Though we taped indoors, the sounds carried across the fields. Later in the day when several neighbors greeted me with amusement, inquiring why exactly Dumnas had been singing during the monsoon at our house, I learned that basketmakers have a distinctive performance style. From the melodies, these listeners also appeared to be able to discern which ballads had been sung.

"The Waterway" was the first ballad the basketmakers sang after having been warmed up with tea. After singing several *dholru*, the two men stepped outside for a smoke. I remarked to the women, "All these seem to be about women. They're about women's suffering [dukh]." Soma Devi, Jounfi Ram's wife, said fiercely, amber eyes intense in her long face, "There's always been women's suffering! It's come down through the centuries." Indeed, the theme of women's suffering weaves through all the *dholru* I taped. Women in these ballads are mistreated in a variety of ways: they are borne off by lustful kings, given far in marriage, scorned or even murdered by callous in-laws.

In Kangra, as in many villages in North India, social structure contributes to women's vulnerability in various ways. A daughter is seen as "goods that belong to another house" and is raised to anticipate leaving her home with an arranged marriage, becoming a member of the husband's joint family instead. On account of the principle of village exogamy, "marrying out," a daughter is frequently married far from her home of birth, thrown at the mercy of in-laws. Because of hypergamy, "marrying up," a bride's original family may have a lower social standing than that of her husband's family, contributing to a

111

sense of inferiority. Given the hierarchy operating within joint families, a daughter-in-law is subordinate not just to her husband but also
to all elders with the family, especially her father-in-law (as "The
Waterway" demonstrates). Among upper castes, women may not re-
marry, but men may, leading to the view of wives as dispensable, and
easily replaceable (as much Kangra women's folklore, and many
dholru, including this one, bitterly articulate). Since the "gift of a virgin" *(kanya dan)* is seen as a meritorious gift for which one should
receive nothing in return, in more orthodox families, parents will not
visit a daughter or accept hospitality from her new home. Instead, it
is a bride's brother who serves as go-between, summoning his sister
for visits home, and escorting her back and forth. The importance of
the brother-sister tie is dramatized in the ballad that follows.

When the men returned from their smoke, I asked if all basketmakers learned such songs. Jounfi Ram said, "Not everyone learns
these songs. Those who want to learn, learn. Those who have good
voices and the interest. Not everyone." He went on to add, "The age
of literacy *[parhe likhe jamana]* is now upon us. People are learning
all kinds of new work. Those who are old-fashioned, who never
learned to read or write, and don't have anything else to do—they still
do these old things." When I asked if the *dholru* changed as they were
passed along, I was adamantly told by all present that they were
transmitted unaltered from the elders. (The presence of multiple
variants suggests otherwise.) "The songs are very old," said Soma
Devi. "They're from the time of kings and queens."

When the basketmakers left, I started to transcribe what I had
taped. For help I turned to Veena Dogra, my Brahman assistant, an articulate and educated woman in her thirties. My friend Urmila Devi
Sud, whom I respectfully called Urmilaji, was also delighted to hear
these ballads on tape, particularly "The Waterway." Urmilaji was
then a woman in her fifties, educated only to primary school but of
boundless learning and curiosity when it came to folk traditions. The
day before the basketmakers were to come, she had given me the plot
outlines of each *dholru* I should expect to hear. This is the outline of
"The Waterway" as told by Urmilaji, and recorded in my fieldnotes
before I heard the basketmakers' rendition:

> "Kulh": about a spring in Garoh, near Dharamshala, where a wealthy
> man was told that if this was to flow, it needed a sacrifice. Not a broom
> [as sacrifice] because this is Lakshmi [goddess of fortune] in a house; not
> a cat, because the sin would not lift for seven lives; not a grandson, be-
> cause the family line would be finished off; but a daughter-in-law. She's

told that the *puja* [worship] will be done by her hands. She gets all ready. As the Nain [female barber] prepares her, someone sneezes. An inauspicious omen. Then the cows low, the birds cry out. She assures them that she'll feed them *puris* [fried bread] on her way back. She is pushed in [to the foundations] and starts to be bricked up. But she implores that her breasts not be covered so her son can suckle, her neck not be covered so that her daughter can embrace her. She is relentlessly bricked up. Then the children go running for their Mama [maternal uncle]. He arrives and he kills the Saura [father-in-law]: it's from his blood that the waterway flows. He [the uncle] takes out his sister and cremates her.

The version that the basketmakers sang did not exactly fit this plot in all details, but Urmilaji was nonetheless delighted. We borrowed her sister's tape recorder, and as the rhythmic beat of the ballad flooded her indoor room, she sang along, stopping to explain, asking me to rewind so she could get the words right. In my notes, I include commentaries from both Veena, Urmilaji, and occasionally one of the singers.

In his Hindi book, *Himachal ki Dholru Lok gathae* (Himachal's *dholru* folk ballads)[2] the Kangra folklorist Dr. Gautam Sharma "Vyathit" reproduces a longer version of this ballad in Pahari, along with a Hindi transcription. As several local people informed me, Dr. Vyathit also adapted this story line for a play that was performed at the Norah Richards open-air theater in my mother's village of Andretta in the late 1980s. The version that I reproduce here is that sung by the basketmakers, Dharmu, Soma Devi, and Samna Devi, on 21 July 1993.

> Sleeping in his bed, the Rana lord has a dream,
> He has a dream, this Rana called Jhaspat.
>
> In the dream appeared the Nadul waterway,
> The waterway that wanders will now come his way.
>
> Sitting in his manor, the Rana discusses this.
> Sitting in his manor, he tells of his dream.
>
> On a Tuesday, the Rana starts work on the waterway.
> On a Tuesday, the Rana presses down
>   the auspicious foundation stone.
>
> "Though dug and shovelled, it all falls in.
> Though bricked and layed, it all tumbles down.
>
> "The waterway flows on,
>   but will not turn and come towards the Rana,
> The waterway, O Rana, demands a huge sacrifice."[3]

113

Sitting inside his manor, the Rana discusses this.
"The waterway, O Rana, demands a huge sacrifice."

"Offer a cat, O Rana,
Offer a broom, O Rana."

"How can I offer a cat, brothers,
        when the murder will cling to seven generations?
How can I offer a broom when this is the
        household's good fortune?"

"Offer the measure for grain, O Rana,[4]
Offer an enormous pumpkin, O Rana."

"How can I offer the measure for grain, brothers, when
        this is the household's storekeeper?
How can I offer a pumpkin when this is the largest fruit?"

"Offer, O Rana, your horse Tegme,
Offer, O Rana, your son Sangar."

"How can I offer my horse, brothers,
        for whom will I then mount?
How can I offer my son, for whom will then rule?"

"Offer, O Rana, your daughter-in-law Rukmani,[5]
Offer, O Rana, this granddaughter Kundala."

"How can I offer a girl when the courtyard will remain a
        bachelor?[6]
How can I offer my grandson, for who will then rule?

"I'll offer my daughter-in-law Rukmani, to be bricked up.
I'll offer my daughter-in-law Rukmani to be bricked up."

Sitting in his manor, the Rana holds counsel.
"I'll offer Rani Rukmani to be bricked up."

With his belt still open, the Rana went with naked feet,[7]
He went into the enclosed courtyard of Rani Rukmani.

Sitting on her bed, Rani Rukmani was embroidering.
She got off the bed and sat on a lower stool.[8]

"In the past, O Father-in-law, you have never visited.
Why have you come here today?"

"Give me your promise, Daughter-in-law,
        and only then will I tell you."
"I promise what you wish, Father-in-law.
    What will you tell me?"

"With your hands will this first worship
        of the waterway be performed,
With your hands, Rukmani, the worship will be performed."

114

"Thanksgiving to my fate, thanksgiving to my fortune,
That with my hands, Father-in-law's
    waterway will be worshipped."

The family priest was called,
The female barber, Nakhro, was called too.

Hurrying and scurrying, the Pandit was agitated.
Hurrying and scurrying, the female barber was agitated too.

"Tell me, oh Rukmani, what work do you order?"
"With my hands, Pandit, the waterway will be worshipped."

When the Pandit consulted the stars, he wept bitterly.
He could see that it would be hard for her to return.

"I'm defeated by my promise, Pandit, what now can I say?
I'm defeated by my promise, Pandit, what now can I say?"

The Rani put one and a quarter mounds of rice in a basket.
The Rani put one and a quarter mounds of frankincense in a
    basket.

When the female barber was braiding the Rani's hair,
    she wept bitterly.[9]
"From your hands, I've accepted much food and water,
    O Rukmani."

"Call for the drummers and the pipers.
Call for four palanquin bearers to carry the palanquin."

Hurrying and scurrying, they appeared.
"Tell us, Rukmani, what work do you order?"

The decorated palanquin was taken out through the gateway.
On that day, the decorated palanquin
    was taken out through the gateway.

"What are you saying to me, O gateway?
When I turn around and come home, my sister,
    I'll see that you are plastered."

As the Rani proceeded, calves and buffalo calves mooed.
A black crow spoke too.

"What are you saying, my calves and buffalo calves?
When I turn around and come home, brothers,
    I'll give you fine grass."

"What are you saying too, O black crow?
When I turn around and come home
    I'll offer you pearls as bird seed."

The Rani's palanquin went towards the waterway,
The Rani's palanquin proceeded to the town of Chadhi.

One hundred and sixty tents[10] were erected
      on the road to the waterway.
When the Rani saw the tents, she was frightened.[11]

When the Rani emerged from the tents,
      she started to worship the waterway.
She did this as she had promised,
      with four masons at hand.

"This moment, brothers, is passing uselessly by."
They grabbed her by the arm and stood her in the waterway.

They surrounded her and put stones down on her feet.
"Go slow with your bricking, brothers,
      don't brick up my feet, good men.
Rani Rukmani needs them to walk to her father's place.

"Go slow with your bricking, brothers,
      don't brick my midriff,
Rani Rukmani needs it for her embroidery.[12]

"Go slow with your bricking, brothers,
      don't brick my breasts.
Rani Rukmani needs them to offer sips of milk.[13]

"Go slow with your bricking, brothers,
      don't brick my neck.
Rani Rukmani needs it for a close embrace.[14]

"Go slow with your bricking, brothers,
      don't brick my mouth.
Rani Rukmani needs it to speak of good and of evil.

"Go slow with your bricking, brothers, don't brick my eyes.
Rani Rukmani needs them to see her father's place.

"Go slow with your bricking, brothers, don't brick my head.
Rani Rukmani needs it to braid her thick hair.[15]

"As you brick me up, brothers, I give you a mighty curse.
In my father-in-law's country, may just
      weeds and intoxicants grow.[16]

"In my father's country, may the finest rice grow.[17]
In my father-in-law's country, may just
      weeds and intoxicants grow."

The news reached her son, Ghunghuru.
The news reached her daughter, Kundala.

"Your mother, Ghunghuru, has been bricked into the waterway."
Weeping and wailing,
   Ghunghuru went to his mother's brother's place.

"Your sister, O Uncle, has been bricked into the waterway."
"Don't ever tell such a lie, O Nephew."[18]

The uncle extinguished the burning fire,
He threw away all the food that was cooking.[19]

He rounded up a huge army and went to the waterway.
He rounded up a huge army and went to the town of Chadhi.

He burned up the town of Chadhi.
He surrounded the waterway.

He killed the father-in-law, Jhaspat, at his sister's head.
He killed her husband, Sangara, at her feet.[20]

Then he also killed the laborers
And the four masons.

For two and a half moments, blood flowed down the waterway.
After that, cold water flowed.

He dug out his sister and embraced her close.
"If I'd known this was to happen, I would never have
   allowed her to be married here.

"Your revenge, O Sister, is still fresh.
Your revenge, O Sister, I have just taken."

He cut sandalwood, and lit her pyre.
He installed Ghunghuru, his nephew on the throne.
He married off the girl Kundala.

In the month of Chaitra, the Rani reached heaven.
In the month of Chaitra, this song was sung.

Musical Transcription

In order to demonstrate that this is really a *song*, not merely a poem,
I present one line that has been musically transcribed. Each line of
text is repeated, and every line follows the same melody.

  For example, this is how the first line appears in Pahari, and how
it sounds in musical notation:

117

Palange jo dhola sute ji Rane jo supana hoia na
Palange sute ni Rane jo supna hoia na

Palange	jo	dhola	sute	ji	Rane
bed	on	man	sleeping	(respect)	Rana

	jo	supana	hoia	na
	to	dream	happened	(na)

Palange	sute	ni	Rane
bed	sleeping	(ni)	Rana

	jo	supna	hoia	na
	to	dream	happened	(na)

"Sleeping in his bed, the Rana lord has a dream."

"Palange"
Transcribed for Kirin Narayan
by Richard C. Miller
8/93

Notes

1. See Jonathan Parry, *Caste and Kinship in Kangra* (New Delhi: Vikas, 1979), pp. 71–72.

2. *Himachal ki Dholru Lok gathae* (Palampur: Sheela Prakashan, 1980), pp. 38–49

3. According to Urmilaji, the masons are reporting here.

4. There are three measures used for grain: a *thimbhi*, a *path*, and a *sarinu*. The *path* is evoked here. These measures, Urmilaji explained, are used when dividing a harvest *(hissa deni)* between a landlord *(bajhiya)* and a tenant *(pau)*.

5. According to Urmilaji, and from the structure of the next verse, it is clear that this line is misplaced here. Rather, it should be "Offer, O Rana, your grandson Ghunguru."

6. Traditional Kangra houses are built around a large courtyard which serves as a setting for ritual events and feasts. In Kangra belief, every courtyard should be host to the wedding of a daughter of the family, else it is referred to as an unfulfilled bachelor.

7. According to Urmilaji, he is not formally dressed because he is in a hurry. Viewing this detail in the context of the larger song suggests an impropriety in relations towards the daughter-in-law, over whom the Rana assumes complete authority

8. She moves to a lower stool, explained Urmilaji, out of respect for her father-in-law so she will not be seated higher than he. In light of a possible unstated sexual overture here, Rani Rukmani's moving from the bed might be seen as a rebuff.

9. According to Urmilaji, in other versions, someone sneezes as the female barber is dressing her hair. This is taken as an inauspicious omen, filling Rani Rukmani with anxiety. In Vyathit's version, it is Rani Rukmani who sneezes: she says, "Oh, sneeze, why are you speaking through my nose? If I return, I will adorn you with a gold nose ring."

10. According to Urmilaji, the tents were put up to line the road as a form of *purdah*, so that when the queen dismounted from her palanquin she wouldn't be seen by any strange men. Urmilaji cited an example from fifty years ago of a local Rana family which was so strict about female seclusion that the newly married bride made visits only in her palanquin. Today, however, the palanquin is used only at the time of marriage, and married women practice veiling with gauzy headscarves when in the presence of certain male elders.

11. Urmilaji explained that the Rani is frightened, since she recalls that the Pandit had said it would be hard for her to return. Seeing the tents, which veil her from the public gaze, and thus from intervention too, perhaps reminds her of her vulnerability.

12. Veena explained that elbows move against the waist while embroidering; Urmilaji added that the midriff is important to bending over embroidery.

13. Other versions, reported Urmilaji, say that her son will sip milk. Indeed, this is what Vyathit's recorded version contains. At the time of a groom's wedding, before he sets out, a mother ceremonially offers him milk: these days it is usually in the form of a steaming steel glass full of milk rather than from her own breast.

14. *Gale lagna*, literally, "to touch necks," indicates an embrace. Urmilaji explained that this is so she can embrace her daughter. In Vyathit's version, Rani Rukmani implores the masons not to brick her shoulders so that she can "meet with," or embrace, her brother.

15. In the past, within the memory of women in their fifties, tight little braids all over the head were worn in Kangra. Hair is still braided this way for a bride at the time of her wedding. Opening the braids in some songs indicates that a woman has become a widow.

16. *Akk, bhang,* and *datura* are three plants that overrun deserted places: they are weeds, reported Urmilaji. All three also grow into thick hedges. *Akk* has a lilac, tubelike flower. *Bhang* is the marijuana plant, and refers to a drink made from the crushed leaves. *Datura* has a white flower and is also used as an intoxicant. Both *bhang* and *datura* are favorite intoxicants used by the Lord Shiva, and as Urmilaji pointed out, this curse implies not only that the place should be deserted, but also that the family line should end. She inquired, "Does [Lord] Shivji have any sons of his own?" Indeed, in Hindu mythology, he is the erotic ascetic who enjoys intoxicants and who has no directly conceived offspring.

17. *Sale* and *jinjhana* are varieties of valued local rices that now, with hybrid seeds flooding the market, are rarely found.

18. The uncle refused to believe this tragic news, explained Veena.

19. Urmilaji explained that when one learns the news of a close relative's death, one must observe a fast, eating just once a day (and then too without asafoetida, onions, or garlic) for the next ten days. The uncle showed that he was observing mourning when he threw out the food he was cooking.

20. I asked Soma Devi where the husband had been when the wife was bricked up. She said, "He must have been there, but what could he do? It was the father-in-law's will." The song, then, speaks to structures of authority in a joint family, where a father-in-law as eldest male may be tyrannical.

"Keregehara" (A Feast for the Well): A Kannada Ballad from South India

From northern India, we move down the subcontinent to the south to the Kannada-speaking area. For the benefit of those readers who may not be familiar with that language, Kannada is a Dravidian language spoken by approximately thirty-five million people, most of whom live in the South Indian state of Karnataka.

In 1989, in a periodical entitled Aniketana: A Quarterly Journal of Kannada Literature for English Readers, published by the Karnataka Sahitya Academy in Bangalore, there appeared three short essays on the ballad which is the subject of this casebook. All three essays have been reprinted in this casebook. The first is simply a text of the ballad. The second and third are literary appreciations of the ballad.

In reading these three essays, the reader should keep in mind that these Kannada literary critics consider the ballad strictly as a remarkable and praiseworthy specimen of Kannada folklore. In that respect they are no different from Greek folklorists who think of the ballad as a Greek product or Romanian folklorists who treat the ballad as a Romanian creation. One suspects that these Kannada writers would be startled but fascinated to learn that "their" ballad was just as popular in many other parts of the world, namely, eastern Europe. By the same token, eastern European folklorists may be equally surprised to read the Kannada discussions. Certainly the tensions of daughter-in-law versus in-laws in the Kannada text differ from the content of most of the Balkans texts. That ultimately is what makes the comparative study of folklore so exciting and important. Each culture, each people, transforms a

Reprinted from Aniketana, No. 2–1 (April-June 1989): 35–38. The ballad was translated from Kannada into English by K. V. Tirumalesh.

piece of folklore into a version which reflects their particular anxieties and concerns.

1

Kallankeri Mallanagowda, he dug a well,
A well, a well, but not a drop of water there,
Not a drop of water there. They asked the book,
They asked the priest. Not any gods' anger
Nor the ghosts'. Give it a feast,
A feast, a feast, of the eldest daughter-in-law, Malavva.
"How can we give the family's eldest?"
"Make a feast," they said,
"A feast of Bhagirathi the youngest."

2

And so she went to her mother-in-law and said,
"Mother-in-law, I'm off to my parents."
"Be off like an arrow and back like an arrow,
Back like an arrow to your home, my dear."
And off she went to her parents' house.
Her father met her at the door.
"Why have you come today, my dear,
Who had not come before?
Why the face and why the tears?"
"My in-laws want to keep us away."
"Keep you away let them do,
You will have a house and farm."
"To the river your house, to the river your farm."
Met her then her mother on the way.
"How come you are here and weeping
Who were not here before?"
"My in-laws want to keep us away."
"Keep you away let them do,
Have my earrings, a pair of them."
"To the fire your earrings, a pair of them."
And then her sister came along.

"Why this sorrow as never before?"
"My in-laws want to keep us away."
"Keep you away let them do,
I'll send my children with you."
"Sister dear, that will not do."
And so the youngest daughter-in-law, Bhagirathi,
Went to her friend and saw her at the door.
"Why these tears as never before?"
"Tell you with fear, tell you with fright."
"Tell me without fear and fright."
"My in-laws want to make a feast,
A feast, a feast of me for the well."
"And so it be, do as they say."
Off like an arrow she had gone
And back like an arrow she had come.

3

She wept and wept as she cleaned the grain.
"Why do you weep, Bhagirathi, as never before?"
"A stone from the grain went into my eye, Father-in-law."
She wept and wept as she cleaned the rice.
"Why do you weep, Bhagirathi, as never before?"
"A stone from the rice went into my eye, Mother-in-law."
They emptied the rice into boiling water,
Emptied the noodles into sugared milk,
Ten cauldrons of water seething and hissing.
"Go wash, Ningavva, go wash, Neelavva."
"Not me, "said Ningavva. "Not me, "said Neelavva.
"Go wash, Gangavva, go wash, Gauravva."
"Not me," said Gangavva. "Not me," said Gauravva.
"You then, Bhagavva, my youngest daughter-in-law."
And so the youngest daughter-in-law, Bhagirathi,
She went and washed, she went
And washed and filled a golden basket,
A golden basket. And she put up her hair,
Put up her hair and walked in front,
Walked in front, and the others behind.
They praised the Ganga, bedecked her with leaves,
Bedecked her with leaves and applied the ash.

Wore her the sari, wore her the flowers,
Wore her the flowers and offered her food.
Offered her food and all of them ate,
All of them ate and the remaining they packed.
They packed and carried the golden basket,
Carried the basket but the gold plate they forgot.
"Go you, Gangavva, go you, Gauravva."
"Not me," said Gangavva. "Not me," said Gauravva.
"Go you, Ningavva, go you, Neelavva."
"Not me," said Ningavva. "Not me," said Neelavva.
"Go you then, Bhagavva, my youngest daughter-in-law."
And so she walked briskly to the well,
Briskly to the well and took the plate.
She climbed a step and the water came up.
She climbed two steps and the water touched her feet.
She climbed three steps and the water touched her knee.
She climbed four steps and the water touched her waist.
She climbed five steps and the water drowned her.
The youngest daughter-in-law, Bhagirathi,
She became a feast for the well.

4

Her husband, Madevaraya, he was in the Forces.
He was in the Forces and had a dream.
His cloth was burnt and his spear broken.
His house collapsed all of a sudden.
The husband, Madevaraya, mounted a naked horse,
Mounted a naked horse and reached home at dawn.
His father and mother saw him and said:
"Give him some water, Gangavva, give him some water,
    Gauravva."
"Why Gangavva, why Gauravva?
Where is my wife, Bhagirathi, gone?"
"Your wife, Bhagirathi, she is gone to her parents, dear."
The husband, Madevaraya, he mounted the naked horse,
Mounted the horse and rode to his in-laws'.
His mother-in-law saw him and said:
"Give him some water, Nimbavva, give him some water,
    Neelavva."

"Why Nimbavva, why Neelavva?
Where is my wife, Bhagirathi, gone?"
"Your wife, Bhagirathi, she is gone to her friend's, dear."
The husband, Madevaraya, he mounted the naked horse
And rode to her friend's house.
The friend saw him and said:
"Give him some water, Balavva, give him some water,
    Basavva."
"Why Balavva, why Basavva?
Where is my wife, Bhagirathi, gone?
"Your wife, Bhagirathi, what can I say?
Your father and mother, they gave her to the well."
The husband, Madevaraya, he mounted the naked horse,
Mounted the horse and galloped in a shock.
He came to the well and wept his tears.
He wept and sighed, sighed and wept.
"A thousand gold mohars will not fetch
A wife like you, there is none!
I bought you pearls, I bought you gems
For you to wear as my wedded wife."
So he said and wept again.
He wept again and jumped into the well.

T. N. SRIKANTAIAH

"Kerege Haara"—A Tribute

In this second essay devoted to the Kannada ballad, some useful glosses are provided by the author. Some folk poetry can be cryptic, and the reader must remember that in this case we are reading the ballad in translation. The reader should also keep in mind that the sacrifice of a young bride for the "good" of the family might be differently perceived in a society which practiced sati *or* suttee, *a custom in which wives were expected to throw themselves on the funeral pyres of their deceased husbands. In that context, it is probably noteworthy that, unlike the European versions of the ballad, where the female victim is unaware of her impending fate and has to be duped into entering the partly built construction, in India, the young bride knows ahead of time that she is the intended victim to be sacrificed. Yet she proceeds even with that knowledge. This is clearly an important cultural difference between the European and the Indic versions of the ballad, a difference consonant with differing worldviews and value systems.*

It is difficult to say where treasure lies. There was a time when educated men thought indifferently, even contemptuously, of the songs of the village folk, sung with the sole purpose of forgetting the weight on their souls. Fortunately, we do not see much of this indifference now. Men of insight have begun to relish the sweetness of these songs, which more than satisfy the expectation of sympathetic critic; in fact they do not need to be patronized. When we read these songs, our patronizing attitude that they should be read sympathetically, as they are written by uneducated village folk, is quelled; our arrogance is replaced by an overriding humility that these songs are indeed great poetry and should be read for our education and refinement.

Fifteen years ago, I read one such poem in Jayakarnataka; it is "Kerege Haara," collected and published by Sri. Betageri Krishna

Reprinted from *Aniketana*, No. 2–1 (April-June 1989): 39–46. This essay was translated from Kannada into English by K. S. Radhakrishna.

Sharma. (It has been included in the second edition of "Kannadada Bhavuta," published by Kannada Sahitya Parishat, recently). As I read and reread the poem, my experience was of a man who had discovered a new star in the firmament of our poetry. I wanted to share my pleasure with others rather than experience it alone. Till now, I have not had the good fortune of hearing it sung by folk singers of North Karnataka. Even if I had, I am sure I would not be able to sing, as my arid voice does not have the richness to reproduce its cadences. I have read and lectured on this poem in many towns of the state; as I have seen it produce a tremendous impact on listeners, young and old alike, irrespective of their sex, my admiration for the poem has grown and my conviction that it is a great poem has become stronger. My purpose here is to introduce this poem to readers.

Many a time a snag shows up and stalls the work taken up in public interest. A tank built to water cattle and farms may not have water springs in its bed; a fortress erected to defend people may crash. In all such cases, our elders thought that there was divine intervention and sought the advice of priests. Only after appeasing the stars and sacrificing animals was the work resumed. These men did not hesitate to make any sacrifice, however difficult and dear it was; for them, the welfare of their village friends was of paramount concern. One such incident is at the backdrop of the poem "Kerege Haara":

> Mallanagowda of Kallanakeri has a tank dug up,
> Has a tank dug up, not a drop of water in it.
> Not a drop of water in it and they have the almanac read.
> They have the almanac read, and question the priest.

The characteristic of village songs, namely, repetition, is seen in the very beginning of the poem; many sayings are repeated twice and are well grafted in the listener's mind. When the priest was asked for his advice, he said that water not filling up the tank had nothing to do with either the wrath of God or evil spirits, but "Mallavva, the eldest daughter-in-law, should be offered as food for the tank," and water would well up. (In the colloquial tongue of North Karnataka, *Ahara* [food] has become *hara*.) Everyone of Gowda's family was worried, naturally, for if the eldest daughter-in-law were sacrificed, how could the clan perpetuate? Sacrifice must be done or else the good work undertaken would not be fruitful. So it was decided:

> Bhagirathi, the youngest daughter in law, to be offered as food,
> Be offered as food, at home so it was decided.

127

But then,

> The youngest daughter wants to go to her home of birth:
> "Mother, I shall to my home of birth go."
> "Go in speed, my dear, come in haste, my dear."

Many things in the sequence of the story are left unsaid, left to the reader's imagination, by the ingenious poet. The elders may not have broached the matter directly with Bhagirathi, but their discussion could not have escaped her hearing. It is probable that she did not ask them about it either, though she was herself the subject of their talk, for it would be against all conventions. But now that she had to sacrifice her own life, it was quite natural that she wanted to visit her parents to seek their help. Her parents-in-law were not bad people, for what could they do? "Tyajet kularthe purusham, Gramasyarthe Kulam tyajet." They were left with no alternative. They approved of her visiting her parents' home and sent her with the advice to "go in speed and come in haste."

> Bhagirathi, the youngest daughter went to her home of birth,
> Ere she reached home, her father arrived.
> "Bhagirathi that never came, why did you come today?
> Why is your face forlorn, why these tears in your eyes?"

Bhagirathi couldn't speak of her sorrow directly. So she said that her parents-in-law intended to keep her in a separate home. "Let them. I shall give you land and home," her father, who could not know the timid, tender heart of Bhagirathi, assured her. She didn't like his arrogance either. She didn't tell him openly what troubled her but replied in pain and hurt, "Throw your land and home into the river." She met her mother and was asked the same thing. Bhagirathi's reply was the same: "My parents-in-law intend to keep me in a separate home." Her father had assured her land and home, and her mother told her she would give her ear pendants. Bhagirathi was not consoled. She said in reply, "Throw your ear pendants into fire." Later she met her elder sister, who promised to send her children with Bhagirathi for protection. Her sister couldn't give her land, home, gold, or silver. She was ready to give what she could to help her sister through the difficulty. (That poor Bhagirathi, so young and tender, didn't have children of her own is suggested.) Having children with her couldn't end her sorrow, could it?

Bhagirathi's parents and sister loved her, no doubt, but couldn't understand the fear and anxiety of this tender, soft-spoken girl. She didn't get the solace she wanted from her parents, and her problem remained unsolved.

> Bhagirathi, the youngest daughter, left her home of birth.
> Left her home of birth and to her friend's house went.
> Her friend, she met at the front door. She was asked,
> "Bhagirathi, why this crying that never was?"

Bhagirathi replied in fear and anxiety, "Shall I tell my friend, shall I?" and her friend comforted her with the words, "Don't fear, my friend, don't be anxious." In these simple words of her friend, Bhagirathi discovered in herself a sense of uncovering which she had not found while talking to her parents and sister. For the first time since leaving her husband's house, she opened up and told her friend directly, "My mother-in-law and my father-in-law intend to offer me as food for the tank." How very deserving of Bhagirathi's trust was her friend! Her clear advice to Bhagirathi was, "Let them if they intend. We shall remain as we are told to." Her words might appear very harsh and cruel, but in reality that was the only course left for Bhagirathi. Her friend was the only one to understand this young girl's sorrow. Only she was able to harden Bhagirathi's determination by leading her in clear words to her future course of action. This she could not have done unless she had great love for Bhagirathi and wished her well always. At last, Bhagirathi's anxiety ended, and now she was resigned to her fate. With this new found firmness, she returned to her mother-in-law's house: "She went in speed, came in haste."

The sequence of events that follow her return is again left undescribed to the listeners, left to their imagination, and we are straight away taken to the day of the great sacrifice. The preparations for the worship of Mother Ganga are underway.

> Cleaning *dhal*, she shed tears.
> "Bhagirathi, why these tears that never were?"
> "The stones in *dhal* fell in my eyes, O Father."

The poet tells many things concisely but in their entirety. In just three lines he suggests: that the conversation was between the father-in-law and his daughter-in-law; that despite her firmness of purpose, tears welled up in Bhagirathi's eyes at the prospect of her certain death; that her father-in-law, though full of love and sympathy for her, was unable in his position to console her and therefore spoke nonchalantly; and that by telling a small lie, Bhagirathi was hardening her purpose. Her mother-in-law asks her the same and is told that stones

129

in the rice fell in her eyes. That was the day of the feast; water was being heated in ten boilers. The elder daughters-in-law, Ningavva, Nilavva, and others, were told to bathe, but they refused as they knew that Goddess Ganga would accept anyone who went to her bathed and well dressed. They all backed out one by one: Ningavva—"I won't"; Nilavva—"I won't"; Gauravva—"I won't"; Gangavva—"I won't."

> "Youngest daughter, Bhagavva, you bathe at least."
> Bhagirathi, the young daughter, has bathed,
> Has bathed and filled the golden basket,
> Has filled the gold basket and made a lovely underpad,
> Has made a lovely underpad, walked in front, in front,
> Bhagirathi in front and all behind her.

Prayers and rich offerings were made at the dry tank bed.

After the feast, things were collected and everyone turned homewards. While returning, the golden basket was forgotten, perhaps deliberately. After treading awhile, the golden basket was remembered and every one of the daughters-in-law was asked to go and bring it. Just as they had earlier refused to bathe, the elder daughters refused to do this; finally:

> "Bhagirathi, the youngest daughter, go fetch it, dear."
> Bhagirathi, the youngest daughter, walked quick and fast.
> Walked quick and fast, took the golden basket.
> Ere she had scaled one step, Gangi touched her feet.
> Ere she had scaled two steps, Gangi drowned her feet.
> Ere she had scaled three steps, Gangi was her knee deep.
> Ere she had scaled four steps, Gangi was her waist deep.
> Ere she had scaled five steps, Gangi had overflowed.
> Bhagirathi, the youngest daughter-in-law, was offered food for the tank.

This valiant girl, who had saved her clan, was taken gently on the lap of Mother Ganga. The acceptance of the sacrifice was as quick and bloodless as the offering of it.

Where was Bhagirathi's husband when these events took place? Didn't he protest or say a word of solace to his wife? The poet is aware of these nagging doubts of the reader. Bhagirathi's husband was not in the village at the time of the sacrifice. "Madevaraya, her husband, was in the army." He learned of his wife's death by water in a dream: "He had a bad dream."

> He felt his upper garment burn, his spear break.
> He felt the villa he had built suddenly crash on him.

The death of his wife and the villa falling are one and the same.

> Madevaraya, the husband, mounted a naked steed,
> Mounted a naked steed, came home in great speed.

His anxiety and worry are very well expressed in his mounting a
naked steed. He did not want to waste the time involved in saddling
the horse. Having had the dream, he jumped on his mount, rode to his
village in great speed.

> Madeva, who had come, his father and mother saw.
> "Gangavva, give him water. Gauravva, give him water."
> "Why should it be Gangavva and Gauravva to give water?
> Where has Bhagirathi, my wife, gone, Mother?"
> "Bhagirathi, your wife, has gone to the home of her birth."

The practice is, the wife gives her husband, who has returned,
water to wash his hands and feet with. Madevaraya's anxiety doubled
when his sisters-in-law were told to give him water. He asked his
mother where his wife had gone that she could not do it. His mother
had no face to tell him the truth and so told him that Bhagirathi had
gone to her home of birth. Yes, Bhagirathi had really been sent to the
home of her birth.

Madevaraya mounted his naked steed and rode at once to his in-
laws' house. There his mother-in-law told Nimbevva and Nilavva to
give him water. (By this time, Bhagirathi's parents must have heard
of her death and become helplessly resigned to their sorrow. The son-
in-law inquired about his wife and was told, "Bhagirathi, your wife,
to her friend's house has gone." At the friend's house, Balavva and
Basavva were told to give him water, and he repeated his inquiry
about his wife. Then Bhagirathi's friend told him with a candor and
simplicity that neither his mother nor his wife's mother could
muster: "Of Bhagirathi, your wife, what shall I say, friend? Your father, your mother, offered her as food for the tank, so it is said." His
suspicions were confirmed, his heart emptied.

What should Madevaraya do now? Should he be angry with his
parents? Could he live without his dear wife? He could think of only
one way to quell the fire that burned in his heart.

> Madevaraya, the husband, mounted the naked steed.
> Mounted the naked steed and rode in agony and fear,
> Came to the tank bund and poured his tears and heaved long sighs.
> "A thousand *varahas* cannot buy such a wife as you were.

Such a wife you were, where did you go leaving me here?
Three hundred *varahas* I paid for ear pendants.
Muttaide that should wear the pendants, where did you go?"
So much did Madevaraya speak and shed his tears,
Shed his tears and then leapt into the tank.

That was his end. The end of the story, too.

What else could Madevaraya have done? Which other course could his love have taken? He leapt into the tank filled to the brim as a result of his wife's sacrifice and put out the fire in his heart. This end of his is as sudden as it is inevitable.

Thus the action implied in every line of "Kerege Haara" has an inevitability that characterizes great works. The tales of the cultured people of the past must have had the same inevitability, considering their social practices. They spoke little, but their lives were refined. Bhagirathi's firmness was noble. Madevaraya's love, boundless. Another feature of the poem is the importance given to Bhagirathi's friend. Her love for Bhagirathi is nearer than that of near relatives; she can speak out and console Bhagirathi, something that Bhagirathi's parents and others cannot do.

Every line of the poem is so good that it is difficult to pick out a few for critical appreciation. A live pearl glitters on its own and does not need the patronage of praise. The anonymous village bard who composed this song was a great bard, indeed. "Kerege Haara" is indeed the Kantihaara of the goddess of Kannada poetry.

The Awareness of Values in Folk Poetry: "Kerege Hara"

The third of the three Kannada essays takes a critical stance with respect to the ballad. In effect, the anonymous folk poet is criticized for not protesting the inherent cruelty involved in human sacrifice. In a way, the essay is reminiscent of Goethe's response to being sent "The Building of Skadar" by Jacob Grimm. He was horrified by the pagan brutality of the ballad, and essentially so is the author of this third Kannada essay. On the other hand, if one does not take a literal or historical view of the ballad, one may appreciate it in metaphorical or symbolic terms. Still, one can applaud a critic who is willing to be critical of folklore rather than simply extolling it on nationalistic or regionalistic grounds.

Our attitude towards folk poetry has undergone a sea-change since its inclusion in folklore. A fundamental doubt has arisen over the question of considering folk poetry as literature. The folklorists are of the view that folk poetry and literature belong to two different mediums of arts; one is passed on from mouth to mouth, and the other exists in written form. The two cannot be judged by the same critical standards. Similarly no critic will judge a folk story as he would judge a modern short story. During such an exercise one would realize that the wide gap between folk poetry and classical poetry often gets blurred. It is due to the fact that both are interlinked from time immemorial. The language, imagery, meter, and rhythm of folk poetry have had a profound influence upon classical poetry. Folk poetry has also influenced classical poetry in the choice of subjects.

All along we have been judging folk poetry from a literary point of view. But this kind of criticism is incomplete and absurd from many points of view. This type of criticism has concentrated on the beauty of imagery, the use of dialect, form, natural characterization, sensi-

Reprinted from *Aniketana*, No. 2-1 (April–June 1989): 47–52. This essay was translated from Kannada into English by S. Naganath.

tive portrayal of emotions, and various other literary values. These attempts have successfully established folk poetry as literature. Whether folklorists want to acknowledge it or not, folk poetry embodies literary values.

A mere acceptance of folk poetry as literature does not make it great literature. Such an assumption is a critical blunder. Through literary values alone we cannot judge the greatness of folk poetry. Therefore a nonliterary value system must be employed to assess its worth, and while judging the worth of a folk poem, sufficient attention must be paid to the value consciousness of the poet. The quintessential nature of the values, universality of the subject, and contradictions within the frame work of art as exhibited by the poet determine the greatness of a folk poem.

There is a special bond between folk poetry and values. Here we infer them as social values. The values cherished by a group of people cease to be relevant to the next generation. A fixed set of values cannot provide solutions to the needs of individuals forever. This is considered by a sensitive person as an obstacle to his development. The individual reserves his right to protest vehemently against the imposition of such values which curtail his liberty and fundamental rights. But unfortunately the voice of rebellion is stifled in folk poetry. There is total acceptance of values without a sign of protest. The pleasure and pain arising out of this situation has led to conformity.

There could be three reasons for this: First is a firm belief in the Indian concept of Karma, which forces an individual to reconcile himself to his situation. He does not question the relevance and meaning of a cruel custom. All the ills of life are traced to one's Karma. Such an individual patiently forbears his misfortunes.

The second reason is that the folk poets understood values in a simplistic fashion. A total comprehension and understanding of the values (vis-à-vis human relationships) were beyond the pale of their imagination and sensitivity. The poets show unbelievable naivety and simplicity in the understanding of values.

The third overriding reason happens to be the folk poets' concern for the collective good of the community. Social justice denied to a few individuals escaped their eagle eye. The poets express their sympathy for the unfortunate victim but refuse to go beyond it. They are least concerned about the inner turmoil and sorrow of the victim. The well-being of the society is more important than the well-being of a few individuals. This is accepted by folk poets as axiomatic.

A good example for this unique phenomenon is the poem "Sacrifice for the Tank" (Kerege Hara). It is held in many quarters that a folk poem is created by a poet for the sake of creation. The folk poet tells the story for its own sake and its beauty. A lot of attention is paid to the narration of the poem. His sole aim is to describe a story in its vivid details. The central meaning of the poem escapes his attention.

I am not saying that these poets failed to understand the values operating at the subconscious level. The important thing is that they did not make a conscious attempt to analyze these factors. But an awareness of values did appear from time to time individually or collectively. While judging the greatness of a folk poem the value consciousness shown by the poet matters a great deal.

Let us evaluate the folk poem "Sacrifice for the Tank" in this context. The whole poem rests on a blind belief. A rich man digs a tank in the village. There is not a drop of water. So an astrologer is consulted for a solution. He advises the rich man to sacrifice his daughter-in-law. This is definitely inhuman and irrational to a modern-day reader, but the folk poet has an implicit faith in this myth. However, as a poet he does not fail to respond to the mental agony of the daughter-in-law.

The news of human sacrifice strikes like a thunderbolt its victim, Bhagirathi, the youngest daughter-in-law of the village rich man. Her husband, Madevaraya, has gone to the war. She is uncertain of his return. She does not protest against the decision made by her father-in-law and mother-in-law. She has more or less reconciled herself to her inevitable fate. She goes to her parents' village seeking solace.

The parents are aghast at the sight of their grief-stricken daughter. They want to know the reason for her grief. She takes shelter under a lie. She tells them that her father-in-law and mother-in-law intend to separate her and her husband from the joint family. The father tries to console his daughter by offering her fertile fields. The mother offers her gold ear-studs. She rejects outright these generous gifts. She does not confide her secret to her parents. There is no sign of protest against her cruel fate. Then she goes to her childhood girlfriend to express her predicament. This friend advises Bhagirathi to reconcile herself to her fate.

After her return to the house of her father-in-law the mental agony becomes more acute. The poet draws our attention to the few drops of tears which Bhagirathi sheds while doing household chores. When asked for a reason she blames it on a speck of dust in her eye. The folk poet is more concerned with the ritual of sacrifice and the gushing of water after the event than with the fate of Bhagirathi.

The husband of Bhagirathi dreams a nightmare and rushes to his village in a hurry on his horse, without a saddle. He meets all the characters of the poem in the same order as described by the poet in the earlier part of the poem during Bhagirathi's sojourn. His parents and Bhagirathi's parents hide the truth from him. It is finally revealed by his wife's friend. His reaction to the news is one of sorrow and not of anger. He does not rebel against the decision of his parents. Instead he goes to the water tank and sheds tears profusely. Madevaraya, filled with uncontrollable sorrow, commits suicide for the sake of his wife by jumping into the tank.

Several questions rise in our minds after reading this poem. The battle-scarred hero has no anger towards his parents. The parents of Bhagirathi, who were prepared to make supreme sacrifices, remain mute and dumb in the face of tragedy. They must have come to know the truth when Madevaraya visited them. They choose to lie to him instead of expressing their anger. None of these characters look upon the sacrifice as an affront and injustice to Bhagirathi. Her death is equated with an accidental death or a death due to sickness. This is, according to them, inevitable and unavoidable. Nobody is blamed for this tragic death.

It is undeniable that the poet has immense compassion and sympathy for the protagonist. He has shown his genuine concern for Bhagirathi in the latter half of the poem. Madevaraya has a true abiding love for his wife. Even if her death had occurred for some other reason, he would have committed suicide because of his unbearable grief. There is no doubt that Bhagirathi was central to his existence. Nevertheless the readers are bound to be shocked by the detachment shown by the poet. This detachment shown by the poet is both a positive and a negative factor. There is no exaggeration of emotional feelings in the poem, except for those lines which express Madevaraya's anguish. The astrologer's verdict assumes the nature of an oracle. Soon after the announcement, the atmosphere of the poem is surcharged with tragic feeling. Bhagirathi's fate is sealed.

There is a total acceptance of traditional values (which prevailed at that time) by all the characters. These people repose their utmost faith unquestioningly in these values. These cherished values give them immense solace in times of crisis. The human sacrifice for water has created a tragic situation. But all the characters feign helplessness. They do not protest against the unjust practices. Rather, their courage and patience is expressed by a total acceptance of the values of the system. The tragic fate of Bhagirathi and Madevaraya pales in significance before the good of the community.

A mere protest alone does not signify anything. The question of protest in the face of unjust and cruel customs like this takes a new dimension. A passive acceptance amounts to lack of imagination and creativity in the poet. To us this faith in human sacrifice to get water is tantamount to ignorance and stupidity. But to the poet and to his characters this custom is laudable. The gushing of water from the ground is a vindication of their faith. This symbolizes the richness and vitality of the community. A blind faith in this custom as such, in its values, epitomizes the creativity, meaningfulness of life, and self-reliance of the people.

All this sounds perfect when we acknowledge the principle that the good of the society is more important than the good of an individual. This leads to an oversimplification of values. Such questions as, Should we not condemn human sacrifice? or, Is it morally right to demand an innocent person's life? escape the poet. If Bhagirathi had embraced her fate willingly, the whole question of values would have taken a different dimension. There is a sea of difference between a coerced act and the willing act of an individual. A number of examples of willing victims of sacrifice could be cited from many folk short stories and poems. But in the poem "Sacrifice for the Tank" the decision is made by Bhagirathi's father-in-law and mother-in-law. Do they have a moral right to make this decision on behalf of the society they represent? In theory one may concede the necessity of such a sacrifice for water. But the cruel society enforces its decision on Bhagirathi in the absence of her husband. In such a piquant situation it is natural to expect Bhagirathi and Madevaraya to rebel against the cruel custom.

The folk poet misses a great opportunity for making a statement against the ritual sacrifice. He fails to understand the crux of the matter. The poet's experience runs parallel to the collective intellectual experience of the community. He lacks a complete awareness of values. He does not respond to the moral dilemmas of the characters in a sensitive manner. The all-pervading moral values escape the notice of folk poets. They stick to a viewpoint and resort to an oversimplification of values. Their innocence and naivety baffle us.

Such critical comments as, "This is good poetry or great poetry," "The anonymous poet who composed this poem is a great poet," and "'Sacrifice for the Tank' is a garland around the neck of the Kannada Muse" make one forget the poem's shortcomings. Our critical attention is focussed on the beauty of folk poetry, its imagery, fine emotions, natural and realistic descriptions, and its universal message. These things may embellish a poem but do not make it truly great. The critic must take into consideration its severe limitations before placing it on a mantle along with other great works of literature. The sensitive critics, who expect good literature to scrutinize an individual and the society closely and evaluate them accordingly, must consider the above points. However beautiful a poem might be, if it fails to examine sensitively the comprehensive value system of society, it cannot aspire to become great literature.

The Value of Innocent Sacrifice:
The Christian Moment in the Poem
"The Erection of Skutari"

Among the various approaches to folklore is one often ignored by academics. That is the approach of "spiritual science" or some other Christian doctrine. According to advocates of such approaches, folklore is shown to contain spiritual messages, usually Christian in content.

One stream of Christian interpretation stems from Rudolf Steiner (1861–1925), the founder of Anthroposophy. Specifically, a lecture he gave in December of 1908 in Berlin set forth some of the principles to be used in understanding European fairy tales. See his The Interpretation of Fairy Tales *(New York: Anthroposophic Press, 1929). Derivative works by Steiner's followers invariably contained the word* wisdom *in their titles, for example: Ursula Grahl,* The Wisdom in Fairy Tales *(East Grinstead, 1972); Rudolf Meyer,* The Wisdom of Fairy Tales *(Edinburgh: Floris Books, 1988). Other representative books include: Norbert Glas,* Once Upon a Fairy Tale *(Spring Valley: St. George Publications, 1976); Madge Childs,* The Other World of Myths and Fairy Tales *(New York: Vantage Press, 1972); Rev. James B. Haggart,* Stories of Lost Israel in Folklore *(Thousand Oaks: Artisan Sales, 1981); Miriam Whitfield,* Fairy Stories . . . Why, When, How *(Castle Rock: Juniper Tree, 1986); and Samuel Denis Fohr,* Cinderella's Gold Slipper: Spiritual Symbolism in the Grimm's Tales *(Wheaton: Theosophical Publishing House, 1991). Not all of these refer explicitly to Steiner, but they all offer Christian readings of European folktales.*

A Christian interpretation of "The Building of Skadar" is offered by the Reverend Dr. Krstivoj Kotur, a native of the former Yugoslavia and a graduate of the University of Belgrade, who occupied

Reprinted from Rev. Dr. Krstivoj Kotur, *The Serbian Folk Epic: Its Theology and Anthropology* (New York: Philosophical Library, 1977), pp. 179–85.

139

the pastorate of St. Peter the Apostle Serbian Orthodox Church in Fresno, California.

King Vukashin collects his brothers, Goyko and Uglyesha, and builds the city of Skutari. Three hundred masters work at the construction, but in the course of three years they are unable to erect the foundations, for what they construct by day, the fairies destroy at night. Finally, the king of the fairies calls from the mountains to King Vukashin that he will not build the city until he finds a brother and sister named Stoyan and Stoya, and buries them in the foundation. Thereupon, the king sends his servant Desimir out into the world with rich treasures to find these children. After searching in vain, Desimir returns. Then the fairies tell the king that one of the wives must be entombed, but the brothers must swear beforehand that they will not betray to the wives what they are about, and indeed, that wife shall be entombed who will be the first to bring luncheon on the following day. "And hereupon they swore by God / That none should betray to his wife."[1]

Both older brothers broke their sworn oath to guard the secret; only the youngest brother, Goyko, kept it. On the next day, when luncheon was to be brought, the wife of Vukashin excused herself because of illness, for it was her turn; the wife of Uglyesha had to bleach linen, so Goyko's wife brought the luncheon. Goyko, in the throes of the most severe torments of the soul, entombed her in the foundation of the walls. As a consequence, she left behind a tiny child yet in the cradle. On the pleas of Goyko's wife, openings were made in the wall so that her breasts were left free so that she might nourish her small son, Jovan. In this way, she quieted her son for the duration of a week, and when she died, milk continued to flow until the child was grown up. Later on, it changed into a spring of miraculous and healing water.

Countless native as well as foreign interpreters of Serbian folk poetry concerned themselves with the origin and the widespread variants of this poem, among the Albanians, Greeks, Bulgarians, Romanians, and other peoples. As can be seen, numerous and different motifs are presented in the poem: the motif of the fairies, who destroy and eventually permit the city to be built; the necessity of human sacrifice in order to continue the construction; the sacrifice of children; the sacrifice of the wife of the king, for whom it is being constructed; the motif of the suckling of the child by the dead entombed mother; the motif of the transformation of the milk into a

spring of miracle-working water; and others. However, we shall not
concern ourselves with these motifs, which, since they are so widespread and could belong to all peoples, are not only Serbian—particularly the motif of the presentation of human sacrifices for the construction of cities, bridges, and large edifices in general. These motifs
are encountered in pre-Christian as well as post-Christian mythologies of many peoples. Neither shall the variants of these poems
amongst different peoples be of interest. The artistic merit and the
poetic treatment of the aforementioned motifs shall be our concern;
a treatment which "bears the unmistakable stamp of the Slavic or,
better phrased, the Serbian spirit."[2] What is particularly of interest is the orientation of the poem in the Serbian variant, especially
with respect to the historical localization of the characters of the
brothers Mrnyavchevich in connection with the religious-ethical
consequences manifested, whence is derived the force of the tragedy
which the poet has artistically treated. Thus, the basic religious-
ethical orientation, which the poet has expressed in the above-
mentioned motifs, is of interest, for

the Serbs have in everything that they have adopted from other nations,
given their spirit and their taste in their forms, their proportions, and
their own ordering of colors; they have treated it in their own way and
imbued it with their own character, so that the Serbian folk art emerges
as something independent and typical.[3]

We cannot accept the opinion of some native as well as foreign interpreters of Serbian folk poetry who see in the poem "The Erection
of Skutari" a remnant of the old heathen thoughts of sacrifice to the
"heathen gods," without which men would be punished for attempting to build something.[4] Nodilo is also of the same opinion, as
he sees in this poem only a strongly expressed heathenism. Goethe
said, as he wrote about Serbian folk poetry:

The oldest poems are distinguished by an already meaningful culture
in superstitious and barbaric feelings; human sacrifices are presented,
and indeed those of the most terrible fashion. A young woman is walled
up so that the fortress of Skutari can be built, which appears to be more
brutal than what we find in the east—that only consecrated holy pictures were provided as a talisman for hidden locations within the foundations of cities in order to secure their invincibility.[5]

However, here it appears that Goethe had insufficient knowledge of
Serbian history, as Ristić notes, or he would have been able to pass

more exact judgment on the Mrnyavcheviches, as the Serbian people did, and for that reason he sees brutality in the poem mentioned. The judgment of the people concerning the Mrnyavcheviches, and consequent thereto the allowing of an innocent creature in the Mrnyavchevich family to be walled up, is the point of this poem, that in the numerous motifs common to all people in the poem "The Construction of Skutari," there is something specifically Serbian wherein the brutality and horror of the indicated motifs are lost.

How the moral judgment of the collective people develops concerning the family of the Mrnyavcheviches, especially concerning King Vukashin, will be discussed elsewhere. Here we would mention only this: The folk genius has denoted all that hinders, chains, and confines their development towards good as a principle of evil in the Mrnyavchevich behavior, since he well knew the qualities of the characteristics of that family through the collective philosophy expressed in folk poetry. The accumulated collective conscience of the people exerts all the force of its historical being to overcome and conquer this principle; it battles with it throughout its entire historical course, for it regards such a principle as a curse.

> The Mrnyavcheviches could not once build the city of Skutari. Justice appears in the figure of the fairies and destroys overnight what has been constructed during the day. They are driven by necessity and they entomb the young wife of Goyko, still living, the mother of a one-year-old male child, the mother of a tiny sprout.[6]

The thoughts presented above are clearly evident from the content of the poem itself. The people believe that a curse weights upon the Mrnyavcheviches on account of their eternal guilt concerning the disintegration of the Serbian state. For that reason the poet permits a tragedy of this type in the poem "The Construction of Skutari." In order to increase the sense of tragedy, the wife of Goyko dies, although he, the youngest brother, has better qualities and more appealing traits than Vukashin and Uglyesha. Apparently this is intentional on the folk poet's part, for only Goyko preserves the oath sworn before God, and indeed is less sinful than the two older brothers. Therefore, Goyko's wife, the being innocent and beloved by him, perishes. The poet has vividly portrayed and so powerfully expressed the occasion of this tragedy, as have many great souls: Shakespeare, Dante, and others who are the most impressive figures of powerfully dramatic spiritual motivations. As the spiritual woe of Goyko for his beloved wife nearly attains its summit, the poet arranges that the hero Goyko breaks forth in tears, as the grief finally has attained its apogee: "And the tears streamed from his face."[7]

Goyko, overpowered by grief, could not look upon the gentle, tender, and innocent countenance of his wife, who in a few moments was to be entombed; he turned his head aside: "Then was the hero sore grieved, / And he turned his head aside."[8] The unbearable, convulsive grief of Goyko's soul is reflected in his movements.

In the description of the suffering of the mortal soul, the poet has actually outdone himself. He has elevated himself to the height of a spirit which expresses the most powerful spiritual emotions by means of physical movements.

> Shakespeare utilizes the averting of the head to express the spiritual emotions of an afflicted soul. The mother of Coriolanus comes over from the Roman side to quench his anger-inflamed soul, and cause him to forget his suffering and not to attack Rome with his army, whereby all will surely find defeat. She introduces everything possible to awaken sympathy within him. Among other things, she says: the gods shall strike you because you have not fulfilled your duty to your mother, where there is a right. *He turns his head to the side.*[9]

We see, therefore, in addition to the apparent brutality, the entombment of a living, innocent being, a completely refined human sensitivity which Goyko demonstrates in regard to his wife. The poet portrays this very vividly: Goyko weeps; however, when his grief has increased even more, he turns his head to the side.

As we see, the poet arranges that an innocent creature in the Mrnyavchevich family is entombed; an innocent being suffers for the sins of others. This is the message of the poem. Thus, we cannot adhere to the view of Stefanović, who maintains that the context of this poem "is of historical characters and the tradition of the Mrnyavcheviches is of secondary importance."[10] On the contrary, the independence of the Serbian variant of this poem is its tie to the folk tradition of the Mrnyavcheviches. They are sinful, but despite that they do not themselves perish; rather, a creature who is innocent and dear to them does. The folk poet here sanctioned the truth of life: the suffering of the righteous and innocent; the thought of any righteousness in the world, or justice, which besets even the innocent members of a guilty family. The drastic actuality, that in this world the good suffer interminably while the evil are not required to, can be mitigated only by the clear and categorical image of the eventual reward in the other world, through the complete Christian assurance that the temporal life of a time is neither the ultimate reward nor the final punishment from God. Moreover, a similar verity of life is effectuated by means of mankind and circumstances, which create this verity themselves. This is best seen in this poem. All this is perfectly clear for the Christian awareness of the folk artist, in which he also provides a deeply Christian reflection: the sin of the Mrnyavcheviches is entirely too large for them to be redeemed thereof through a personal sacrifice or the price of one of them. Therefore, a higher sacrifice—that of an innocent person—is necessary. Is this not a complete analogy with the redemption of the sinful human race by the Son of God? Mankind could not enter into a new relationship and unity with God through its own sacrifice because of the immeasurability of its sin, its alienation from God, its monstrous sinfulness, and the inordinate depravity of its nature. As a consequence, the incomparably great sacrifice, the death of the innocent Son of God, was necessitated.

In its Christian reflection of the poem now lies its value and, simultaneously, the greatness of the folk poet. The heathenish motif of human sacrifice on account of affection for a higher, good power and aversion to evil forces receives a pure Christian tone. Thus, that which is presented here is not a sacrifice "for the heathen gods," but one for the satisfaction of the higher, divine justice, in whose powerful accents is reflected a higher religion, a pure ethic: sin and the priceless sacrifice for the redemption of that sin.

Notes

1. Vuk Stefanović Karadžić, *Srpske Narodne Pesme*, Vol. 2 (Vienna, 1843), p. 26:95.
2. Svetislav Stefanović, *Studije o narodnoj poeziji*, 2 vols., 2nd ed. (Zagreb, 1937), p. 307.
3. Tih. R. Djordević, *Naš narodni život* (Belgrade, 1923), p. 146.
4. T. Maretić, *Naša narodna epika*, Vol. 4 (Zagreb, 1909), p. 714.
5. Svetomir Ristić, *Duševni pokreti u našem narodnom pesništvu s obzirom na Homera, Dantea i Sekspira* (Belgrade, 1920), p. 66.
6. Ristić, *Duševni pokreti*, p. 36.
7. Karadžić, *Srpske Narodne Pesme*, p. 26:157.
8. Ibid., p. 26:172.
9. Ristić, *Duševni pokreti*, p. 68, regarding *Coriolanus*, act 5, scene 3.
10. Stefanović, *Studije*, p. 307.

Moral Vision in the Serbian Folk Epic: The Foundation Sacrifice of Skadar

There is another reading of the ballad with Christian overtones. This time the interpretation is offered by Professor Zora Devrnja Zimmerman, Professor of English at Iowa State University. However, she also proposes alternative meanings, for example, the immurement symbolizing the historical subjugation of the Serbians by the Turks. These interpretations certainly may well apply to the Serbian versions of the ballad, but would surely be questionable were they to be imposed upon the versions from North and South India. Once again, it is a matter of whether the analysis of an item of folklore can be successfully undertaken without full knowledge and consideration of other versions of that same item.

The confusing contexts and purposes of a folk poem and its complicated oral and textual history often persuade contemporary audiences that philosophical meaning in the poem is neither palpable nor significant. Such is the apocryphal nature of "Zidanje Skadra" (The Founding of Skadar). Efforts to discern meaning in this Serbian folk poem, first collected in 1804 by Vuk Stefanović Karadžić, are plagued by historical ambiguities and religious inconsistencies.[1] For instance, characteristics properly belonging to the epic, the legend, the romance, and even the ballad appear disconcertingly in the narrative's poetic form. While the plot records the founding of present-day Scutari in Albania, by recounting the decisions of idealized historical figures who lived in the fourteenth century, it also documents social roles and customs reflecting the political and economic environment of eighteenth-century Serbia. The religious beliefs incorporated by the poem range from pre-Christian notions associated with the practice of foundation sacrifice to others celebrating the Christian miracle. The poem can be classified as an etiological tale, an oral epic, and

Reprinted from the *Slavic and East European Journal* 23 (1979): 371–80.

a religious legend. But these disquieting and disorderly aspects of the poem's genealogy and form should not distract audiences from the narrative's expression of traditional moral ideas about human behavior—ideas which have managed to survive generations of chaotic transmission. Traditional folk poetry has not been sufficiently or specifically examined for its communication of moral ideas. Nevertheless, it is possible to clarify how one simple yet complex folk poem, "The Founding of Skadar," defines and illustrates moral ideas.

Ethnographers consider "The Founding of Skadar" to be the major South Slavic variant of the Master-Mason foundation sacrifice legends.[2] These international legends vary both in poetic form and in historical data. A major difference in form, for instance, immediately distinguishes various versions: the Bulgarian, Hungarian, and Romanian texts appear as ballads, the Serbian texts as epic poems. The national origin of each is indicated by specific localizations in time and place. In spite of these distinctions, the Master-Mason legends are united by their attention to the practice of sacrificial immurement. Vuk's version of "Skadar," the oldest collected version of the legend and the first to achieve literary notoriety,[3] describes the human immurement associated with the construction of Fort Skadar (Scutari) during the first half of the fourteenth century. Collected from one of his principal informants, Rǎsko, a singer from the town of Kolašin in Serbia, Vuk's text is interesting to us not only because it preserves a significant account of a human sacrifice, an account that contributes to our understanding of cultural history, but also because that experience is preserved for us in a plot based on religious beliefs. At first these beliefs appear to be an amalgam of nineteenth-century Christian concepts and pre-Christian mythology. Upon closer study, the apparent contradictions dissolve. A sequence of moral ideas can be traced in the poem which explains human behavior according to a consistent, traditional causality. This causality emerges in all versions of the Master-Mason legends: poetic techniques elicit a moral structure as a result of transforming localized historical experience into the symbolic. By examining how poetic techniques express moral ideas in "Skadar," the motivation which originally developed and later preserved the Master-Mason legends may be illuminated.

The role of a traditional narrative in a particular culture can often be traced through the form a narrative assumes. An animal tale composed in prose, for instance, may play a markedly different role from the lyrical ballad. Most versions of the Master-Mason legend occur in the form of ballads. The Serbian versions do not. Although typical European ballad characteristics appear in the Serbian texts—dramatic motifs, leaping and lingering, dialogue, and partial use of incremental repetition—the versions follow traditional Serbian epic criteria: the poems are decasyllabic and trochaic; enjambment does not occur; there are no refrains, line cycles, or stanzas; internal and end rhymes appear occasionally, while alliteration, assonance, and consonance are highly developed. The typical Serbian folk ballad depends on melodic rhythms, refrains, stanzas, enjambment, and varied metrical patterns, none of which appears in the epic. Most interesting of all, Serbian epic songs focus on the story being told rather than the melody; epics communicate information believed to be important. The epic's emphasis on plot is confirmed by the assertions of early Yugoslav ethnographers, who maintained that epics were composed originally for chanting, the traditional instrument providing ceremonial emphasis only.[4] Formal epic characteristics apply to Vuk's version of "Skadar," the oldest Serbian version, indicating that the Serbians considered the foundation-sacrifice motif to possess epic significance. The Serbians value their traditional epics as records of cultural history: during four and a half centuries of domination by the Ottoman Turks, the epics preserved descriptions of customs, beliefs, heroes, and crucial historical events. Perhaps the classical ballad may function in a comparable manner for the Hungarians and Romanians. What is conclusive, however, is that the story of "Skadar" was believed to contain essential cultural material worthy of being preserved and honored in the form of a national epic.

Confirmation of the legend's importance in cultural history can also be found in the historical accounts of the sacrificial immurement of living human beings. For over a century, ethnographers have conscientiously investigated hundreds of reported cases. Such sacrifices appear to have been commonplace throughout the civilized world for millennia. Westermarck, in a 1906 study, cited instances of foundation sacrifices at Germany's Maulbronn Monastery, the Bridge Gate walls of Bremen, and the Elizabeth Bridge of Halle, among others.[5] In an 1898 treatise on foundation sacrifice, Sartori listed hundreds of cases in dozens of cultures. Muenster Cathedral of Strasbourg, France, numerous Buddhist monasteries in Thailand and Cambodia, the Palace at Dahomey, Africa, the City Gate of Tavoy in Tenasserim, Burma, the Temple of Quetzalcoatl in Mexico, the Cathedral of Schleswig in Schleswig-Holstein, Denmark's Roeskilde Cathedral, the city walls of Antioch, Turkey, of Alexandria, Egypt, as well as the cultural centers of the Phoenicians and Carthaginians, and the foundation walls of most ancient settlements on the Danube—these are among the many immurement sites Sartori discusses.[6]

Even though this apparently common ritual has been historically documented, no written literature has been preserved which analyzes the impact of this practice on the development of culture. The only material that even begins to suggest the psychological implications of the practice is the Master-Mason collection of oral ballads and epic poems. This distinction makes these accounts invaluable. Vargyas, Stefanović, and Leader have demonstrated convincingly that the more than two hundred international versions, based perhaps on only two or three major variants, were distributed throughout southeastern Europe (predominantly Albania, Bulgaria, Greece, Hungary, Romania, and Serbia), and that master texts must have been circulating by the mid-fourteenth century.[7]

The Master-Mason ballads and their variants provide us with a body of literature on foundation sacrifice which interprets and recreates the human drama of this widespread phenomenon.[8] As such, the songs' conclusions on the causes and effects of the practice should be seriously studied. To date, comparative ethnographic research on the ballad group has investigated structural variation, motif-frequency, linguistic and stylistic methods of oral composition, migration and proliferation of versions, and general sociohistorical background. No study has focussed on religious and psychological motivation or symbolization in an individual version. The content of each version reflects how events are rationalized and interpreted by a social group. It may be that these remarkable legends were preserved precisely because of their psychological and religious interpretations of ritual immurement. In the collection studied by Vargyas, events directly contributing to moral dilemma recur most frequently, suggesting that these texts successfully preserved moral beliefs whether or not that was the primary intention of the tradition.

The basic plot features of most versions in the six cultural collections noted above do not vary in any radical way. The most consistent variation among these texts is the localization of the legend. Several sites recur frequently. In the Hungarian "Clement-Mason," the immurement takes place in the still-existing foundation walls of Fort Deva, situated on the Maros River in southeast Hungary.[9] In Romania the legend, called "Manole, the Master-Mason," generally involves the founding of a monastery in Argeschtal. Bulgarian texts describe the building of a bridge over the Struma River. Once assumed to be the master text, but later disproven, the Greek version tells of the construction of a bridge over the Arta River. The main Serbian tradition preserves the legend of Fort Skadar on the Bojana River;

most Albanian versions refer to the same site. When considered from an artistic perspective, these localizations—often fervently defended as historically true—provide the all-important concrete setting for the moral dilemma. Such concrete descriptions and immediate sense data characterize folk literature; they are essentially mnemonic. Without these concrete images, the Master-Mason legends might not have survived. Yet it must be remembered that the localization is not the story. The story consists of the folk analysis of the immurement.

A sacrificial immurement of a woman—usually a young mother—is recorded in all the major cultural collections of the Master-Mason legends. This sacrifice most often occurs as a sequel to a motif which explains the repeated collapse of an important edifice in the process of construction as the work of angry superhuman powers. A sacrifice is planned in order to appease these powers. The selection of the scapegoat and the events which determine that selection form the plot in these ballads. The sacrifice is always effective: the construction is completed with no further disturbance. This conclusion depends upon an unquestioning acceptance by the culture of a single religious principle: when mortals presume to rival divine creation with their own, they will incur the wrath of the gods. Belief in this notion conflicts with personal ambition, so strategies of appeasement inevitably follow. In the Master-Mason legends, progress is allowed only after the penalty for trespass onto divine territories is paid. The penalty is a sacrificial offering. This religious principle appears in all the major texts and should be given primary attention when the motivation or the development and preservation of the songs is studied.

Each version presents localized settings, characterizations, customs, and, consequently, localized solutions to an ethical dilemma. Each version judges and rationalizes the immurement, always described as profoundly disturbing. A most interesting aspect of these rationalizations is their essential determinism. They emphasize the necessity of the immurement, a conclusion which may have dispelled anxiety in both singer and audience. If the release of cultural anxiety is one of the effects of the tradition, then we may ask why the tradition intentionally preserves this anxiety by preserving the songs. This paradox may indicate again that the religious interpretation of the immurement may be the essential feature of the legend, the feature which tradition seeks to preserve.

In Vuk's text, traditional beliefs eventually resolve the dilemma in a unified, consistent manner, providing us with a sequence of ideas that reveals how folk tradition transforms historical experience into organized, symbolic experience:

> For three years, the three royal Mrnjavčević brothers—Vukašin, Uglješa, and Gojko—and three hundred laborers try to lay the foundations of a fortress at Skadar (Scutari) on the Bojana River. The efforts are directed by Rade, a master-mason.[10] Every night a Vila destroys what was built during the day.[11] She advises King Vukašin to not squander his wealth but to offer a sacrifice: to immure in the foundation walls a brother and sister whose names are Stojan and Stoja.[12] Vukašin sends a servant to search for and bring back the brother and sister. After a three year search, he returns without success. King Vukašin, ignoring the Vila's warning, begins to build once more. This time the Vila announces that the brothers must sacrifice one of their wives if they want the foundation walls to be erected. She stipulates that the wife who comes on the morrow to bring the men their daily meal should be immured. The brothers vow to each other not to divulge this secret to their wives but to leave the decision to fate. Both Vukašin and Uglješa break their vows; Gojko does not. The next day it is Vukašin's wife's turn to bring the meal. Under a pretense of being ill, she asks Uglješa's wife to go instead. Uglješa's wife also refuses, feigning illness, and Gojko's wife is asked. Gojko's wife, who explains that she must bathe and care for her infant son, nevertheless is persuaded to bring the meal. When she arrives at the construction site, Gojko is grief-stricken upon seeing her but powerless to warn her. She is led to the foundation by the elder brothers and placed in a gaping hole by the workers who proceed to build the walls up to her knees, then to her waist. At first she believes them to be joking; later, she pleas to be released but to no avail. Her final request to the master-mason, that he leave openings for her breasts and eyes, is granted. Her infant son is then brought to her to be nursed each day. She nurses him long after her voice has withered, for over a year, and even to this day, the milk still flows down the walls, working wonders and curing women with no milk.[13]

As the poem opens, we immediately enter the closed, *a priori* world of traditional folk religion. No one—neither singer, nor audience, nor internal character—questions the existence of superhuman forces or the fact that mortals choose to conflict with these forces. Vukašin could choose not to build Skadar. But, like Agamemnon, who sacrifices his daughter Iphigenia so that he can embark with his troops to wage war on Troy, Vukašin cannot relinquish his original plan, his personal ambition. The original decision to build a fortress without the approval of the vila constitutes an implicit religious transgression—a trespass upon forbidden territories—and Vukašin must pay a penalty. (Perhaps the custom of consulting various oracles and performing ceremonial offerings before choosing a building site had been ignored.) Such a trespass alludes to classical Greek notions of hubris. Aeschylus wrote that human beings cannot progress without committing hubris. Human ambition advances civilization but it also brings about suffering. In short, mortals are punished for their defiance of the gods, but defiance gives knowledge. Vukašin's act of hubris becomes more grievous when, unable to perform the necessary sacrifice of Stojan and Stoja, he disregards the decree of the vila. Not only does Vukašin defy the gods when he begins construction again but he also brings about the second, fatal, decree as a penalty for his vanity. In his arrogance, he believes that the effort to comply is a sufficient gesture. ·

In Vuskašin we are given a prototypical aggressive hero, a hero who believes he is powerful enough to bargain with gods. This belief that human beings are different from other creatures, that they alone can intervene in the processes of nature, is ancient and contemporary. "The Founding of Skadar" documents the belief in the efficacy of a contract between human beings and superhuman forces—a sacrificial contract. By drawing up a contract, a change in the status of a people becomes formalized. The contract establishes a power hierarchy. Such bargaining is characterized in folk tradition by the belief that for the gods the gain equals the loss but for mankind the gain outweighs the loss. Thus, the great irony in this legend, and in many myths, appears in the realization that humans will not sacrifice unless they are assured of far greater gain. In effect, mortals believe they can outwit the gods. Like Prometheus, who thought that he could trick Zeus by disguising a sacrificial offering, Vukašin believes he will emerge the victor. It is always clear that for Vukašin the fortress has priority. His behavior is locked into a predictable system, a system which folk tradition has learned to recognize.

The tone of the poem implies that Vukašin's decision to offer a sacrifice rather than to abandon the project is immoral. Vukašin agrees to offer a sacrifice because it will further his own ambition. The consequences of this ambition are indirectly analyzed by the events in the central portion of the poem: the story of the brothers and their wives. We shift here from a general historical point of view to a more immediate one. The betrayal of the oath by the older brothers and the deception of the innocent by their wives determine the choice of victim. Had the brothers left the selection to chance, there would have been no individual guilt. But Vukašin and Uglješa, by breaking their vows, choose to become directly responsible, to accept the burden of guilt. Again, Vukašin believes he can outwit the vila and keep himself, his wife, his fortune, and his plans intact. The actions of the two elder brothers are condemned as immoral by traditional values. But, the evil-doers in the poem are not directly punished. In many oral narratives deceivers and renegades are appropriately penalized, sometimes by their fellows, most often by superhuman powers. In this poem, Vukašin's cunning is seen as a necessary evil. And the acts of deception, although reprehensible, occur as acts of self-preservation. In comparison with his brothers' actions, Gojko's allegiance to his oath, his morality, represents unusual and idealized behavior. The sacrificial victim, who was to have been randomly chosen, becomes, because of her innocence, the only possible choice among the participants. The circumstances become especially tragic when Gojko determines that innocence and thus the martyrdom of the victim by his righteous behavior. The conclusion becomes evident: immoral behavior is rewarded, moral behavior is punished.

Gojko suffers for the evil of others and becomes the ethical hero. By keeping his vow, he succeeds in controlling his instincts. He is a man who believes in principles. He does not bargain with the gods or try to outwit them; he accepts their demands. This does not mean that Gojko lacks ambition or that he loves less, but only that he obeys moral principles. Gojko's ability to transcend human weakness and to live according to moral obligations distinguishes him from other men, and he is victimized accordingly. The good and the innocent are sacrificed to the gods, and the sacrifice is accepted. Gojko's reward, tradition insists, is the sanctification of his behavior and of his wife's immurement in cultural memory. He becomes a model, an ideal hero for future generations, whereas Vukašin, the aggressive, crafty, dominant leader, and Uglješa, the follower, the common man, are remembered as unprincipled, instinctive creatures. Gojko's symbolic role is supported by the fact that he is the only invented figure in the royal Mrnjavčević family, a fact which allows for more intense identification by the audience.

That a mother is sacrificed and that her sacrifice is preserved and celebrated in oral tradition are worthy of comment. (Only a few of the Master-Mason variants refer to other immurements, and those are of children.[14]) The belief that women are sacrificed for the preservation of society—"to the house"—is an ancient maxim known to women all over the world. A woman, especially a mother, represents the future. She is an absolute in the human struggle for survival and self-preservation. By being the "foundation" of society herself, the woman is one of the highest sacrifices mankind can offer. In the

"Skadar" legend, the offenders must sacrifice that which they value most; only in this way can they be punished. By sacrificing one of the wives, the progeny of that marriage is also sacrificed. The goodness of Gojko and his wife is therefore rewarded in an extraordinary fashion by the miracle which allows their progeny to survive.

Traditional thinking discriminates between moral and immoral behavior in this legend, but it also tragically concludes that evil is a necessary fact of human existence, that we cannot always resist temptation. Those who transcend greed and selfishness will be abused by others, but such transcendence will be honored by the gods and preserved in cultural memory. Folk poetry preserves and defines cultural memory. The poetic process, which is inseparable from the verbalization of experience, ensures that moral patterns are recognized and evaluated by the people. Poetry gives an order to the apparently random interrelationships between natural events and human behavior. The poet renames and restructures experience according to a generalized abstract perspective. In effect, he transforms a historical experience into the symbolic. In this transformation, not only is human experience given an order but the ordering is generalized. Such ordering, the advent of which was apparently dependent upon language, may underlie the development of abstract religious principles, such as the Greek notion of hubris.

Not only is the poet able to organize an experience according to his understanding of it but also, through such techniques as polarization, ironic reversals, and concrete imagery, his audience is able to identify with and participate in that transformed experience. Through identification the audience perceives the experience from a different standpoint, since a distance has been created between the self and the experience. This distance objectifies the experience and, as a result, the audience can recognize the structure of the experience in the abstract. The process is described in the classical theory of catharsis. Catharsis, a releasing or purifying of emotion, cannot occur, Aristotle said, until fear and pity are aroused in an audience. Fear and pity are brought about by identification and then purged as a result of identification. This freeing sensation must take place before the audience can recognize the objectified patterns, the abstract moral or religious principles, dramatized by the poet.

In the tragedy of "The Founding of Skadar" we can recognize the poetically transformed experience and the abstract ideas which this transformation seeks to define. The emotional confusion and the moral perplexity accompanying the historical practice of foundation sacrifice need to be dispelled, and this is accomplished through the audience's identification with Gojko and his bride. Once fear and pity have been purged, the objective patterns in human behavior and the causes and effects of the catastrophe can be analyzed. Vukašin's vanity and greed are directly blamed for the events; and since Vukašin, as a historical figure, has become a symbol, it is his moral character which comes under attack. But such a character triumphs in this world, the poet says, and the innocent, the good, must suffer. At first Gojko may be thought a fool because of his trust, integrity, and obedience, but he emerges a hero in the end. Through the closing miracle, a motif which reflects Christian philosophy, his ideal behavior is celebrated and his bride's innocent sacrifice sanctified. Both attest to the poet's, and the folk's, vision of redemption. It is through the miracle of the ever-flowing milk that the audience is comforted. If the struggle between Vukašin and the vila actually does portray the archetypal conflict between mortals and immortals, then the sanctification of the sacrifice may indicate the ultimate triumph of faith.[15]

"The Founding of Skadar" provides us with a consistent and complex interpretation of human experience. The poem transforms historical data into symbolic events and figures, a transformation which elucidates moral patterns in human behavior. We know that the historical practice of immurement persisted for centuries in every part of the known world. Guilt-ridden cultural memories about foundation sacrifices may have encouraged efforts to articulate and rationalize the experience and to preserve for future generations the philosophical meanings that the events embodied. The reinforcement that "The Founding of Skadar" gives to the traditional Christian beliefs in an ultimate reward for suffering and the triumph of good over evil—beliefs that can be traced in plot organization and character development—may explain why the epic was so highly valued by the Serbians during the Turkish domination. The immurement, in this context, can represent the subjugation of the Serbian peoples at the time, and the survival of the infant, the ultimate survival of the nation. The importance of the sacrifice motif in the literature associated with this period would seem to support such an interpretation. Through identification and cartharsis the audience is brought to understand the sacrifice as a strategy of appeasement finalizing the ageless conflict between mortals and gods, a conflict initiated by human ambition. The miracle sanctifies the suffering of the innocent and confirms that such innocence transforms the sacrifice into an act of ultimate redemption.

Notes

1. Vuk Stefanović Karadžić, *Srpske Narodne Pjesme*, 2nd ed., 4 vols. (1823; rpt. Belgrade: Prosveta, 1953), Vol. 2, no. 25.

2. Lajos Vargyas, "Forschungen zur Geschichte der Volksballade in Mittelalter: Die Herkunft der ungarischen Ballade von der eingemauertcn Frau," *Acta Ethnographica* 9 (1960): 1–88. Vargyas gives summaries of all motifs occurring in master-mason ballads collected up to 1960.

3. First translated into German by Talvj (Terese Albertini Luise von Jakob Robinson, 1797–1870), the published text appeared in 1825 in *Über Kunst und Altertum* 5 (1825), against the better judgment of Goethe, who was shocked by the poem's barbarity—despite Jakob Grimm's strong defense of its value. Goethe's discussion of Serbian poetry may be found in *Gedenkausgabe der Werke, Briefe und Gespräche*, ed. Ernst Beutler, 27 vols. (Zurich: Artemis-Verlag, 1948–71), 19: 530–46.

4. For full descriptions of gusle performances, see Matthias Murko, *Tragom srpsko-hrvatske narodna epike: Putovanje u godinama 1930–32*, 2 vols. (Zagreb: Jugoslavenska akademija znanosti i umjetnosti, 1951); Karadžić, *O Narodnim Pesmama*, ed. Dobrašinović (Belgrade: Prosveta, 1964); Albert Bates Lord, *The Singer of Tales* (New York: Atheneum, 1968).

5. Edward A. Westermarck, *The Origin and Development of the Moral Ideas*, 2nd ed. (London: Macmillan, 1912), 461–66.

6. Paul Sartori, "Über das Bauopfer," *Zeitschrift für Ethnologie* 30 (1898): 1–54.

7. S. Stefanović, "Legenda o zidanju Skadra," *Studije o narodnoj poeziji*, 2nd ed. (Belgrade, 1937), 245–314; Ninon Leader, *Classical Hungarian Ballads* (Cambridge: Cambridge University Press, 1967), 2–30.

8. See for example Donna Shai, "A Kurdish Jewish Variant of the Ballad of 'The Bridge of Arta,'" *Association for Jewish Studies Review* 1 (1976): 303–10. The religious function of the foundation sacrifice is analyzed by Mircea Eliade, *Zalmoxis: The Vanishing God*, trans. Willard R. Trask (Chicago: University of Chicago Press, 1972).

9. Leader, *Classical Hungarian Ballads*, 5, reports that according to legend the castle was built by the Davian king Decebalus. The ruins are known in various legal documents from the time of the Arpad Dynasty; Leader's earliest reference is A.D. 1269.

10. Historically, Rade, the master mason, appears to have been a noted architect—see Karadžić, *Pjesme*, 2: 123.

11. The vila is a wood-nymph possessing specific magical powers. She is usually beneficent to mortals but can do harm if provoked. See my article "The Changing Roles of the Vila in Serbian Traditional Literature," *Journal of the Folklore Institute* 3 (1979): 167–175.

12. Stojan and Stoja are the masculine and feminine proper names derived from *stojati*, "to stand, to be erect, to be immovable."

13. Witnesses say that a chalky liquid oozes from Skadar's walls even today—from holes through which Gojko's wife purportedly nursed her son. Women mix this chalky substance with water and drink it. The liquid is said to restore milk to women who cannot nurse, and to relieve pain associated with full breasts.

14. See Vargyas, "Forschungen zur Geschichte der Volksballade in Mittelalter," 1–88.

15. The legend's psychological and moral meaning inspired the winner of the Emily Clark Balch Prize in Fiction; see Margaret Edwards, "The Fountain of Milk," *Virginia Quarterly Review* 53 (1977): 400–17.

RUTH MANDEL

"Sacrifice at the Bridge of Arta":
Sex Roles and the
Manipulation of Power

*The study of gender has revolutionized the fields of anthropology
and folklore among other academic disciplines. In view of the
prominent role played by women in the ballad, not to mention the
nuances of the walling-up imagery, it was only a matter of time
before a feminist approach was utilized in connection with the
ballad.*

*Anthropologist Ruth Mandel, who teaches in the Department of
Anthropology, University College, London, concentrates on the
modern Greek versions, that is, on "The Bridge of Arta." Using the
Lévi-Straussian nature-culture dichotomy (with woman as nature,
man as culture), she makes a persuasive analysis of the Greek
ballad. She also has recourse to the notion of liminality (which derives ultimately from Arnold Van Gennep's classic* The Rites of Passage*) and again argues convincingly for the bridge as a symbol of
liminality.*

*This sophisticated essay suggests that there may be more to be
said in the way of analysis of the ballad of "The Walled-Up Wife."
Whether or not Mandel's analysis would apply equally well to Serbian, Hungarian, Bulgarian, and other versions of the ballad remains to be seen.*

*For an entrée into the burgeoning feminist folklore literature, see
Rosan A. Jordan and Frank de Caro, "Women and the Study of Folk-
lore,"* Signs: Journal of Women in Culture and Society *11 (1986):
500–18; Joyce Ice, "Women, Folklore, Feminism and Culture,"*
New York Folklore *15 (1989): 121–37; Margaret Mills, "Feminist
Theory and the Study of Folklore: A Twenty-Year Trajectory toward
Theory,"* Western Folklore *52 (1993): 173–92; and Susan Tower
Hollis, Linda Pershing, and M. Jane Young, eds.,* Feminist Theory

and the Study of Folklore *(Urbana: University of Illinois Press, 1993).*

> If we remember, too, that the traditional societies saw the human
> dwelling as an *imago mundi*, it becomes still clearer that every work of
> foundation symbolically reproduces the cosmogony.
> —Mircea Eliade, *Zalmoxis: The Vanishing God*

This paper will try to demonstrate how the story of the woman sacrificed and immured in the foundation of the bridge of Arta symbolically reproduces Greek cosmogony and notions of culture and nature.
This will be made evident by examining the gender-linked concepts
of nature and culture which form the background for the sacrifice
that takes place. Ultimately it will be shown how the woman's role
as a mediator between households and the worlds of the living and
the dead imbues her with an essential liminality to the extent that
she concurrently is the instantiation of both nature and culture.

The Greek woman has been perceived by scholars in many different lights. She is the idealized mother-Panayía (Virgin Mary) figure,
the wife-sister-daughter repository of male honor, and the sister or
daughter who is a financial burden requiring a substantial dowry, to
name but a few. Most of the roles she assumes and is assigned im-
plicitly identify the woman in relation to her male kin. Through a
symbolic approach,[1] an examination of the ballad "The Bridge of
Arta" provides an excellent vehicle for exploring the various roles
and meanings of woman, and woman-as-sacrificial-victim, as they
unfold in the song.[2]

Drawing also on the theoretical contributions of structuralism
and ritual analysis, I will focus upon, first, the basic opposition of in-
clusivity vs. exclusivity expressed in Greek by the terms *dikós* and
ksénos (insiders-outsiders)[3] and, second, the notion of liminality.
The *dikós-ksénos* opposition as discussed by Vassiliou and Vassiliou
("*Philotimo*," passim), Campbell (*Honour*, passim), and Herzfeld
("Segmentation," passim) is understood to be pervasive and central
to the Greek cosmology as a salient distinction that Greeks make in
the course of meaningful social action.

As might be expected, the category of *dikós* is often congruent
with the "family" (delimited in varying ways), but in many instances,
as will become clear below, it is important to discern between the two
terms, *dikós* and *family*, because they are each context-dependent,

relative, and therefore not isomorphic categories. The *dikós-ksénos* opposition proves particularly useful when a meaningful distinction emerges between consanguines or blood relations, and affines or relatives by marriage.

In light of the importance of the distinction between the categories *dikós* and *ksénos*, the nebulous territory lying between the two emerges as equally important. Many anthropologists have explored this territory, referring to it as ambiguous, marginal, or liminal. It is often addressed in the domain of the sacred. For instance, in Durkheim's discussion of the nature of the sacred, he distinguishes between two opposed sorts of sacredness, the propitious and the unpropitious. He describes this in terms of purity, positing that

> the pure and the impure are not two separate classes, but two varieties of the same class, which includes all sacred things. . . . The pure is made out of the impure, and reciprocally. It is in the possibility of the transmutations that the ambiguity of the sacred consists" (*Elementary Forms*, 458).

It is this same ambiguity that Victor Turner addresses. Liminality was first propounded as such by Turner, who, drawing on Van Gennep's *Rites of Passage*, developed his theory. Briefly, it speaks to what Mary Douglas *(Purity and Danger)* and others have called marginality. It can apply to specific rituals as well as to more or less permanent statuses. Friedrich describes it as "dynamic or processual in that it involves crossing over (out of or in to) relatively stable or fixed structures or "grids." Or it may involve operating "betwixt and between" the margins of these recognized and accepted categories, rules, groups, and structures" (Friedrich, *The Meaning of Aphrodite*, 132). Liminality is that which lies in the interstices, in the margins, or that which is transitional and mediates between two distinct spheres or statuses. This paper explores the interplay of the *dikós-ksénos* dichotomy and the notion of liminality pervasive throughout "The Bridge of Arta." It indicates especially the central role of the woman as a figure who necessarily embodies multivocal expressions of liminality given the realities of the social structure which assigns her an ambiguous position regarding her incorporation into households.

The ballad in question is found throughout the Balkans and has been the subject of many studies.[4] In Greece it is most commonly known as "Τῆς Ἄρτας τό γιοφύρι" (The Bridge of Arta), and it provides a text rich in symbols and drama that carry much cultural currency with regard to the themes just mentioned. The plethora of versions, many of which vary significantly, contains enough consistency for the following thematic sketch. The story of the ballad begins with a group of master builders and apprentices who have been trying in vain to construct a bridge over the river at Arta, each day building it only for it to collapse at night. They lament their futile labors. Finally, they are informed, by either a bird or the demon-protector (τό στοιχειό) of the bridge and river, that the bridge will not stand unless a person is built into it. The demand often specifies that the victim cannot be just anyone, such as an orphan or stranger; only a member of the family of the first master builder is acceptable. Sometimes the demand names the wife from the start. The first master dispatches a bird to summon his wife. He instructs the bird to tell his wife to come slowly to the bridge. The bird misapprehends, telling her to come at once. An exchange takes place between the bird and the wife regarding her clothing. Arriving at the site she asks the workers why her husband looks so forlorn and depressed. When she is told that it is because his wedding ring has fallen into the arch the loyal wife offers to retrieve it. Once down at the bottom of the foundation she realizes the ruse, as the builders begin to shovel mortar and heave stones at her. She curses, bemoaning her fate. One of the more typical curses is:

> τρεῖς ἀδερφάδες ἤμασταν κι οἱ τρεῖς κακογραμμένες
> Ἡ μιά 'χτισε τό Δούναβη κι ἡ ἄλλη τόν Αὐλώνα,
> κι ἐγώ ἡ πλιό στερνότερη τῆς Ἄρτας τό γιοφύρι.
> Καθώς τρέμ' ἡ καρδούλα μου, νά τρέμει τό γιοφύρι·
> κι ὡς πέφτουν τά μαλλάκια μου, νά πέφτουν οἱ διαβάτες.

> We were three sisters, all three ill-fated.
> One of us built the bridge over the Danube, another at Avlona,
> and I, the youngest, the bridge of Arta.
> As my heart is shaking, so may the bridge shake;
> and as my hair is falling out, so may those passing over fall off.

In some versions her husband, the master builder, beseeches her to revoke the curse, reminding her of a brother in a foreign land who might chance to cross it. She complies, issuing a revised curse, ending the ballad.

The very clothing of the wife, mentioned in the passage when she speaks with the messenger-bird, is subject to ambiguity. The wife wishes to know if she is being summoned to the bridge for auspicious or inauspicious purposes, so she will know how to dress appropriately. The opposition of *ta hrisá*, the gold finery, vs. *ta mávra*, the black clothing of mourning, corresponding to *yiá kaló* and *yiá kakó*, for good and for bad (or evil), respectively (Cowan, "Bridge of Arta"), is mediated by the bird's puzzling answer: "*kai kaló, kai kakó, éla ópos eísai*" (both good and bad, come as you are). In other words, neither good nor bad, and both good and bad are implied. This is the "betwixt and between" suggesting the "out of the ordinary" situation, the nebulous and liminal shades of gray that characterize the narrative. Good and bad, however, are seemingly reversed.

Reversals can symbolize things being askew, sometimes made more evident in the song by paradox and category dissonance. A common feature to nearly every version is the wrong, backwards message delivered by the bird sent to fetch the wife.[5] As noted above, when the bird is told to tell the wife to come slowly, it tells her instead to hasten. A Dodecanese version has a rather complex message to be relayed. She is not to comb her hair on Saturday, not to change on Sunday, and to go to the bridge Monday morning. The bird commands her to perform the opposite things. This sequence is reminiscent of marriage rituals (Cowan, "Bridge of Arta"), a theme much larger than that into which the scope of this paper permits inquiry. Suffice it to say here that in the Balkans and throughout Europe the themes of death and marriage have many parallels and that death is often referred to in marriage metaphors and vice versa (Eliade, *Zalmoxis*).

Finding herself at the bottom of the arch looking for the ring, the woman sometimes tells the workmen to pull her up, as the whole world is upside-down and she has not found anything. Her world is indeed *anáyira*, upside down; messages are delivered wrongly and, as will become clear below, someone else will assume all her duties and obligations against her will. The normal social order of the cosmos is severely threatened. The intensity of this lack of order, further emphasized in the revocation of the curse proferred by the victim, draws on paradoxes from the natural world. In one she says: "'If rugged mountains should tremble so shall the bridge / If wild birds should fall so shall they fall who cross the bridge.'" Since neither do mountains tremble nor do wild birds fall prey to capture (in normal times) we can understand the woman's exclamation about the whole world being upside-down both as a literal statement reflecting her experience in the narrative and as symbolic of the generally disordered, dangerous, and threatening situation implied by her imminent death.

The bargaining passage between the first master and the demon presents a puzzling and seemingly contradictory element. An exchange which Megas calls κυνικός ὑπολογισμός (shameless calculation) between the *stoiheió*-demon and the first master proceeds thus:

> What will you give, Master, so I will support the bridge?
> —If I give you my father, I'll not have another.
> What will you give me, Master, so I will support the bridge?
> —If I give you my mother, I'll have no other.
> What will you give me, Master, to make the bridge stand?
> —If I give you my brothers, I'll not have more.
> What will you give, Master, and I will make the bridge firm?
> —If I give my children, I won't have others.
> What will you give, Master, and I'll make your bridge stable?
> —If I give my wife, a better one I'll find!
>
> (from Pontos)

So, while the wife is *dikí*, insider enough to be considered part of the kin of the first master, she is sufficiently *kséni*, outsider to be considered less valuable, even replaceable. It is her liminal and relative status as less *dikí* to her husband than are his consanguineal kin—his parents, siblings, and children—which qualifies her as inferior, structurally unequal, and ultimately expendable.

However, other versions specify, instead of the master's "calculation," that only the sacrifice of the wife of the first master will allow the bridge to stand. Such is this stanza from Crete: "Build in neither blind man, nor cripple, nor passerby; / Only the beautiful wife of the first master . . ." Here the opposition implies not that the wife is of lesser value than the others, as was the case in the previous passage; rather, it is her greater value over an orphan, stranger, or passerby that serves as the determining criterion. In both instances her uniqueness marks her: first, it renders her replaceable, and, then, it privileges her over physically marred persons and strangers who are more *ksénoi*, suggesting relative spheres of social distance.

It can be stated therefore that it is the wife's relative *kséni* status to her husband compared with her in-laws which victimizes her in the former example, while the reverse is the case in the latter, where her *dikí* status relative to her husband is the salient factor. Here we see a paradox: the woman is expendable, yet her incorporation into the patrilineal unit is essential to ensure its continuity. Her presence is required to secure the foundation of both the lineage and the bridge—yet not to sustain it.

An analogous passage to the bargaining one just discussed is found at the end of many versions in the victim's curse and her revocation of it. We have just seen how her husband, the first master, discerns between his consanguines and his affines in selecting the victim. In a like manner the wife's curse often reflects the same sentiment. Her initial curse usually is sufficiently general to include all persons who will cross the bridge. For example: "'As my eyes run with tears, so may the river overflow, / As my heart trembles, so may the bridge shake . . .'" Upon either remembering or being reminded of her brother in a foreign land, *ksenitiá,* she modifies it: "'All who fall off will be unharmed— / All but those kin of my husband; / Of them, not even one shall remain.'" Again, the blood relatives are privileged over those by marriage, with particular importance shown the brother.[6] Here again we note the woman's unique position of feeling both *dikí* and *kséni,* included and excluded, from two sets of kin, underscoring her essential liminality throughout the narrative.

Female liminality is evident in nonfamily domains as well, and is often associated with power. It is the woman in Greek society whose role it is to mediate between the worlds of the living and the dead. The women are the chief managers of death, singing the "words of fate," the *moirológia,* "death laments." Since death and events surrounding it are considered dangerous, it follows that those who directly deal with death both court danger and are dangerous. And, accompanying this dangerous status of women is power.

Hubert and Mauss *(Sacrifice: Its Nature and Function)* have discussed the intrinsic power of words during a sacrifice. This power is particularly germane in "The Bridge of Arta," when the victim curses. It is terribly important to the builders that she rescind the curse. She, after all, is about to enter the world of the dead, where contact may be established with their dead ancestors. Should she be sacrificed involuntarily, leaving a curse behind her, the consequences for the living could be grave indeed.

Many Greek proverbs attest to the woman's innate danger. One of the best-known, τά τρία κακά τοῦ κόσμου: πῦρ, γυνή, καί θάλασσα (the three evils of the world: fire, woman, and the sea) expresses succinctly the ambiguity of these three "evils," since it is clear that each of the three has its life-sustaining qualities as well. (Also, the notion of female "pollution" is much discussed in the literature.[7])

Much of the woman's danger and power derives from her sexuality. Durham, referring to another area of the Balkans, Montenegro, states that three options are open to women: marriage, life in a convent, or a symbolically neuterized, masculinized permanent virgin status. Each of these three states limits, regulates, and restricts the woman's sexuality. She is, in effect, either tamed, jailed, or symbolically castrated. A woman's sexuality, if loose and uncontrolled, is thought to be dangerously threatening, so it must be captured and regulated within the ideally, at least, acceptable norms. Keeping the woman in check necessarily implies the belief in the latent power she embodies. The powerful sexuality and fertility are required, then, to immure her into the bridge. The victim's potency is increased in precisely this domain: the conjoining of her fertility and motherhood with her sexuality and femininity (cf. Friedrich, *The Meaning of Aphrodite*). Her beauty is often mentioned in the narrative, but her status as a proven fertile woman is even more striking.

Many versions place her in a dialogue with her husband when she has realized her fate, pleading with him to pull her up from the depths of the arch. She invokes only that which is symbolic of her role as a mother and wife. "My child is in the cradle, pull me up," she says. "You gave birth to him but others will raise him," is his answer. "Throw me the chain," she says, "I have bread rising in the trough." "Others will knead it, others will eat it," replies the husband. And so on. In this dialogue both he and she call attention to her fertility and her creative powers—exactly what the bridge needs if it is to stand. In a few versions the victim has the workmen promise to leave a hole in the bridge's arch for her breast so that she may continue to suckle her child, even after her death. Thus the mother's milk, a prepotent symbol of the woman's fertility, her generative and creative powers, will be captured within the construction, assuring its success.

This creativity—suggesting fertility, motherhood, and sexuality, all perceived as natural powers—belongs to the woman's domain. The corresponding male domain, then, is that of the craftsmen of culture. However, the production of this male culture relies on the appropriation of female nature. This can happen only through destruction: her sacrifice. Male culture lacks the self-creative ability inherent in female nature and therefore must take it from the woman. Culture appropriates nature, then, through an inversion or destruction (culture:nature :: killing:vitality). The sacrifice of the woman makes this possible, as she belongs to both worlds. The men are intent on sacrificing her because she has something they need, to wit, creative, natural powers. Ultimately she is vulnerable to the men and the sacrifice precisely because of her dual nature; it is when the men invoke her socialness—here, the salient brother-sister tie—that she is transformed into a willing victim.

If man is to take on nature—first, by conquering the river in the form of a bridge and, second, by the ultimate act of destruction of woman-as-nature—there is a cost that must be paid. That cost is the tragic loss of the social woman—the wife, the mother.

It is this identical creative power that permits her to serve alternately as the foundation of, first, the lineage and, second, the bridge. But she can no longer actively participate as the foundation of lineage if the bridge is to be built. Instead, she must be sacrificed for the sake of the foundation of the cultural bridge.

Culture, lacking the creative ability inherent in nature, must invert social and cultural order through the pivotal act of sacrifice. In other words, culture, without a positive nature, can construct itself only by deconstructing nature, by destroying and thereby encompassing nature. In the process, culture relinquishes a valued and cherished cultural as well as natural object: the woman. And the woman, sacrificed for the sake of her natural powers and qualities, ultimately can be sacrificed only by means of her cultural and social qualities. Thus the men cannot tame pure nature, but must sacrifice a part of their own cultural and social world, the wife-sister-mother, as well.

The success of the construction, contingent upon the sacrifice of the wife of the first master, has ample precedent. Eliade has summarized the principle underlying sacrifice at construction rites:

> . . . to last, a construction . . . must be animated, that is, receive both life and a soul. The "transference" of the soul is possible only by means of a sacrifice; in other words, by a violent death. We may even say that the victim continues its existence after death, no longer in its physical body but in the new body—the construction—which has been "animated" by its immolation; we may even speak of an "architectonic body" substituted for a body of flesh. (Eliade, *Zalmoxis*, 183)

It is unclear whether the wife is sacrificed to the *stoiheió* or actually becomes the *stoiheió* of the bridge, which corresponds to Eliade's "animated . . . architectonic body." Hubert and Mauss concur with Eliade: "In the building sacrifice, for example, one sets out to create a spirit who will be the guardian of the house, altar, or town that one is building or wants to build and which will become the power within it" (*Sacrifice: Its Nature and Function*, 65). A key idea here is that of creative death. Eliade maintains that the original schema upon which all construction rites are based included "immolation of a living being, followed by a creation, that is, his metamorphosis into a substance that did not exist before" (*Zalmoxis*, 186–87). A violent death, a sacrifice, begets creativity.

The bridge itself represents a liminal construction. It is a fragile link between two places but is neither of one place nor of the other. It lies between territorial boundaries, both linking them and accenting their separateness. The bridge, contiguous to both banks of the river, belongs to neither.

In a like manner, the mode in which liminality articulates with the *dikós-ksénos* opposition is mediated by the woman. In her peculiar position she is at once both part of two family groups and part of neither. She is both *kséni* and *dikí* in varying degrees and contexts to her consanguineal and to her affinal relations. In the contexts of the household the woman serves as the link between family members—intrahousehold, interhousehold (natal and marital), and intercosmic (worlds of living and dead)—yet she is neither of nor out of the family. Necessary but threatening, the woman, quintessentially liminal, stands at the interface between *dikós* and *ksénos.*

We have seen as well a male-female dialectic at play. The men who exercise power and control over the woman's sexuality and fertility in the world of the living at the same time recognize their vulnerability to the woman's power as she enters the world of the dead. It is her implicit and primary liminality between *dikós* and *ksénos*, between nature and culture, and as the mediator between the worlds of the living and the dead, that is magnified in the song and around which its many symbols are made meaningful.

Notes

This paper has benefitted from the comments and criticism of several people. I would like to thank Michael Herzfeld, Kostas Kazazis, Gail Kligman, and Dan Segal for their helpful suggestions at various incarnations of the paper. At an early stage Jane Cowan's research and insights were important influences. The responsibility for its present form remains my own.

1. This approach follows David Schneider's theory of culture as that integrated system of symbols and their meanings. See especially Schneider, *American Kinship*, and "Notes Toward a Theory of Culture."

2. The passages cited in this paper were selected because of their relevance to the themes herein discussed. In the versions used, no criteria such as geographic origin, for example, were privileged; rather, selection was dependent on availability of texts.

3. The terms *ingroup* and *outgroup* were first used by Sumner in his *Folkways* in 1906. Sumner set out principles explaining how ingroup and outgroup relate to "ethnocentrism." Many studies on ethnocentrism stem directly from his theory. For a thorough critique, see LeVine and Campbell, *Ethnocentrism.*

4. Most if not all of the many published studies of this song address exclusively questions of diffusion and origin. As this line of thought and research is not relevant to the argument presented here, I have chosen not to deal with that body of literature.

5. In Balkan folklore, birds often represent the link between the worlds of the living and the dead. The world of the dead is seen as an inversion of the world of the living. I owe this insight to Gail Kligman.

6. There is ample precedent for the close brother-sister tie. Durham writes: ". . . it is firmly fixed in the mind of the peasant that the sister is a man's nearest relation. Her first duty, as Antigone said of old, is to her brother. The wife is a mere outsider from another family" (*Tribal Origins*, 222). She cites the saying, "A man feeds his son for himself, but his daughter for another man" (ibid.). Thus the inherent conflict of the woman's position is evident.

7. The *lehóna*, the mother of a newborn, and the menstruating woman are considered particularly vulnerable and dangerous as evidenced by the many restrictions regulating their behavior and the beliefs surrounding their statuses. For more on this, see Blum and Blum, *Dangerous Hour*.

References

Blum, Eva, and Richard Blum. *The Dangerous Hour*. London: Chatto and Windus, 1970.

Campbell, J. K. *Honour, Family and Patronage*. Oxford: Oxford University Press, 1964.

Cowan, Jane K. "The Bridge of Arta: Song, Sacrifice and the Wife of the First-master." Unpublished paper, 1976.

Douglas, Mary. *Purity and Danger*. London: Routledge and Kegan Paul, 1966.

Durham, Mary E. *Some Tribal Origins, Laws, and Customs of the Balkans*. London, 1928.

Durkheim, Emile. *The Elementary Forms of the Religious Life*. New York: The Free Press, 1915.

Eliade, Mircea. *Zalmoxis: The Vanishing God*. Chicago: University of Chicago Press, 1972.

Friedrich, Paul. *The Meaning of Aphrodite*. Chicago: University of Chicago Press, 1978.

Herzfeld, Michael. "Segmentation, Cognatic Kinship and the Domain of Political Anthropology." Paper delivered at the American Anthropology Association meeting in Cincinnati, Ohio, 1979. Cited with the author's permission.

Hubert, H., and M. Mauss. *Sacrifice: Its Nature and Function*. Chicago: The University of Chicago Press, 1973.

LeVine, R. A., and D. T. Campbell. *Ethnocentrism*. New York: Wiley, 1972.

Megas, George. *To Tragoudi tou Yefyriou tis Artas*. In *Laografia, Deltion tis Ellinikis Laografikis Etairias*. Tomos KZ' (27). Athens, Greece, 1971.

Schneider, David M. *American Kinship: A Cultural Account.* Englewood Cliffs, N.J.: Prentice-Hall, 1968.

Schneider, David M. "Notes Toward a Theory of Culture." *In Meaning in Anthropology,* ed. Basso and Selby. Albuquerque: University of New Mexico Press, 1976.

Sumner, William G. *Folkways* (Boston: Ginn, 1906).

Turner, Victor. *The Ritual Process: Structure and Anti-Structure.* Chicago: Aldine, 1969.

Van Gennep, Arnold. *The Rites of Passage.* Chicago: University of Chicago Press, 1960.

Vassiliou, V. G., and G. Vassiliou. "The Implicative Meaning of the Greek Concept of Philotimo." *Journal of Cross-Cultural Psychology* 4 (1973): 326–41.

The Ballad of "The Walled-Up Wife": Its Structure and Semantics

The majority of the essays in this casebook have been concerned with the ballad of "The Walled-Up Wife" in the former Yugoslavia, in Greece, or in India. However, the ballad is just as popular in other east European countries, for example, Bulgaria. Bulgarian folklorist Lyubomira Parpulova, after examining 180 Bulgarian versions of the ballad, proposes a number of different approaches to the ballad's content. After briefly considering a structural analysis inspired by Russian folklorist Vladimir Propp's classic The Morphology of the Folktale *(Austin: University of Texas Press, 1968), Parpulova turns to what she terms "deep semantics," or semiotics. However, after all is said and done, she ends by seeming to prefer a form of "myth-ritual" interpretation, suggesting that the ballad may derive from a ritual, namely, a rite of passage involving "ritual separation." Readers should note that this myth-ritual interpretation is quite different from the earlier "foundation-sacrifice ritual" championed by many of the nineteenth-century students of the ballad.*

The ballad about the walled-up wife is familiar to all Balkan peoples and to the Hungarians. It has attracted the interest of folklorists since last century. A number of studies, articles, and two monographs have been devoted to it.[1] The books by G. Megas and I. Taloş contain carefully collected bibliographies, as well as reviews of different opinions and investigations. They give a good idea also of the methods of investigation used and the main conclusions reached so far.

The studies by A. P. Stoilov[2] and M. Arnaudov[3] are representative of the investigation of the Bulgarian material especially, although they were written a long time ago. A new investigation is needed which would take into account the numerous recent field record-

Reprinted from *Balkan Studies* 25 (1984): 425–39.

ings as well as the new methods used in folklore study. The present article does not aim to fulfill this role. Rather, it aims to prove the need for such an investigation and to contribute towards it in some measure.

In the course of work, 180 Bulgarian variants were analyzed in detail. Of these, 96 are published, and 84 are recordings made in connection with the preparation of a volume to be entitled *The Bulgarian Folk Ballad.* The materials were collected in the period 1970– 1981 and are now in the Archives of the Institute of Folklore at the Bulgarian Academy of Sciences. All the texts were subjected to structural analysis in accordance with the principles outlined below. These principles and the concrete methods of analysis had to be elaborated because of the obvious inadequacy of previous attempts to reveal the structure of the ballad. The main weakness of these attempts consists in the investigators not giving sufficient attention to the question of separating the different levels in the structural analysis. And when they had such intentions, they did not carry them out with sufficient accuracy or with sufficient consistency.

1

On the basis of the work done within the Soviet school of thought in the field of structural typological investigations, and, especially, on V. Propp's seminal book, *Morfologia skazki,* the "obligatory structure-forming elements" were established for all Bulgarian texts that can be attributed to the ballad type The Walled-Up Wife, i.e., the aim was to find *the morphological invariant* of the type. The analysis revealed that, disregarding the plainly incomplete texts, the songs invariably display the following elements, or, in other words, that the morphological invariant of the type is:

I. *Agents:* A. Man-husband-father-builder with assistants; B. Woman-wife-mother (suckling mother); C. Child-son-suckling; D. Being (force)-supporter-unifier.

II. *Objects:* E. Building which cannot be completed unless it is linked with the being-unifier; F. Victim.

III. *Actions:* G. Building: a. unsuccessful; b. successful: 1. realizing the need for sacrifice; 2. immolation-immurement; 3. transformation into being-unifier.

2

We do not propose to proceed with the structural typological analysis, although all index cards are available. That would mean introducing new facts but no new ideas in this short paper. Rather, we propose to try to use the possibilities of structural semiotic analysis, since in this respect the ballad has been least adequately studied. The reason for this may be in the inherent limitations of the comparative historical method employed by previous investigators. The latter focus their attention mainly on the individual texts and their connections in space and time, only incidentally and almost reluctantly referring to other folk creation. They seem content with a literal reading of the text, unwilling to extend their researches into the field of deep semantics.

A typical example is the debate between G. Megas and K. Romeos concerning the interpretation of the image "bridge as narrow as a hair" encountered in the Greek ballads.[4] In order to refute Romeos' suggestion that this image is probably related to the idea of a bridge, as narrow as a hair, over which the souls of the dead pass on their way to the beyond—an idea familiar from other Greek songs and beliefs—Megas cites an informant who maintained that this was the actual name of a bridge near his village. Obviously, this is no argument against Romeos' view. Whether the informant is or is not aware of the meaning of a given motif, that is no proof that the motif has no such meaning. It would be logical to formulate the question: why was the bridge near the village named that way? Was it only because it was a narrow bridge, as Megas is suggesting? The point is that Romeos' idea meets with a difficult problem: is the image of the "bridge as narrow as a hair" a primary feature or was it introduced later under the influence of other songs, as the plot was being elaborated and associated with already existing formulas?

A literal reading of the text may result in ignoring parts of that text when they are unclear from the point of view of the usual direct derivation of the ballad from construction rites. More often than not, the scholars enumerate, at great length, customs in connection with the immuration of a living being in the foundations of a building, and argue whether the custom should be interpreted as sacrifice to the "genie of the place" or as the creation of a spirit-protector of the construction. They do not, however, ask the question, what lies at the root of the rites themselves? Why not assume a third possibility, for instance, a myth lying at the root of both the rite and the ballad—or its prototype—with the link between song and rite as derivative and at the same time strengthening because of the tendency to take the ballad out of the sphere of the fantastic and the miraculous and bring it closer to the realities of daily life?

Thus, attracted by the obvious link between song and construction rites, most researchers seem not to be paying sufficient attention to the song of the little bird in the Greek ballad: "The bridge shall not last unless you wall up a living being; but not an orphan, nor a widow's child; let it be Master Yani's wife!" Or, "but not an orphan, neither a stranger, nor a traveller," "but not a madman, nor a fool," or "but not a blind man, neither a lame man, nor a traveller."[5] And it is this song that expresses an opposition to the concrete choice of victims (socially weak members of the community or foreigners) for different forms of constructional human sacrifice, probably practiced in the past and preserved as legend.

G. Megas is inclined to explain this contradiction with the demands of artistic form. He believes that sacrificing the loved one is the dramatic element of the piece and that sacrificing the master builder, which would be more just and hardly less dramatic, is avoided because that would bring the action to an end. But then, why is it that the substitution is never effected through the child, but rather through the wife? This would not minimize the dramatic effect while allowing the action to go on. L. Vargyas cites Georgian and Mordovian songs about immurement as well as central European and east European legends, and in both cases a child[6] is walled up.

Why is it that the Balkan variants never use this motif, although as a possible ancient practice it must have been familiar, as witness the Greek songs referred to above? Could it be that the reason for the unusual yet invariable recurrence of the wife-victim is to be found in the deep semantics of the plot? It appears to be the case that in the songs about the walled-up wife, the woman-wife-mother has some meaning which does not come from the common rites during construction alone (they are indifferent as to kind of sacrifice), nor does it come only from the requirements about dramatic elements in artistic form.

K. Romeos and I. Taloş put forward the idea of a link with funeral rites and with beliefs about life beyond the grave on the basis of the image of the bridge as narrow as a hair and some functions of the Greek ballad (it is performed in lamentations and in ritual dancing, "Roussalya," on the second day of Easter). How can this interpretation contribute to an understanding of the semantics of the ballad type? As a parallel to the Greek "hairlike bridge," in a group of Bulgarian variants from the Pomorie District (Nos. 15, 54, 55, 56, 57, 53) there appears another image: "the bridge over the Tundzha River—a ladder to the sky." M. Arnaudov was not familiar with this group of variants. The image in question does not seem related to the Greek songs known to us and probably did not appear under their influence. Its meaning is: connection, a path to the great beyond, the world of the dead, the world of supernatural beings, of the gods. The image combines the vertical and the horizontal notions about the location of "the beyond"—up in the sky and beyond the river/the sea.[7]

Somewhat similar notions can be found in another group of Bulgarian variants from the Gyumyurdzhina area.[8] Here the husband walls up his wife in "Dimna grada" and consoles her saying that she will turn into a fig tree and her milk will continue to feed her child. The tree, with its mythical meaning of "axis of the world," also carries the semantics of the link between the worlds and is synonymous with the ladder in the sphere of mythical semantics. The life-giving moisture trickling from the tree may be reminiscent of one of the essential characteristics of the cosmic tree and the tree of life. And the fig tree is one of the botanical varieties associated with these two mythical notions.

Clearly, funerary rites, customs, and beliefs cannot fully explain the significance, the central position, of the woman-wife-mother in the structure of the song type. They only convince us that the construction which is "built by day, falls at night" is closely linked with specific mythical images and ideas. This confirms our doubts about the derivation of the plot from construction rites, customs, and beliefs practiced in life.

Let us, therefore, turn to the mythical notions and texts of a cosmogonic nature. There we find both the bridge and the big construction (town, church, monastery) used as images with an indisputable mythical semantics, meaning the "center of the world," and thus related to the semantics of the world axis, or, meaning the cultivated, ordered world, the cosmos, as opposed to the wild, unordered world, chaos. I. Dobrev[9] has shown this in an excellent manner with reference to Bulgarian Christmas and some Easter songs. Of special interest are the Christmas songs which picture Christ as the builder of bridges for sinful souls. This shows that Bulgarian folklore was familiar with the symbolic interpretation of the bridge. In some Ukrainian Christmas songs, God, Saint Peter, and Saint Paul are presented as demiurges. And in the Bulgarian Christmas songs, Master Petur cuts down the wonderful tree, "bozhur durvo," to make the gates of heaven. In the Bulgarian variants of "The Walled-Up Wife" from the southeastern parts, the name Pavel predominates as the builder of the mysterious construction, but there are also obvious traces of the name Petur (in the abbreviated forms Peicho, Pencho,

Becho). The name Petur is regularly present as the name of one of the two brothers of Master Pavel, when they are mentioned at all. There seem to be traces of it in the name of the wife—Petranka (Petruna, Petriyka). How far the appearance of these names in the ballad is a reflection of a later Christianized folk cosmogony is difficult to say. But there is no doubt that the similarity merits attention.

Also, I. Dobrev points out interesting parallels with the bridge Bifrost ("the shaking road") from ancient Scandinavian mythology, and with the construction of the walls of Midgard.[10] We find similar images in Iranian mythology where the souls of the dead, on their way to "the beyond," pass over the bridge Chinvat, which is shaking. A comparison with cosmogonic imagery confirms the impression that the construction in the songs of the type of "The Walled-Up Wife" was associated with mythical constructions.

Such an association is suggested by the victim's curse: that the bridge shakes and that the travellers fall off the bridge. This feature of the Bulgarian variants is seen as due to the influence of Greek songs.[11] Similarity to mythical constructions may be seen in the variant from the Belogradchik area,[12] where the master builder bets God to build a town; in the variant from the Shumen area,[13] where sacrifice is needed to complete the dome of the construction, which is a borrowing from the ballad type God Is Building a Monastery. Mythical constructions may explain the peculiarities of the construction in the Tetovo variant[14] (with walls from copper coins and windows from gold), and the gold walls in the variant from the village of Hahnyovo, No. 76, the Rhodopes. They remind us of the construction in the Christmas night with gold poles and silver stakes, as the Sun-foster-father and the Moon-foster-mother provide light for the master builder; of the church that Saint Georgi started building with copper coins and completed with gold coins.[15]

It has been pointed out that the construction of Midgard was the price for the hand of the goddess Frigg. The bridge Chinvat was guarded by the maiden Modgud. Yet the connection with the ballad of "The Walled-Up Wife" is remote. The motif with Frigg reminds one more of the fairy tales where the hero must build a bridge, a road, or a palace in order to win the king's daughter.

M. Eliade suggests that the plot of "The Walled-Up wife" is based also on some cosmogonic legends about the creation of the world from the body of a giant, specifically pointing out those variants in which this primordial being is a woman.[16]

According to the Soviet folklorist L. Baiburin, ". . . on the plane of semantics, constructional sacrifice was linked with the whole complex of beliefs about the sacrosanctity of the house, about the possibility to "derive" it from the body of the victim, about the mutual transcoding between sacrifice, house and structure of the world."[17]

Bulgarian folklore is familiar with the theme of the creation of the world from the body of a woman: the eyes of the dead *samodiva* (fairy) become lakes, her body grows into a tree, her hair, into clover;[18] on the spot where the innocent slandered sister was killed by her brother there appears a church-monastery.[19] A maid warns her loved one not to fell a tree because he would thus cut her body, not to drink water because he would thus drink her tears.[20] Of particular interest is the song recorded in the village of Beguntsi, Plovdiv District, in 1975, now in the Archives of the Institute of Folklore. It is about a maiden who wants to accompany her sweetheart in the army, but he refuses because, when her body would be *uzun kyupriyka* (narrow bridge), her eyes, wells, her hair, a forest, she would allow the whole army to pass, drink, and lie in the shade, but him. Again we can see that, despite the similarities between some images and themes, the connection with "The Walled-Up Wife" is quite remote.

We propose to look at the marriage theme and symbolism. There are numerous examples of mythical symbolic constructions there. Let us take, by way of an example, the song about the maiden walled up in a tower by her brothers, who want to protect her from the marital intentions of a young man. At her request, storms and rains destroy the tower, she is released and marries the young man. This song has been referred to in studies of "The Walled-Up Wife" because of the clearly expressed theme of the immured woman. However, no special attention has been paid to the dominating marriage theme, or to the relationship between the structures of "The Maiden in the Tower" and "The Walled-Up Wife." The idea of violent immurement is realized by means of a different structure. It is a maid that is walled up, and it is her brothers that wall her in, not her husband or her husband's brothers. The immurement is followed by the destruction of the building and marriage, unlike the walled-up wife, who remains forever in the building and her only worry is how she would feed her child. In similar songs we see a maiden who builds the tower herself, walls herself in, and from the inside negotiates with the matchmakers. These songs seem to be linked with the customs and rites related to premarital (or during initiation rites) ritual separation of maids.[21] The common characteristic features of the songs of the two types are that immuration is followed by destruction of the building, the unmarried state is succeeded by the married state. They should not be confused with the songs about "The Walled-Up Maiden" which developed from the ballad of "The Walled-Up Wife" as a result of its increasingly close connection with the common customs and beliefs related to the construction of new buildings.[22]

We propose a deep semantics for the songs of the type "Maiden in the Tower," with identical structuring of images and actions, which can be found explicated in a wedding song from the district of Demir Hisar (Thrace). It is sung as the bride is being braided:

> When they were braiding your hair, young one,
> Was your brother by you, young one,
> Was he holding a thin kerchief, young one,
> Was he building two buildings, young one?
>
> He was, dear girls, he was,
> He was building, dear girls, two buildings.
> There came, dear girls, my two brothers-in-law,
> They wrecked, dear girls, the two buildings,
> And then, dear girls, they took me away.
> (*BFC*, 5: 517)

If we borrow A. Van Gennep's[23] terminology, this is clearly a "rite of passage" with a ritual separation (immuration, imprisonment in a building), followed by ritual integration (destruction of the building, release). The main characters are also clearly shown: the bride's brothers, at the first stage, and the bridegroom's brothers, at the second stage.

In a song performed during the making of the wedding bread or banner in the village of Sitovo in the Rhodopes, the bride is rocking in a swing over yards and over bridges and the bridegroom rocks the swing (*BFC*, 5: 504). Here the bridge and the swing are unified in location on the basis of their mythical semantics: mediators found on both sides at the same time, metaphors of the transition itself. The bridge has a similar metaphoric role, and, in addition, it shakes, in a song performed when the bride gives the presents, in the Plovdiv area.

> The groom's brother is leading the bride
>   along the bridge,
> All the bridges start shaking.
> The groom's brother speaks to the bride:
> "Don't, Magdana, do not shake!
> Wait till you start shaking
> Before father-in-law, before mother-in-law."
> (AIF, No. 3, 1: 25, Tsalapitsa)

There is another interesting song which pictures the life of the married woman. In it the infant-suckling is invariably present:

> Dark prison before the eyes,
> Heavy iron in the arms.
> The dark prison—the husband,
> The heavy iron—the child.
>
> (*BFC*, 5: 588)

This song is performed at setting off to bring the bride, in Ser (Macedonia). It presents the young bride-mother locked in a prison, and the prison is decoded as married life.

To sum up, some songs present the creation of the world from the body of a woman, sometimes explicitly decoded as bridge, i.e., mediator. Others, connected with ideas about the world of the dead and about death, present the bridge as a metaphor of the transition from the world of the living into the world of the dead; or, they present death as integration-immuration in the town, the building of the world "beyond": God builds a monastery,[24] *samodiva* builds a town,[25] the dead build heaven.[26] Still others, probably associated with initiation rites, present the passage from childhood to marriageable age as walling-up in a tower/town and release from it. Still others connect the bridge and the town with wedding and married life.

It is obvious that most of these notions are associated with the so-called rites of passage: marriage and childbirth, initiation, funerary rites. However, none of them has a monopoly over the mythological images of the bridge, town, big construction, immuration. Rather, these images are employed in each of the said ritual complexes to mark either the transition itself or one of its stages. Immuration turns out to be an action of ambivalent semantics: on the one hand, it is the equivalent of separation; on the other, of integration, creation of something new—cosmos, family.

Let us return to the invariant of the plot under discussion. It will be seen that both in regard to the agents and to the objects of the actions, the structure comes closest to the use of these images in marriage symbolism. This may explain why in a song from Tetovo (this song has baffled scholars persistently) the bride gladly agrees to be walled up in the building with walls of copper and windows of gold, which her husband is erecting, only asking him to leave a small window for her face so that passersby may watch her.

The Greek variants commonly have the motif about the fate of the heroine's two sisters walled up in bridges or in a church and a monastery. If the interpretation of the semantics advanced here is valid, this motif expresses the inevitability of a woman's fate: to be transformed into the foundations of a new construction, a new world, a new family. This, no matter how noble, is not always very pleasant, as is shown in that Bulgarian song about a woman's married life.

The Bulgarian variants of The Walled-Up Wife type never use the motif about the fate of the three sisters, although it must have been familiar to the folksingers in the South. They prefer to develop the plot further with the motif of the child-suckling, which is not present in the Greek songs. Both motifs logically derive from the deep semantics of the plot. With the "three sisters" the connection is more direct, while with the "child-suckling" the situation is more complicated. It probably involves the belief, shared by the Bulgarians and other peoples, that the marriage is complete only after the delivery of the first child.[27]

The theme of the child-suckling in the Bulgarian variants often has a continuation, usually in prose, which tells about the milk trickling from the construction; or, that a brew from the white traces of this milk can be used as a cure by women who have no milk; or, that on certain days the water in the river under the bridge turns into milk, and so on. Clearly, the fact that the wife is nursing mother is rather important and receives special motifs.

We do not maintain that there is necessarily a direct link between the walled-in nursing mother and the customs, well known to anthropologists, of separating the mother and child for a shorter or a longer period after childbirth.[28] Still, we would like to draw attention to these parallels as well.

Could it not be that such ritual separation gave rise to the theme of the walled-up wife-mother (nursing mother), just as the ritual separation of girls probably gave rise to the theme "maiden in a tower"? Another interesting detail is the motif of The Child Nurtured by Nature, attached to the plot of "The Walled-Up Wife." We encounter this motif in the songs about marriage between shepherd and *samodiva*[29] (the *samodiva* flies away after the delivery of the first child), and about the mother who joins the *samodivi*, leaving her child behind.[30] Another parallel which, although it is not directly linked with the plot of "The Walled-Up Wife," evidently points to similar notions, can be found in the folktale "The Children with the Wonderful Features" (AT 707). The children are put in a basket and thrown into the river, the mother is buried alive up to the waist and released only when the children grow up and return safely.[31]

We started from the question about the structure of the type The

Walled-Up Wife and arrived at the formulation of its morphological invariant. In its turn, it helped up to reach the conclusion that the deep semantics of the song comes from "the rites of passage" which use "the construction code" to express their basic content, and, more specifically, from the complex of rites and beliefs related to marriage and the delivery of the first child.

Abbreviations

AEIM	Archives of the Ethnographic Institute and Museum (Archiv na Etnografskia Institut i Muzei)
AIF	Archives of the Institute of Folklore (Archiv na Instituta za folklor)
BFPP	*Bulgarian Folk Poetry and Prose* (Bulgarska narodna poezia i proza)
BFC	*Bulgarian Folk Creations* (Bulgarsko narodno tvorchestvo)
CFC	*Collection of Folk Creations* (Zbornik narodni umotvorenia)
PSSPh	*Proceedings of the Seminar of Slavic Philology* (Izvestia na seminara za slavyanska filologia)
V.	village
E.M.	Evgenia Mitseva
K.M.	Katya Mihailova
L.B.	Lilyana Bogdanova
L.D.	Lilyana Daskalova
L.P.	Lyubomira Parpulova
S.B.	Stoyanka Boyadzhieva
S.S.	Stefana Stoykova
Y.K.	Yordanka Kotseva

List of Used Unpublished Bulgarian Variants of "The Walled-Up Wife"*

1. Matsa, V., Topolovgrad area, 1972. At harvest time, early in the morning. Stoyana Boneva, 61. AIF. L.B.**

*A list of the published variants can be found in I. Taloş (pp. 326–35). From that list, No. 81 should be excluded—it is, in effect, the reprinted text of variant No. 20, as well as Nos. 82–87, which are résumés of published songs and can be found in Volume 5, not volume 6, of *PSSPh*.

**The initials stand for the names of field folklorists who recorded the songs; cf. Abbreviations, above.

2. Boyana, V., Sofia area, 1973. At the wedding feast. Verka Boneva, 77. AIF. L.B.

3. Stoikite, V., Devin area, 1981. Huba Stoeva, 83. AIF. S.B.

4. Hursovo, V., Blagoevgrad area, 1978. Katerina Kyuchukova, 67. AIF. S.B.

5. Gorna Grashtitsa, V., Kyustendil area, 1971. At the horo. Tsvetana Chulkova, 65. AEIM. S.S.

6. Kremikovtsi, V., Sofia area, 1977. Tsveta Baltiyanova, 71. AIF. L.B.

7. Malko Turnovo, Chirpan area, 1980. Ivana Koleva, 66. AIF. L.B.

8. Chokoba, V., Sliven area, 1981. At a party *(moabet)*. Suba Ignatova, 69. AIF. S.B.

9. Lyulin, V., Yambol area, 1972. At harvest time. Stanka Nikolova, 50. AEIM. S.S.

10. Mihalich, V., Svilengrad area, 1976. At the Easter horo. Maria Darakchieva, 70. AIF. S.S.

11. Ilinden, V., Gotse Delchev area, 1979. At the horo, in winter. Irina Yurukova, 71, AIF. S.B.

12. Marten, V., Rousse area, 1980. At a party *(moabet)*. Yordan Stoyanov, 80. AIF. L.P.

13. Pavel, V., Svishtov area, 1970. Atanasa Georgieva, 59. AEIM. S.S.

14. Hrabrovo, V., Provadia area, 1977. Yordanka Boeva, 53. AIF. S.B.

15. Kozichino, V., Pomorie area, 1975. At *sobat*. Petra Shteryuva, 65. AIF. L.P.

16. Kyulevcha, V., Shumen area, 1970. Yordanka Ilijkova, 56. AEIM. S.S.

17. Tserovo, V., Blagoevgrad area, 1978. At a working bee. Gergana Edipova, 41. AIF. S.S.

18. Gradina, V., Veliko Turnovo area, 1981. At a working bee. Pena Slavcheva, 82. AIF. K.M.

19. Matsa, V., Topolovgrad area, 1972. At harvest time. Yova Gyorgyova, 83. AEIM. L.B.

20. Vulcho Pole, V., Svilengrad area, 1976. At the horo at new constructions. Elena Vangelova, 54. AIF. L.B.

21. Dubovets, V., Svilengrad area, 1976. At the horo. Petra Dimitrova, 50. AIF. S.B.

22. Levka, V., Haskovo area, 1972. At the horo. Elena Andonova, 60. AEIM. L.B.

23. Koren, V., Haskovo area, 1976. At the horo. Lenka Marinkova, 60. AIF. S.S.

24. Koren, V., Haskovo area, 1976. At the horo. Vanka Karaboideva, 56. AIF. L.B.

25. Dositeevo, V., Haskovo area, 1972. At harvest time, in the morning. Mara Uzunova, 60. AEIM. L.B.

26. Garvanovo, V., Haskovo area, 1972. At a working bee. Vuchka Vancheva, 55. AEIM. S.S.

27. Chernogorovo, V., Haskovo area, 1972. At *medzhia*, out in the street. Vana Gospodinova, 54. AEIM. S.S.

28. Filevo, V., Purvomai area, 1972. Kera Nacheva, 61. AEIM. S.S.

29. Kurdzhali, area, 1969. Stoyanka Markova, 77 (born in the village of Chadurlii, Gyumyurdzhina area). AEIM. S.S.

30. Petlyovo, Kurdzhali area, 1976. Vana Bulcheva, 57. AIF. L.B.

31. Mudrets, V., Harmanli area, 1981. At sunrise during harvest time. Marina Zhurnalova, 62. AIF. K.M.

32. Cherepovo, V., Harmanli area, 1976. At harvest time, before noon. Krustina Bogdanova, 67. AIF. L.B.

33. Belopolyane, V., Ivailovgrad area, 1976. At a show horo. Mara Apostolova, 84 (born in the village of Kyuchebunar). AIF. L.B.

34. Svirachi, V., Ivailovgrad area, 1976. Kera Pehlivanova, 44, and Despina Zangocheva, 36. AIF. S.B.

35. Plodovitovo, V., Chirpan area, 1980. Vida Dimova, 58. AIF. L.P.

36. Bratya Kunchevi, V., Stara Zagora area, 1972. At a party. Elena Avramova, 44. AEIM. L.B.

37. Ruda, V., Stara Zagora area, 1980. Stoyana Marinova, 56. AIF. L.B.

38. Rakitnitsa, V., Stara Zagora area, 1980. Mariyka Stoyanova, 63. AIF. L.B.

39. Rakitnitsa, V., Stara Zagora area, 1980. At *sobat*. Ivanka Petkova, 67. AIF. L.B.

40. Mlekarevo, V., Nova Zagora area, 1981. In the morning at harvest time. Stana Vulkanova, 65. AIF. L.P.

41. Radevo, V., Nova Zagora area, 1981. Toward evening at harvest time. Kuna Petkova, 59. AIF. K.M.

42. Radevo, V., Nova Zagora area, 1981. At the horo. Rada Decheva, 67 (learned from settlers from Western Thrace, now in Turkey). AIF K.M.

43. Bozadzhii, V., Nova Zagora area, 1981. At a party. Kosyo Kosev, 70. AIF. L.B.

44. Novoselets, V., Nova Zagora area, 1981. At harvest time. Kina Stancheva, 63. AIF. S.B.

45. Slamino, V., Yambol area, 1975. At a party. Stoyana Boneva, 63. AIF. L.P.

46. Nedyalsko, V., Yambol area, 1972. At the horo. Donka Muradova, 76. AEIM. L.B.

47. Zlatinitsa, V., Elhovo area, 1975. At a party *(moabet)*. Karamfila Peeva, 67. AIF. L.B.

48. Ruzhitsa, V., Bourgas area, 1975. At a working bee. Yanka Kaludova, 56. AIF. L.P.

49. Draka, V., Grudovo area, 1975. In the morning at harvest time. Sofia Krusteva, 63, and Maria Stankova, 68 (born in the village of Arpach, Lozengrad area). AIF. L.B.

50. Vratitsa, V., Aitos area, 1975. In the morning at harvest time. Velika Petrova, 65. AIF. S.S.

51. Chernograd, V., Aitos area, 1975. At a party *(moabet)*. Dimitra Markova, 56. AIF. L.B.

52. Prosenik, V., Aitos area, 1975. At table. Dobra Stoyanova, 52. AIF. L.B.

53. Prosenik, V., Aitos area, 1975. At *sobat*. Stanka Kutsarova, 70 (born in the village of Dobrovan). AIF. L.B.

54. Medovo, V., Pomorie area, 1975. At *sobat*. Stoika Krusteva, 65. AIF. S.B.

55. Panitsovo, V., Pomorie area, 1975. At parties, weddings, at Shrovetide. Ivanka Lefterova, 53 (born in the village of Morsko). AIF. L.B.

56. Kozichino, V., Pomorie area, 1975. At *sobat*. Kalya Stoyanova, 67. AIF. S.B.

57. Kozichino, V., Pomorie area, 1975. At *sobat*. Petra Zheleva, 64. AIF. L.P.

58. Dobrinovo, V., Karnobat area, 1975. In the morning at harvest time. Yordana Ivanova, 60. AIF. S.B.

59. Zheleznik, V., Karnobat area, 1975. Pena Andonova, 53. AIF. L.B.

60. Zimen, V., Karnobat area, 1975. Ivanka Hristova, 55. AIF. S.B.

61. Sanstefano, V., Karnobat area, 1975. At table. Ganka Shivacheva, 70. AIF. S.S.

62. Trapoklovo, V., Sliven area, 1972. At *sobat*. Mariyka Andreeva, 66. AEIM. L.B.

63. Srednogorovo, V., Kazanluk area, 1980. Gena Paünova, 81. AIF. K.M.

64. Boryana, V., Varna area, 1977. At the fair. Nikolina Nikolova, 70. AIF. S.B.

65. Bluskovo, V., Varna area, 1977. At a party *(moabet)*. Marinka Lazarova, 72. AIF. S.B.

66. Golitsa, V., Varna area, 1977. At *sobat*. Maria Miteva, 67. AIF. S.B.

67. Golitsa, V., Varna area, 1977. At *sobat*. Mariyka Velikova, 43. AIF. S.B.

68. Nova Cherna, V., Rousse area, 1980. Yordana Kostandinova, 67 (born in the village of Cherna, North Dobrudzha). AIF. L.B.

69. Vasil Levski, V., Silistra area, 1980. At a working bee. Stoyanka Miteva, 59. AIF. S.S.

70. Davidkovo, V., Smolyan area, 1981. Nevena Ivanova, 55. AIF. S.B.

71. Bukata, V., Smolyan area, 1981. Sevda Rushanova, 31, and Zorka Cholakova, 37. AIF. S.B.

72. Mogilitsa, V., Smolyan area, 1981. Minka Yurukova, 52. AIF. S.B.

73. Mogilitsa, V., Smolyan area, 1963. Ava Karaisenova, 56. AEIM. S.S.

74. Mogilitsa, V., Smolyan area, 1963. Safia Peteska, 38 (born in the village of Arda). AEIM. S.S.

75. Konarsko, V., Yakoruda area, 1979. Mitko Mandzurski, 45. AIF. L.D.

76. Hahnyovo, V., Razlog area, 1979. Fatime Kaluchova, 63. AIF. S.S.

77. Banichan, V., Blagoevgrad area, 1979. Ilinka Hadzhieva, 65. She learned the song from a Bulgarian-Mohammedan woman from the village of Slashten. AIF. S.B.

78. Breznitsa, V., Gotse Delchev area, 1979. At the horo. Tinka Pudarska, 53. AIF. L.B.

79. Luki, V., Gotse Delchev area, 1979. At the Easter horo. Elena Gramatikova, 75. AIF. L.B.

80. Nova Lovcha, V., Gotse Delchev area, 1979. At the horo. Elena Velikova, 53. AIF. E.M.

81. Gaitaninovo, V., Gotse Delchev area, 1979. At the horo. Sarakinya Murganova, 70. AIF. Y.K.

82. Luki, V., Gotse Delchev area, 1979. At the horo. Ilinka Popova, 70 (born in the village of Paril). AIF. L.D.
83. Breznitsa, V., Gotse Delchev area, 1979. Gulub Zaimov, 55. AIF. L.D.
84. Boyana, V., Sofia area, 1973. At the horo. Petra Pankova, 71. AIF. L.B.

Notes

1. G. A. Megas, *Die Ballade von der Arta-Brücke: Eine vergleichende Untersuchung.* 150, Institute for Balkan Studies (Thessaloniki, 1976), 204 pp; I. Talos, *Meşterul Manole* (Bucureşti, 1973), 470 pp.
2. A. P. Stoilov, "Zazizhdane na zhivi chovetsi v osnovite na novi gradezhi" (Immurement of live human beings in the foundations of new constructions), *Periodichesko spisanie na Bulgarskoto knizhovno druzhestvo 13* (Sofia, 1902): 179–213.
3. M. Arnaudov, "Vgradena nevesta" (The walled-up wife). In *Studii vurhu Bulgarskite obredi i legendi,* 2nd ed., Vol. 2, 221–460 (1st ed., Sofia, 1924/; 2nd ed., 1972).
4. Megas, *Die Ballade von der Arta-Brücke,* pp. 72, 115.
5. Cf. Arnaudov, "Vgradena nevesta," pp. 351, 352, 354, 355.
6. L. Vargyas, *Researches into the Medieval History of Folk Ballad* (Budapest, 1967), pp. 178–79.
7. More about this image and its semantics in Bulgarian folklore, in L. Parpulova, "Simvolichni obrazi v Bŭlgarskia folklor" (Symbolic images in Bulgarian folklore), *Literaturoznanie i folkloristica v chest na akademic Petŭr Dinekov,* ed. A. Stoykov et al., pp. 378–82 (Sophia: Izdatelstvo na Bŭlgarskata akademiya na naukite, 1983).
8. Cf. Arnaudov, "Vgradena nevesta," pp. 339–40; *Narodni pesni ot severoiztochna Bulgaria* (Folk songs from Northeast Bulgaria), comp. R. Katsarova, I. Kachulev, and E. Stoin (Sofia, 1962), No. 875, Svetlen, Popovo District (settlers from the area around Soflu, now in Turkey).
9. Ivan Dobrev, *Proizhod i znachenie na praslavyanskoto konsonantno: diftongichno sklonenie* (Origin and significance of the protoslavonic consonantal and diphthongal declension) (Sofia, 1982), pp. 43, 64–66 ("Master Petur"), 73, 79, 82, 88, 92, 101, 106–7, 183, 193–94, 199–202, 209–10.
10. F. Buslaev, *Skazanie Novoi Eddy o sooruzhenii sten Midgarda i serbskaya pesnya o postroenii Skadra: Istoricheskie ocherki russkoi narodnoi slovestnosti.* Vol. 1 of *Russkaya narodnaya poezia* (1861), pp. 301–7.
11. Arnaudov, "Vgradena nevesta," p. 411.
12. V. Stoin, *Ot Timok do Vita* (Sofia, 1928), p. 953, No 3631.
13. Arnaudov, "Vgradena nevesta," pp. 348, 421.
14. Arnaudov, "Vgradena nevesta," p. 306.
15. Dobrev, *Proizhod i znachenie,* pp. 202, 210.
16. M. Eliade, "Master Manole and the Monastery of Arges," in *Zalmoxis:*

The Vanishing God, 164–90 (Chicago and London: University of Chicago Press, 1972).

17. A. Baiburin, "Stroitel'naya zhertya i svyazannie s neyu ritual'nie simvoli u vostochnih slavyan," in *Problemi slavyanskoi etnografii* (Leningrad, 1979), p. 162.

18. *BFC,* 4: 137, the Byala Slatina area.

19. *BFPP,* 4: 370, the Veles area.

20. *BFC,* 7: 491, the Elin Pelin area.

21. Cf. L. Parpulova, "Bulgaro-ukrainski paraleli v sistemata na folklornata simvolika" (Bulgarian-Ukrainian parallels in the system of folk symbolism), *Slavyanska filologiya* 18 (1983): 265–75.

22. Cf. *Knizhtsi za prochit* 7–9 (Solun, 1891): 212; *CFC,* 46: 53, No. 77, Koprivshtitsa; *CFC,* 50: 138, No. 28, Ruzhdene, Drama area; AIF, Corna Banya, Sofia area, 1974, rec. by L. Bogdanova.

23. A. Van Gennep, *The Rites of Passage* (1960, 1961; Chicago: University of Chicago Press, 1975), pp. 10–11.

24. *BFPP,* 4: 95.

25. *BFPP,* 4: 54.

26. *BFPP,* 4: 101.

27. R. Ivanova, "Obrednoto vreme v Bulgarskata svatba" (Ritual time in the Bulgarian wedding) *Bulgarian Folklor* 2 (1982): 6–7; Van Gennep, *Rites of Passage,* p. 129.

28. Van Gennep, *Rites of Passage,* pp. 46–47.

29. *BFC,* 4: 114, 115.

30. *BFC,* 4: 128.

31. A. Van Gennep gives interesting data about customs connected with the separation of the mother after the birth of twins: ". . . all rites of passage become more complex in abnormal cases, especially if the mother has given birth to twins. Among the Basoko, in the Congo, the mother is confined to her cabin until the two children are grown; she is allowed to speak only to members of her family; only her mother and her father have the right to enter her cabin; any stranger who sets foot in it is sold as a slave; and she has to live in complete chastity. The twins are kept apart from other children, and all dishes and other utensils employed by them are taboo. The house they live in is marked by two posts placed one on each side of the door and overhung with a piece of canvas. The threshold is adorned with many little stakes which are driven into the ground and painted white. These are the rites of separation.

The transitional period lasts until the children are more than six years old. Then comes the rite of reintegration . . ." (p. 47).

ALAN DUNDES

The Ballad of "The Walled-Up Wife"

We have come a long way from the first reporting of the ballad of "The Walled-Up Wife" by Vuk Karadžić in 1815 to the detailed monographs and articles devoted to the ballad in the twentieth century. The history of the scholarship of this ballad in some ways parallels the development of folkloristics as a discipline. First there was fieldwork, that is, the collection of texts, in the nineteenth century. What theory there was concerned possible origins. In the case of "The Walled-Up Wife," the origin was thought to be foundation sacrifice as a special form of myth-ritual theory. A variant of the preoccupation with origins took the path of claiming nationalistic priority. A great many of the studies of the ballad seemed to be inclined towards "proving" that the ballad belonged originally to a particular country or people.

In the twentieth century, as the theoretical emphasis in folkloristics shifted from diachronic to synchronic, the origins question was put aside somewhat in favor of issues of structure, function, and meaning. We can see this clearly demonstrated in the series of essays included in this casebook.

What can we learn from these essays? For one thing, they absolutely confirm the importance of the comparative method in folkloristics. The failure of Balkan folklorists to take account of Indic versions of the ballad (as well as the failure of Indian folklorists to relate their ballad to the eastern European texts) should be obvious enough. Nationalistic-inspired essays which consider only the versions found in the native land of the writer are almost certainly doomed to be superficial and incomplete. An item of folklore, ideally speaking, should be considered in all its variant forms. Only with the full panoply of versions available can one begin to tackle the ultimate task of discerning meaning(s) in that item. What are the possible meaning(s) of the ballad of "The Walled-Up Wife"? The following essay is an attempt to consider this question, but it is only a

Reprinted from the *Journal of American Folklore* 108 (1995): 38–53. Reprinted by permission of the American Folklore Society.

beginning, not the end. The debate about the significance of "The Walled-Up Wife" is bound to continue.

The governing intellectual paradigm in nineteenth-century folkloristics was the historical reconstruction of the past, modelled in part on the parallel disciplines of archaeology and philology. There were, to be sure, competing forms of diachronic searches for origins, but most involved some type of historical-comparative-diffusionistic bias. Synchronic concerns with structure, function, context, performance, and the like would not emerge until the next, that is, the twentieth, century.

Among the most prominent nineteenth-century folklore theories of origins was the so-called Indianist hypothesis. One of the acknowledged starting points of the argument that much of European folklore had originated in India was Theodor Benfey's (1809–1881) introduction to the first German translation of the *Panchatantra* in 1859. Champions of the "Indianist" school of folkloristics included William Clouston (1843–1896), Joseph Jacobs (1854–1916), and Emmanuel Cosquin (1841–1919), among others. The influence of Max Müller (1823–1900), a leading Indologist (despite the fact that he never once set foot in India), and the Aryan-migration notions that he espoused gave further credence to the Indianist school inasmuch as it was believed that "the Aryan peoples emigrated from India and carried their language and myths with them" (Dorson 1968:178). The Indianist theory has gone the way of most nineteenth-century folklore theories. In other words, it has been relegated to a long footnote in the history of nineteenth-century folkloristics. It is not my purpose here to attempt to resuscitate the Indianist theory, but I cannot forbear noting that the theory was primarily applied to folk narrative with special emphasis on myths and folktales. The ballad genre seems to have been pretty much ignored by those advocating Indic origins.

"The Walled-Up Wife"

One of the most famous ballads in the world in terms of the amount of scholarship devoted to it is surely "The Walled-Up Wife." Found widely reported throughout the Balkans, it has intrigued and bedeviled east European folklorists for more than 150 years. Romanian folklorist Ion Taloş, who has devoted a book-length monograph to the ballad (1973), has this to say about it: "The song about the mason's wife is a ballad of rare beauty, perhaps the most impressive in world folklore" (1987:400). This echoes the sentiment of Jacob Grimm, who called the ballad "one of the most outstanding songs of all peoples and all times" (Dundes 1989:156).

The basic plot involves a group of men who seek to construct a castle, monastery, or bridge. Through supernatural means, whatever is constructed during the day is undone at night. A dream revelation or some other extraordinary means of communication informs the would-be builders that the only way to break the negative magic spell is to sacrifice the first woman (wife or sister) who comes to the building site the next day. When the chief architect's own young wife arrives, she is duly immured. Often the process is thought to be a joke or game by the female victim until a poignant moment in the ballad when she suddenly realizes that she is being sacrificed by her husband and his colleagues. In some versions, she begs for an aperture to be left so that she can continue to nurse her baby. Sometimes a milky spring marks the site of the alleged event, a site where infertile women or mothers suffering from a lack of lactation later come in the hope of obtaining a folk medical cure. This brief synopsis does not by any means do justice to this powerful ballad (and legend), but it should be sufficient to identify it for those not familiar with it. Since the ballad is apparently not in the English and Scottish canon and does not appear in western Europe generally, it is not particularly well known among folklorists in western Europe and the United States.

In eastern Europe, in contrast, however, it is extremely common and well known. In Serbia, it has the title of "The Building of Skadar"; in Hungary, it is often called "Clement Mason"; in Romania, it is "Master Manole"; in Greece, it is "The Bridge of Arta"; and so on. The numbers of collected texts of this ballad are truly staggering. Greek folklorist Georgios Megas based his study of the ballad on 333 Greek versions (Megas 1976:5), for example. Bulgarian folklorist Lyubomira Parpulova analyzed 180 Bulgarian versions of the ballad (Parpulova 1984:425). When one adds the numerous Hungarian, Romanian, Serbian, and Albanian versions to the Greek and Bulgarian texts, we are dealing with a ballad for which we have more than seven hundred texts available.

The ballad of "The Walled-Up Wife" has fascinated some of the leading folklorists of the nineteenth and twentieth centuries. One of the earliest versions was a Serbian text of "The Building of Skadar" collected by Vuk Karadžić (1784–1864), the founder of Serbian folkloristics. He began publishing his *Narodne srpske pjesme* in Vienna in 1814. At that time, Jacob Grimm (1785–1863) was serving as a delegate to the Vienna Congress (from October 1814 to June 1815), and he eventually wrote a review of Karadžić's first volume of folksongs (Wilson 1986:112). In 1824, Karadžić sent a new edition of the folksongs to Grimm, who was so delighted with "The Building of Skadar" that he began to translate it. He sent his translation to Goethe in May of the same year, but Goethe was appalled by what he considered to be the heathen-barbarity of the ballad (Dundes 1989:156; Milović 1941:51). Grimm would later discuss the ballad as a prime example of "foundation sacrifice" in his *Teutonic Mythology* (1966: Vol. 3, 1143). But that was just the beginning of the enormous mass of scholarship devoted to the ballad. Among the dozens—note the use of the plural—of monographs on the topic, there are major studies by such distinguished scholars as Cocchiara, Eliade, Megas, Taloş, and Vargyas. Much of the earlier scholarship has been ably surveyed by Vargyas in his magisterial essay "The Origin of the 'Walled-Up Wife,'" which is chapter 3 of his excellent *Researches into the Mediaeval History of Folk Ballad* (1967:173–233). Vargyas, arguably one of the leading ballad authorities of the twentieth century, continued his detailed and meticulous investigation of the ballad in his *Hungarian Ballads and the European Ballad Tradition Vol. 2* (1983:18–57). Vargyas considers virtually all texts available in print and reviews their contents, not to mention summarizing the incredible number of essays and monographs on the ballad, written, I might add, in a bewildering variety of languages.

If one wished to describe the bulk of scholarship treating the ballad, one could say that two principal features characterize the literature. From Jacob Grimm on, there has been a host of essays using the ballad to illustrate a conventional myth-ritual thesis that the story represented a survival from an actual practice of the past of offering a human sacrifice in order to appease supernatural spirits who were believed to be involved in or threatened by the proposal to build some kind of structure, for example, a bridge. An example of the logic adduced: the river goddess will be deprived of "food" by a bridge that will permit all passengers to cross the stream safely. Hence a human sacrifice must be offered to appease the goddess (Mitra 1927:41). Famed comparativist Reinhold Köhler's 1894 paper (first published in 1873) is representative, but one could easily cite many others, including Gittée 1886–1887, Krauss 1887, Feilberg 1892, Sartori 1898, Sainean 1902, De Vries 1927, O'Sullivan 1945, Cocchiara 1950, and

Brewster 1971. (See also Taloş 1973:25.) The second observable trend in the scholarship is the persistent attempt to establish a national origin for the ballad. Through a modified form of the comparative method, folklorists have sought to "prove" that the ballad originated in one locale rather than another. Zihni Sako ends his discussion of Albanian versions with the unequivocal statement: "It seems to us that the original source of the ballad is Illyria, that is, Albania" (1984:165). Similarly, Georgios Megas ended one of his several essays on the ballad this way: "I hope that it is clearly demonstrated from the publication of my full-fledged investigation that Greece must be considered as the cradle and homeland of our ballad" (1969:54, my translation). Megas reiterated this position at the very end of his 1976 monograph on the ballad when he (rightly) rejected the idea that polygenesis could be responsible for the different versions of the ballad found throughout the Balkans, and (wrongly) concluded that the single origin of the ballad *must* have been the Greek territory in early Byzantine times (1976:179). It is not difficult to see a high correlation between the hypothetical country of origin and the nationality of the researcher! (For a convenient chronological summary of the longstanding origins debate, see Vargyas 1967:178–79 and its continuation 1983:55–57; for other comprehensive accounts of previous scholarship devoted to the ballad, see Dundes 1989:153–55; Megas 1976: 125–79; and Taloş 1973). I am by no means the first to underscore the extreme nationalistic bias in ballad origin scholarship. Ballad specialist David Buchan, in his essay "British Balladry: Medieval Chronology and Relations," has this to say about Child 73, "Lord Thomas and Fair Annet": "Grundtvig thought its origin Danish, Gerould thought its origin British, Doncieux thought it French, which perhaps tells us more about the ethnocentricity of ballad scholars than about 'Lord Thomas'" (Buchan 1978:104). As to why the ballad as opposed to other genres of folklore should have been the focus of nationalistic proprietary "wars," one can only speculate that the ballad's hallowed status vis-à-vis other folklore genres—either as the detritus of glorious epics of the past or alternatively as a relatively late medieval elitist creation, not related to any primitive origins—might account for ardent nationalistic scholars' eagerness to claim exclusive "ownership" of such treasures. Also since two or more neighboring nations appeared to have the "same" ballad, it was perhaps almost inevitable that it would become a natural bone of contention.

For more than a century, there has been a brisk many-sided debate among Balkans folklorists as to which country had the right to claim "credit" for originating "The Walled-Up Wife" ballad. It may be difficult for some modern folklorists to appreciate just how heated the debate was over which of the numerous nationalistic competing claims was "correct." One illustrative example may suffice to indicate the intensity of the furor. In 1863 the noted Hungarian collector of folksongs, János Kriza (1811–1875), a Unitarian minister from Transylvania influenced in part by Herder and Percy, published a collection of folksongs. He called the songs "the collection of the flowers of the mind of the Székeley people—its wild roses, if I may so describe them" (as quoted in Ortutay 1973:498). In that collection, entitled *Vadrózsák* (Wild Roses), Kriza included a Hungarian version of "The Walled-Up Wife" ballad: "Kömives Kelemennë." Almost immediately upon publication of the collection, one Julian Grozescu (whose name clearly suggests Romanian origin) accused Kriza of having plagiarized this ballad and one other from a Romanian source. These accusations became the basis of a famous court trial in Budapest. Although Kriza was not guilty of plagiarism, the *Vadrózsa* lawsuit saddened him for the rest of his life. Ortutay's comment on the matter is of interest in the present context: "It has come to light on the basis of more recent collections and European comparative ethnographic research that the charges of plagiarism brought against Kriza were unfounded, and that the two ballads in question, like the others, constitute an integral part of both Hungarian and European folk-poetry, including the Romanian. It is obvious today that the accusations were groundless; they were inspired by the awakening Romanian nationalism, Hungarian nationalism defended itself against them" (Ortutay 1973:501).

An Indianist Origin via the Gypsies

None of the many scholars involved in the dispute over the origin of "The Walled-Up Wife" was aware of the fact that the ballad was extremely popular in India as well. (For references to published texts in Telugu and Kannada, see Dundes 1989:165 n. 25.) The first hint of a possible Indic origin of the ballad came from Francis Hindes Groome (1851–1902), who included the "Story of the Bridge" in his 1899 *Gypsy Folk-Tales*. Groome had translated into English a somewhat-garbled Gypsy version reported by Alexandre G. Paspati (1870: 620–23). Of particular interest is Groome's endnote, which begins with an apology: "I hesitated whether to give this story; it is so hopelessly corrupt, it seems such absolute nonsense. Yet it enshrines beyond question, however confusedly, the widespread and ancient belief that to ensure one's foundation one should wall up a human victim" (Groome 1899:13). Later in the same note, Groome makes the following observation: "The Gypsy story is probably of high antiquity, for two at least of the words in it were quite or almost meaningless to the nomade [sic] Gypsy who told it" (cf. Paspati 1870:190–91). Groome continues: "The masons of southeastern Europe are, it should be noticed, largely Gypsies; and a striking Indian parallel may be pointed out in the Santal story of 'Seven Brothers and Their Sister'" (Campbell 1891: 106–10). "Here seven brothers set to work to dig a tank but find no water, so, by the advice of a *yogi*, give their only sister to the spirit of the tank. 'The tank was soon full to the brim, and the girl was drowned.' And then comes a curious mention of a Dom, or Indian vagrant musician, whose name is probably identical with *Doum*, *Lom*, or *Rom*, the Gypsy of Syria, Asia Minor, and Europe" (Groome 1899:13). To my knowledge, this is the only suggestion in print that there might be a connection between the Balkans ballad of "The Walled-Up Wife" and a cognate story in India.

In 1925, B. J. Gilliat-Smith published another Gypsy version of "The Song of the Bridge" in the *Journal of the Gypsy Lore Society*. The text was accompanied by a learned comparative note by W. R. Halliday. Halliday summarily dismisses Groome's suggestion of a possible Indic parallel: "Actually the parallel does not extend further than the building of a tank by seven brothers and the drowning of their sister (not the wife of one of them), in order that the tank may fill with water. The similarity, in fact, is derived merely from the common origin of the two stories in the belief in the necessity for Foundation Sacrifice, which we have noted to be world-wide. *I have personally no doubt whatsoever* that the *Song of the Bridge* is a localized form of story arising out of this wide-spread custom and *belongs properly to the Balkan area*" (1925:111, emphasis added). Halliday was dead wrong in failing to see that the Indic narratives were cognate with the Balkans ballad. But then again, every scholar who has written on the ballad has also failed to consider the many Indic versions of the narrative. (Vargyas too dismissed the two Gypsy texts [1967:194] as being of little or no consequence.)

Objective readers who take the time to read through the hundreds of Balkans texts *and* the Indic versions can easily see for themselves that they are unquestionably part of a common Indo-European tradition, although the ballad apparently never became popular in western Europe. (It is worth noting that folklorist A. H. Krappe [1894–1947] posited an Indic origin for a legend involving the foundation sacrifice of a child (rather than a wife-bride), a legend that may or may not be cognate with "The Walled-Up Wife" [Krappe 1927: 165–80].) Given the possible/probable Indic origin of the ballad, the Gypsy texts, garbled though they may be, support this hypothesis inasmuch as the origin of the Gypsies is presumed to be India. A Bulgarian-Gypsy text of the ballad reported in 1962 (Čherenkov 1962) tends to confirm the traditionality of the narrative among Gypsy groups. If this is so, then all the petty arguments between Balkans folklorists about which country's versions are the earliest become more or less beside the point. The moral of this exemplum is that the comparative method can be effective only when *all* available versions of a ballad or folktale are taken into account.

Consider one of the issues raised in Halliday's dismissal of a possible Indic parallel. The Indic text involves the drowning of a "sister" of the water-tank builders rather than "the wife of one of them." But as Vargyas observes, "The victim is not always a wife: in the Serbian, Albanian, and Roumanian she may be the sister of the builder. This appears to be a secondary element" (1967:202). It should also be noted that in many modern Indic texts the victim is a daughter-in-law, that is, a wife. So both the wife and sister appear as victims in the Indic texts. The "sister instead of wife" argument therefore cannot constitute a legitimate objection to the cognation hypothesis.

Formulaic Evidence

Not only are the Balkans ballad and Indic song-tale plots cognate, but also there are formulaic features that provide indisputable evidence of the genetic relationship between the two sets of texts. In the Balkans, the entombment of the female victim is often described in a moving series of lines in which the poor girl is ever so gradually covered, typically from the lower body to the upper body, from toe to head, so to speak. The girl speaks of being walled up to the knees, to her breast, to her throat; or knees, breast, eyes; or knees, waist, breast, and throat (Vargyas 1983:46–48). In the Romanian text analyzed in such depth by Mircea Eliade (1907–1986), "the wall rose ever higher, burying her, up to the ankles, up to the calves, up to the ribs, up to the breasts . . . up to the eyes" (Eliade 1972:168).

Let us briefly consider three Santal folktales. In the first, "The Magic Fiddle" (Campbell 1891:52–56), the sister is sent to get water, but the water vanishes when she tries to scoop some up into her pitcher. Gradually the water "reaches to my ankles, . . . to my knee, to my waist, to my breast, to my neck, . . . [to] a man's height," and the girl drowns. In a second tale (Campbell 1891:106–10), the girl goes to fill her pitcher "but she could not do so, as the water rose so rapidly. The tank was soon full to the brim, and the girl was drowned." In a third Santal tale, entitled "How Sabai Grass Grew" (Bompas 1909:102–6), the sister is sent to the tank to draw water. "Directly the girl drew near to the bank the water began to bubble up from the bottom; and when she went down to the water's edge, it rose to her instep." Gradually the water rises to her ankle, knees, waist, and neck. "At last it flowed over her head and the water-pot was filled, but the girl was drowned." In a modern Kannada text published in 1989, the water touches the daughter-in-law's feet, knee, and waist:

> She climbed a step and the water came up
> She climbed two steps and the water touched her feet
> She climbed three steps and the water touched her knee
> She climbed four steps and the water touched her waist
> She climbed five steps and the water drowned her
> The youngest daughter-in-law Bhagirathi
> She became a feast for the well.
> (*Aniketana* 1989:37)

In a previously unpublished version from northern India collected in 1991 (Kirin Narayan, personal communication, 1994), the beleaguered female victim begs her brothers: "Don't brick up my feet . . . my midriff . . . breasts . . . neck . . . mouth . . . eyes . . . head." This version is even closer to the southeastern European texts, inasmuch as the woman in this instance is bricked into the foundation of a waterway under construction. (It's included in this book on pages 113–17.)

The demonstration of this formulaic parallel alone—even without the obvious plot similarity—would obviously offer strong support for the proposed Indic origin of the Balkans ballad.

What is especially fascinating in the light of the likely Indic source for the ballad is the fact that a number of the Balkans texts end with the formation of a magical spring that contains either pure water or nourishing milk (Vargyas 1967:203). In the Romanian version cited by Eliade, Manole, the master builder, is so saddened by the sacrificial death of his beloved young wife that he kills himself: "and from the woodwork high on the roof, he fell, dead; and where he was shattered a clear fountain sprang up, a trickle of water, salt with his tears" (Eliade 1972:169). The "spring" motif could well be an instance of what folklorists call peripheral distribution or marginal survival.

Certainly the "spring" motif is reminiscent of the water-tank image so common in the Indic versions. For that matter, even the suicidal jump may not be a Romanian innovation. In a Kannada text, for example, the bereaved husband wept and "jumped into the well" (*Aniketana* 1989:38).

The Pitfalls of Parochial Nationalism

It is truly sad to think of so many eminent folklorists writing lengthy essays and learned monographs on this ballad in total ignorance of the Indic texts. It is especially distressing for those scholars who tried so hard to find the "origin" of the ballad and were misled (1) by wrongly limiting the areas of their comparative efforts—that is, failing to consult available Indic texts in print, and (2) by yielding to an excessively emotional and ideological nationalistic bias. The methodological lesson to be learned seems simple enough. The comparative method cannot possibly succeed if whole sets of cognate versions of an item of folklore are ignored. Folklorists who insist upon working in narrow, parochial, nationalistic mindsets are no better than unsophisticated anthropologists who are utterly convinced that a tale or song they collect from "their" people or "their" village is absolutely unique when in fact it is but one version of a narrative to be found among many peoples. The impressive veneer of comparativism found in the numerous monographic treatments of "The Walled-Up Wife" ballad cannot cover the egregious error of having failed to take Indic cognate texts into account.

To be sure, Indian folklorists are no less parochial. They are just as unaware of the massive Balkans scholarship on the ballad as Balkanologists are unaware of the ballad's existence in India. Accordingly, Indian scholars analyze "their" local version of the ballad (see Govindaraja 1989; Srikantaiah 1989) without reference to any other versions just as, say, Romanian scholars analyze only the Romanian text of the ballad (see Anghelescu 1984; Filiti 1972).

Another instructive illustration of the consequences stemming from excessive nationalistic zeal concerns aesthetics. Invariably, investigators claim that their "national" version of the ballad is the most beautiful. Romanian scholar L. Sainean contended, for example, "From the point of view of beauty and comparative originality, the Serbian and Romanian versions take first place; the Bulgarian songs, because of their loose form, give the impression of being detached fragments; the Albanian traditions are pale imitations of the Greek or Serbian ballads . . . the Hungarian variants seem to echo the Romanian ballad" (1902:360–61, as translated in Eliade 1972: 174). Not surprisingly, Hungarian scholars disagreed with this assessment. Vargyas notes, "I think the examples shown make it clear on the uniform evidence of several details that the Hungarian formulation shows the purest form," although to be sure, he does suggest a Bulgarian rather than a Hungarian origin (1967:222, 228; 1983:37). Of course, it is the height of ethnocentric subjectivity to claim that one national version of a cross-culturally distributed folksong is more "beautiful" or "esthetically pleasing" than that of another nation. The texts from India are surely every bit as poignant and eloquent as those from the Balkans—and remember, these were not even known to the myriad of Balkanologists making esthetic assessments of the relative merit of ballad versions. Again, it can hardly be coincidence that the national version adjudged best or purest just happens to come from the same nation of which the scholar making the judgment is a citizen!

Parochial nationalism also turns out to be a critical factor in the few attempts to interpret the ballad. Greek scholars, seizing upon the "bridge" motif in "The Bridge of Arta," have suggested that the ballad may have originated from the mythological hair bridge, over which the souls of the dead are required to pass on their way to the afterlife (Beaton 1980:122–24; Megas 1976:72). The problem here is that other versions of the ballad involve a castle, monastery, or water tank, rather than a bridge. So while the mythological hair bridge may appear plausible to those who know only the Greek "Bridge of Arta" tradition, it is highly implausible in the light of the total range of ballad variants. (It would also require that "The Bridge of Arta" be the original form of the ballad, which seems unlikely given the many versions from India.)

Another striking instance of a nationalistic interpretation of the ballad is Zimmerman's suggestion that "The Founding of Skadar" with its "immurement" can "represent the subjugation of the Serbian peoples at the time" of the Turkish domination. Moreover, "the survival of the infant" would accordingly represent "the ultimate survival of the nation" (Zimmerman 1979:379). It is certainly possible that the ballad could have such allegorical significance to nationalistic-minded Serbs, but this reading could scarcely apply to the Albanian, Bulgarian, Greek, Hungarian, Romanian, and Indic versions of the ballad.

Cross-Cultural Interpretation

What is needed in international folkloristics—as opposed to nation-alistic folkloristics—are interpretations of items of folklore which could in theory apply to most if not all of the versions of those items of folklore. This is not to deny the importance of identifying oico-types and analyzing those oicotypes in terms of national or regional personality characteristics. But it does stress the inevitable limita-tions of nationalistic readings of folklore items with cross-cultural distribution. (One can compare Geertz's classic reading of the cock-fight in Bali with a cross-cultural interpretation of the same event [Dundes 1994:94–132, 241–82].) Clearly the comparative method con-tinues to be essential for establishing the distribution pattern of any particular item of folklore. But merely demonstrating historical-geographic trait distributions is no substitute for searches for the meaning(s) of folklore. It is one thing to note that the ruse of sending the wife-victim into the foundation to retrieve an intentionally dropped wedding ring is "encountered in the Bulgarian, Greek, Al-banian and Serbian versions" (Vargyas 1983:37), but what is the sig-nificance, if any, of this motif? And how does it relate to the possible overall meaning(s) of the ballad?

Over the past 150 years of thinking about this ballad, the only "cross-cultural" theory to be consistently applied is that of myth-ritual. Specifically, it has long been assumed that the ballad is a sur-vival-reminiscence of human sacrifice, a ritual required to appease otherwise hostile supernatural spirits who for various reasons op-pose the building of some ambitious construction. What this theory utterly fails to illuminate is why the victim to be sacrificed must be *female*. In theory the supernatural spirit could just as well be ap-peased by the sacrifice of a male victim. In fact, the myth-ritual the-ory of foundation sacrifice explains very few of the actual details of the ballad plot. How, for example, does the myth-ritual theory ac-count for the ring-dropping device to induce the wife-victim to enter the foundation? The myth-ritual theory also suffers from being a *lit-eral* one; that is, it is predicated upon the notion that the construc-tion ritual is historical. This is why so many Balkans scholars have spent so much time trying to locate the actual monastery or bridge that supposedly inspired the story (see Sapkaliska 1988:170; Zim-merman 1979:374). If the ballad did originate in India, as now seems probable, all those efforts would appear to be in vain. (They do, how-ever, show how ballads and legends in their paths of diffusion tend to become localized in a particular place, tied to a particular topographic feature in the landscape.)

A few women scholars have sought to find metaphorical meaning in the ballad. Zimmerman proposes a Christian reading of the ballad in which "the traditional Christian beliefs in an ultimate reward for suffering and the triumph of good over evil" are emphasized (1979: 379). It is not entirely clear how these values are reflected in the sacrifice of a woman in a wall. Zimmerman also refers to "guilt-ridden cultural memories about foundation sacrifices," indicating that she has not completely abandoned the standard myth-ritual theory (1979:379). In her analysis of "The Bridge of Arta," Mandel argues a Lévi-Straussian opposition of nature and culture. Specifically, uncreative male culture "relies on the appropriation of female nature" (Mandel 1983:180). Although Mandel identifies women with nature, she also insists that women are liminal "between nature and culture" and act "as the mediator[s] between the worlds of the living and the dead" (1983:182). It is not immediately apparent how women can be both nature *and* mediating figures *between* nature and culture. However, Mandel's suggestion that the ballad deals with the men's attempt to "exercise power and control over the woman's sexuality and fertility" has merit (1983:182). But when she speaks in similar terms of the "bridge" as a liminal construction—"contiguous to both banks of the river" but belonging to neither (1983:181), she falls into the nationalistic parochial pitfall of thinking only in terms of the Greek versions of the ballad. The bridge may well be liminal, but what about a castle or a water tank? Once again we see the theoretical difficulties arising from interpreting an item of folklore in terms of just one culture (or one set of versions), when that same item of folklore is found in many different cultures. It is noteworthy that Mandel, in typical anthropologist fashion, dismisses all the many published studies of the song because they address only "questions of diffusion and origin" and hence are deemed "not relevant to the argument presented here" (1983:175 n. 4).

Another interesting interpretation is offered by Lyubomira Parpulova when she has recourse to Van Gennep's celebrated rites of passage. Parpulova gives the myth-ritual theory a new life when she argues that the ballad reflects a ritual of transition. But she, too, cannot escape the older theoretical bias. She suggests, rather than looking for a rite that underlies the ballad, "why not assume . . . a myth lying at the root of both the rite and the ballad?" And she speaks further of the "the different forms of constructional human sacrifice, probably practiced in the past and preserved as legend" (Parpulova 1984:427). She hints at a possible connection of ritual separation of women (e.g., during childbirth) with the ballad, although she maintains that there may not necessarily be a direct link (1984:435). One serious problem with the linkage to childbirth is that not all the ballad texts refer to either a pregnant victim or an infant to be nursed through the wall. Still, Parpulova does cite a Bulgarian song in which a prison "is decoded as married life" (1984:433), and she insightfully suggests that the walling up may express "the inevitability of a woman's fate: to be transformed into the foundations of a new construction, a new world, a new family" that "is not always very pleasant" (1984:434).

Toward Multiple Interpretations

As I have previously argued, we can view "The Walled-Up Wife" ballad as a metaphor for married life in all those societies in which it is sung (Dundes 1989). By entering marriage, the woman is figuratively immured. She is kept behind walls—to protect her virtue and to keep her confined. The ring-dropping ruse—which none of the earlier critics has addressed—would certainly support this feminist metaphorical interpretation. The husband drops the ring into the foundation and persuades the faithful wife to go in after it. It is the act of searching for a wedding ring which seals her fate literally and figuratively. The fact that a man is willing to sacrifice his wife in order to build a bigger and better castle, bridge, water-tank shows the second-class status of women in such societies. In that male chauvinist world, women's role is to stay protected from the outside world and to concentrate upon nurturing her infants (preferably sons)! The fact that women living near Skadar in modern times seek the chalky liquid from the walls to mix with drinking water in order "to restore milk to women who cannot nurse" continues to underscore women's nurturant role (Zimmerman 1979:380). The ideal wife nurtures males—either by bringing food to her husband working on a construction site or by giving suck to her newborn son.

Whereas myth-ritual totally fails to explain why it must be a female victim in the ballad, the present hypothesis would explain why it must be a woman who is sacrificed. Marriage is a trap—for women. That is the ballad's message. She must sacrifice everything, her mobility—she is transfixed—and even her life. The only aperture—in some versions—is a tiny window through which she can continue to suckle her infant son.

I believe this is a plausible metaphorical reading of the ballad of "The Walled-Up Wife," but is it the only possible reading? Certainly not. And this brings us to a final issue in our brief consideration of the ballad's significance. Nineteenth-century folklorists, if they thought about the meaning of folklore at all, invariably proposed some monolithic hypothesis. While they understood perfectly well the multiple existence of folklore texts, they did not realize that meanings could also be multiple. As variation is a hallmark of folklore texts, so is it also to be found in folklore interpretations.

Ever since Propp delineated the various dramatis personae in the magic tale (Aarne-Thompson tale types 300–749) in 1928, folklorists have had the methodological tools to explore the possibility of investigating the crucial matter of perspective or point of view in folktales or ballads. Any given folktale or ballad may give priority to one of several vantage points. Perhaps the most obvious distinction concerns whether the tale is told from the perspective of the hero or of the victim, assuming they are two different characters. (Propp made an important differentiation between hero-victims, who saved themselves, and hero-seekers, who saved victims [1968:36].) Although, in theory, a tale could be told from the villain's point of view, this is more common in written literature than in oral tradition.

In my analysis of the folktale source of Shakespeare's *King Lear*, I tried to demonstrate that an originally girl-centered folktale was retold by Shakespeare from a male parent's point of view (1976). In the same way, A. K. Ramanujan revealed that the Indic Oedipus tale was told from the mother's viewpoint rather than the son's (1983). Similarly, Jack Zipes has brilliantly shown how the female-centered tale of "Little Red Riding Hood" was recast by male collectors, namely, Perrault and the Grimm brothers, so as to satisfy the agenda of male ideology. (In the original oral tale, the heroine saves herself through her own cleverness—an example of Propp's hero-victim—whereas in the Perrault and Grimm "rewrites," the heroine is either eaten up by the wolf or else saved by an intervening male woodsman [Zipes 1993:30–34, 375–78].) Finally, Jim Taggart in his splendid *Enchanted Maidens* (1990) proved from his own field materials from Spain that there were distinct male and female versions of the same tale type, a differentiation that could frequently be correlated with the gender of the tale-tellers. Bengt Holbek in his magnum opus devoted to the European fairy tale also sought to distinguish "Masculine" and "Feminine" tales (1987:161, 417).

What this suggests in terms of the ballad of "The Walled-Up Wife" is that there are at the very least two distinct possible perspectives:

199

one would be that of the victim, the wife who is immured, and the second would be that of the male builder. It is obviously a matter of opinion as to whose story the ballad tells. Is it the tragic fate of the female? Or the tragic grief of the builder-widower? Just as there is no one correct "text" of an item of folklore, there is no one correct "interpretation" of an item of folklore. Folklorists must accustom themselves to accepting multiple interpretations just as they have learned to accept the existence of multiple versions of texts.

As mentioned above, I have proposed a feminist reading of the ballad which argues that the plot provides a deadly metaphor for marriage from India to the Balkans in which a wife is forced to give up her freedom and mobility by the demands of her husband and his family (e.g., in patrilocal residence). A new bride was expected to become fully assimilated and integrated into her husband's world, often becoming initially a virtual slave or servant to her husband and her in-laws. But if we look at the ballad text from the builder's perspective, we may get quite a different reading. All versions of the ballad involve one or more males engaged in some kind of construction enterprise. This is true whether the goal is the building of a bridge, a castle, a monastery, or a dam (to hold water). I have somewhat facetiously called this a male edifice complex (Dundes 1989: 161). But the key motif is that whatever is constructed during the day is deconstructed at night. Folklorists know this as Motif D2192, Work of Day Magically Overthrown at Night. Now, it is perfectly obvious that we are dealing with fantasy here, inasmuch as buildings do not disappear night after night after repeated daily attempts to put them up. Thus if we consider the motif in metaphorical or symbolic terms, we must ask, what could it mean to have something raised during the day to be razed at night? If we use the verb *erect* instead of *raise*, perhaps the symbology might be clearer. Men fear that they may not be able to sustain an *erect*ion, especially at night, a time for love-making. In terms of males versus females, males may try to express their masculinity by denying any dependence upon women. Boys become men by means of rites of passage (normally administered by males, not females) in which they formally repudiate any hint of maternal control. The most surprising feature of such rites of passage, as Bettelheim (1962) and others have suggested, is that the men frequently imitate or emulate female procreative behavior. In the ballad, men force a sacrificial woman to be enclosed in a man-made construction—just as men were originally enclosed in a female womb. That the male symbolism is not completely successful is hinted at by those versions of the ballad where the woman, though immured, is permitted to suckle her *male* baby through an aperture. Still, the male message in the ballad concerns the importance of creating a *permanent erection*, and one that, in imitation of the female, can contain a human being within it. The fallacy of the "phallicy" is that the male womb results in the death of its occupant, whereas female wombs—if all goes well—contain new life. In that sense, the ballad represents wishful thinking on the part of males, that they can create remarkable edifices just as women procreate, but the sad reality is that the male hubris brings only death to the female. Male death is opposed to female life, and the male insistence upon erecting his edifice complex or complex edifice means that his obedient, subordinate female must sacrifice her life for that male enterprise.

Keep in mind that one need not choose between the female or male interpretations of "The Walled-Up Wife." The ballad as sung in India more often reflects the female victim's point of view as opposed to the Balkans, where the story is seemingly most frequently told from the male builder's perspective. In any event, perhaps neither the female nor the male interpretation may be deemed valid, but they are surely a welcome alternative to the simplistic, literal myth-ritual building-sacrifice theory that has dominated the scholarship devoted to this extraordinary ballad up to the present time. Both these interpretations also are, unlike the earlier parochial nationalistic readings of the ballad, applicable to the ballad in *all* its versions, not just to the versions found in Serbia, or Hungary, or Romania. Moreover, rather than tying the ballad to an unproven myth-ritual hypothesis of human sacrifice, these interpretations link the ballad to the ongoing traumatic relations prevailing in the battle of the sexes, which would help explain why the ballad continues to be a painful and poignant reminder of the difficulties of balancing a career and marriage for males, and of achieving freedom of movement and opportunity for females in India and in the Balkans.

The future of the ballad's popularity in India and the Balkans may be in question. The "liberation" of women—the very word *liberation* refers to the basic complex of ideas which generated the ballad in the first place, a complex that insisted that women were *not* free, *not* liberated—may in time make the ballad's message obsolete. As more and more women become builders of bridges, castles, and dams, perhaps it will be men who will be forced to become the "victims" of their wives' ambitions.

201

References

Anghelescu, Serban. 1984. "The Wall and the Water: Marginalia to 'Master Manole.'" *Cahiers Roumains d'études littéraires* 4: 79–83.

Aniketana. 1989. "Keregehara—A Feast for the Well." *Aniketana* 2(1): 35–38.

Beaton, Roderick. 1980. *Folk Poetry of Modern Greece.* Cambridge: Cambridge University Press.

Bettelheim, Bruno. 1962. *Symbolic Wounds: Puberty Rites and the Envious Male.* New York: Collier Books.

Bompas, Cecil Henry. 1909. *Folklore of the Santal Parganas.* London: David Nutt.

Brewster, Paul G. 1971. "The Foundation Sacrifice Motif in Legend, Folksong, Game, and Dance." *Zeitschrift für Ethnologie* 96: 71–89.

Buchan, David. 1978. "British Balladry: Medieval Chronology and Relations." In *The European Medieval Ballad: A Symposium,* ed. Otto Holzapfel, 98–106. Odense: Odense University Press.

Cammiade, L. A. 1923. "Human Sacrifices to Water Spirits." *Quarterly Journal of the Mythic Society* 13: 693–94.

Campbell, A. 1891. *Santal Folk Tales.* Pokhuria: Santal Mission Press.

Čherenkov, L. N. 1962. "A New Version of the Songs of the Bridge." *Journal of the Gypsy Lore Society* 41: 124–33.

Cocchiara, Giuseppe. 1950. "Il ponte di Arta: I sacrifici nella letteratura popolare e nella storia del pensioro magico-religioso." *Annali del Museo Pitrè* 1: 38–81.

De Vries, Jan. 1927. "De sage van het ingemetselde kind." *Nederlandsch Tijdschrift voor Volkskunde* 32: 1–13.

Dorson, Richard M. 1968. *The British Folklorists.* Chicago: University of Chicago Press.

Dundes, Alan. 1976. "To Love My Father All: A Psychoanalytic Study of the Folktale Source of *King Lear.*" *Southern Folklore Quarterly* 40: 353–66.

Dundes, Alan. 1989. "The Building of Skadar: The Measure of Meaning of a Ballad of the Balkans." In *Folklore Matters,* ed. Alan Dundes, 151–68. Knoxville: University of Tennessee Press.

Dundes, Alan. 1994. *The Cockfight: A Casebook.* Madison: University of Wisconsin Press.

Eliade, Mircea. 1972. "Master Manole and the Monastery of Argeş." In *Zalmoxis: The Vanishing God,* 164–90. Chicago: University of Chicago Press.

Feilberg, H. F. 1892. "Levende begravet." *Aarbog for Dansk Kulturhistoire,* 1–60.

Filiti, Grégoire. 1972. "Hypothèse historique sur la genèse de la ballade de Maître Manole." *Südost-Forschungen* 31: 302–18.

Gilliat-Smith, B. J. 1925. "The Song of the Bridge." *Journal of the Gypsy Lore Society* (3rd series) 4: 103–14.

Gittée, Aug. 1886–1887. "Les rites de la construction. I. La victime enfermée." *Melusine* 3: 497–98.

Govindaraja, Giraddi. 1989. "The Awareness of Values in Folk Poetry." *Aniketana* 2(1): 47–52.

Grimm, Jacob. 1966. *Teutonic Mythology.* 4 vols. New York: Dover.

Groome, Francis Hindes. 1899. *Gypsy Folk-Tales.* London: Hurst and Blackett.

Holbek, Bengt. 1987. *Interpretation of Fairy Tales: Danish Folklore in a European Perspective.* FF Communications No. 239. Helsinki: Academia Scientiarum Fennica.

Köhler, Reinhold. 1894. "Eingemauerte Menschen." In *Aufsätze über Märchen und Volkslieder*, 36–47. Berlin: Weidmann.

Krappe, Alexander Haggerty. 1927. "The Foundation and the Child's Last Words." In *Balor with the Evil Eye*, 165–80. New York: Institut des Études Françaises, Columbia University.

Krauss, Friedrich S. 1887. "Das Bauopfer bei den Südslaven." *Mitteilungen der Anthropologischen Gesellschaft in Wien* 17: 16–24.

Mandel, Ruth. 1983. "Sacrifice at the Bridge of Arta: Sex Roles and the Manipulation of Power." *Journal of Modern Greek Studies* 1: 173–83.

Megas, Georgios A. 1969–1970. "Die Ballade von der Artas-Brücke." *Zeitschrift für Balkanologie* 7: 43–54.

Megas, Georgios A. 1976. *Die Ballade von der Arta-Brücke: Eine vergleichende Untersuchung.* Thessaniniki: Institute for Balkan Studies.

Milović, Jevto M. 1941. *Goethe, seine Zeitgenossen und die serbokroatische Volkspoesie.* Leipzig: Harrassowitz.

Mitra, Sarat Chandra. 1922. "On Some Vestiges of the Custom of Offering Human Sacrifices to Water-Spirits." *Quarterly Journal of the Mythic Society* 12: 397–405.

Mitra, Sarat Chandra. 1923. "Further Note on the Custom of Offering Human Sacrifices to Water-Spirits." *Quarterly Journal of the Mythic Society* 13:589–90.

Mitra, Sarat Chandra. 1927. "On the Indian Folk-Belief about the Foundation-Sacrifice." *Man in India* 7: 30–41.

Ortutay, Gyula. 1973. "János Kriza." In *Festschrift für Robert Wildhaber*, ed. Walter Escher et al., 492–501. Basel: Verlag G. Krebs.

O'Sullivan, Sean. 1945. "Foundation Sacrifices." *Journal of the Royal Society of Antiquaries* 75: 45–52.

Parpulova, Lyubomira. 1984. "The Ballad of the Walled-Up Wife: Notes about Its Structure and Semantics." *Balkan Studies* 25: 425–39.

Paspati, Alexandre G. 1870. *Études sur les Tchinghianés.* Constantinople: Antoine Koroméla.

Propp, Vladimir. 1968. *The Morphology of the Folktale.* Austin: University of Texas Press.

Ramanujan, A. K. 1983. "The Indian Oedipus." In *Oedipus: A Folklore Casebook*, ed. Lowell Edmunds and Alan Dundes, 234–61. New York: Garland.

Sainean, L. 1902. "Les rites de construction d'apres la poesie populaire de l'Europe Orientale." *Revue de l'Histoire des Religions* 45: 359–96.

Sako, Sihni, 1984. "The Albanian Entombment Ballad and Other Common Balkan Different Versions." In *Questions of the Albanian Folklore*, 155–65. Tirana: 8 Nëntori.

Shapkaliska, Teodora, 1988. "Die Einmauerung von Lebewesen in Bauwerken als Motiv in der Makedonischen Volksballade." In *Ballads and Other Genres*, 167–71. Zagreb: Zavod za istrazivanje folklora.

Sartori, Paul. 1898. "Über des Bauopfer." *Zeitschrift für Ethnologie* 30: 1–54.

Srikantaiah, T. N. 1989. Kerege Haara—A Tribute. *Aniketana* 2(1): 39–46.

Taggart, James M. 1990. *Enchanted Maidens: Gender Relations in Spanish Folktales of Courtship and Marriage*. Princeton: Princeton University Press.

Taloş, Ion. 1973. *Mesterul Manole: Contributie la studiul unei Teme de folclor european*. Bucureşti: Editura Minerva.

Taloş, Ion. 1987. "Foundation Rites." In *The Encyclopedia of Religion*, Vol. 5, ed. Mircea Eliade, 395–401. New York: Macmillan.

Vargyas, Lajos. 1967. *Researches into the Mediaeval History of Folk Ballad*. Budapest: Akadémiai Kiadó.

Vargyas, Lajos. 1983. *Hungarian Ballads and the European Ballad Tradition*. Vol. 2. Budapest: Akadémaiai Kiadó.

Wilson, Duncan. 1986. *The Life and Times of Vuk Stefanović Karadžić 1787–1864*. Ann Arbor: Michigan Slavic Publications.

Zimmerman, Zora Devrnja. 1979. "Moral Vision in the Serbian Folk Epic: The Foundation Sacrifice of Skadar." *Slavic and East European Journal* 23: 371–80.

Zipes, Jack. 1993. *The Trials & Tribulations of Little Red Riding Hood*. 2nd ed. New York: Routledge.

Selected Bibliography

Index

A Selected Bibliography:
Suggestions for Further
Reading on "The Walled-Up Wife"

Arnaudov, M. "Vagradena nevesta" [The walled-up young wife]. *Sbornik za narodni umotvorenija i narodopis* 34 (Sofia, 1920): 247–528. A substantial sampling of fifty-seven Bulgarian versions of the ballad.

Cocchiara, Giuseppe. "Il ponte di Arta: I sacrifici nella letteratura popolare e nella storia del pensiero magico-religioso." *Annali del Museo Pitrè* 1 (1950): 38–81. Reprinted in *Il Paese di Cuccagna e altri studi di folklore* (Torino: Paolo Boringhieri, 1980), 84–125. This distinguished Italian folklorist argues for a myth-ritual (foundation sacrifice) interpretation of the ballad.

Dundes, Alan. "The Building of Skadar: The Measure of Meaning of a Ballad of the Balkans." In *Folklore Matters*, ed. Dundes, 151–68. Knoxville: University of Tennessee Press, 1989. A summary of the enormous scholarship devoted to the ballad plus a feminist-inspired reading of the text.

Leader, Ninon. *Hungarian Classical Ballads and Their Folklore.* Cambridge: Cambridge University Press, 1967. Includes a useful detailed discussion of the Hungarian ballad "Clement Mason" (pp. 19–44) somewhat superseded by Vargyas's writings on the same ballad.

Megas, Georgios A. *Die Ballade von der Arta-Brücke: Eine vergleichende Untersuchung.* Thessaloniki: Institute for Balkan Studies, 1976. 204 pp. This important monograph by the leading international Greek folklorist consists of two parts. The first (pp. 19–121) is a modified historic-geographic study of more than three hundred Greek versions of the ballad, while the second (pp. 123–77) surveys all the previous scholarship on the ballad.

Sako, Sihni. "The Albanian Entombment Ballad and the Other Common Balkan Different Versions." In *Questions of the Albanian Folklore*, 155–65. Tirana: The '8 Nentori' Publishing House, 1984. Professor Sako assumes human sacrifice underlies the ballad, which he claims is of Albanian origin.

Sulițeanu, Ghizela. "Muzica baladei 'Mesturul Manole.'" *Revista de Etnografie si Folclor* 16 (1971): 97–116. In one of the relatively few studies of the music (as opposed to the text) of the ballad, an attempt is made to establish a morphologically based typology of the melodies of the Romanian versions of the ballad.

Taloş, Ion. *Meşterul Manole: Contributie la studiul unei teme de folclor european.* Bucharest: Editura Minerva, 1973. 469pp. A monumental study of the Romanian versions of the ballad, which also includes comprehensive coverage of most of the previous Balkans scholarship. Taloş also wrote an excellent update of scholarship published after his book in "Die eingemauerte Frau: Neuere Forschungsarbeiten über die südosteuropäische Bauopfer-Ballade," *Jahrbuch für Volksliedforschung* 34 (1989): 105–16.

Vargyas, Lajos. *Researches into the Mediaeval History of Folk Ballad.* Budapest: Akadémiai Kiadó, 1967. 303pp. Chapter 3, "The Origin of the 'Walled-Up Wife'" (pp. 173–233), is a magisterial survey of the scholarship on the ballad's origins and is primarily concerned with possible paths of diffusion of the ballad in the Balkans. Vargyas's superb overview is extended in his later book *Hungarian Ballads and the European Ballad Tradition*, Vol. 2 (Budapest: Akadémiai Kiadó, 1983), 18–57.

Index